BISON
BOOKS

THE OVERLAND ROUTE.

On the Trail to the California Gold Rush

Alonzo Delano

INTRODUCTION BY J. S. HOLLIDAY

University of Nebraska Press
Lincoln and London

∞

First Nebraska paperback printing: 2005

Library of Congress Cataloging-in-Publication Data
Delano, Alonzo, 1806–1874.
[Life on the plains and among the diggings]
On the trail to the California gold rush / Alonzo Delano; introduction by J. S. Holliday.
p. cm.
Originally published under title: Life on the plains and among the diggings. Auburn, N.Y.: Miller, Orton & Mulligan, 1854.
ISBN 0-8032-6649-9 (pbk.: alk. paper)
1. West (U.S.)—Description and travel. 2. Delano, Alonzo, 1806–1874—Diaries. 3. Pioneers—West (U.S.)—Diaries.
4. Overland journeys to the Pacific. 5. Frontier and pioneer life—West (U.S.) 6. Indians of North America—West (U.S.)—History—19th century. 7. California—Gold discoveries.
8. California—Social life and customs—19th century. 9. Frontier and pioneer life—California. I. Title.
F593.D33 2005
917.8—dc22   2004028366

This Bison Books edition follows the original in beginning chapter 1 on arabic page 13; no material has been omitted.

J. S. HOLLIDAY

Introduction

During the 242 years preceding the discovery of gold in California, the westering pressure of American families pushed the frontier of settlement from the shores of the Chesapeake Bay in 1607 to the banks of the Missouri River by 1849. Sustained and hastened by the rewards of the virgin continent—fertile soil and vast forests watered by innumerable streams amid a profusion of natural bounty—this migration of husbands, wives, and children (with their Bibles), pushed ever westward, across the Appalachian Mountains, into Pennsylvania and the Northwest Territory of Ohio and Indiana, and on to Missouri and Texas. Despite Indian hostility, disease, and suffering, the settlers' perseverance and hunger for land had created the thirty United States by 1849.

Throughout those more than two centuries of westward expansion, the presence of women and children instilled confidence that the wilderness promised a better living, to be earned as years of labor yielded ever more bountiful harvests. That was the lure of The West: cheap, if not free, land available to anyone ready to plow new furrows.

To temper the hope and optimism that nurtured westward migration, no one set forth a more realistic assessment than the West's own first president, Andrew Jackson, who admonished in 1834: "The planter, the farmer, the mechanic and laborer all know that their success depends on their industry and economy and that they must not expect to become suddenly rich by the fruits of their toil."

In 1849 the news from California of gold—free for all—challenged the ethos pronounced by President Jackson and known for generations before him to be true. Suddenly California promised that those who journeyed there would be "rich by the fruits of their toil." And just as amazing, their toil would be brief, for the news from the goldfields reported the treasure to be not only free for the taking but abundant and easy to dig up, if not simply to pick up.

Therein lay the true motive force of the rush to California—the gold belonged to no one, in astonishing contrast to the world's storied past.

For thousands of years gold had been sought and found, controlled and plundered by pharaohs, kings, emperors, czars, pirates, and whomever else had swords and power. How amazing, how attractive it was that in 1849 California had no ruler, no governing authority, no institutions or property owners to claim possession of this most sought-after treasure. The world rushed in, free to find California's gold, to dig for it, and to take it home—no license needed, no tax to be paid. Free for all: that was the wonder of California.

So it was that in 1849 and for many years thereafter, California attracted a wave of emigration unlike any westward expansion of previous centuries. By the scores of thousands, men left their families at home ("back in the states") and set off for El Dorado. They promised they would return within a few months, surely within a year. That was the central fact, the all-shaping influence. These fathers, husbands, brothers, and sons would be separated from their mothers, wives, sisters, and daughters. California would be a new place, a masculine society—free from the moral authority of women that had ruled the societies of their fathers and grandfathers.

As well, California's economy would not be based on the toil of cultivating the soil, with traditional, hard-earned rewards. Rather California's gold promised immediate gain, sufficient to finance a better life back home. Gold to pay off the mortgage on a farm in Indiana, to pay back money borrowed from a father-in-law in Baltimore, to provide escape from the subservient role of a younger brother in Massachusetts, to win the hand of a sweetheart in Georgia.

In an age when the vast majority of Americans spent every day of their lives in the city, village, or county of their birth, the California gold rush (as in a time of war) sent many thousands of men far from their families and the rules of home. As they set off on their long journeys (whether by overland trails or by sea voyages), they joined their good-byes with promises to send letters whenever possible or to keep diaries of the enterprise to be read on their triumphant return. More than filial obligation or emotional attachment motivated writing such records. That spring of 1849 Americans in all the thirty states shared a sense of history in the making, of being witness to or participants in an epochal event. All the nation's leaders—the president, local officials, clergymen, lawyers, bankers, editors—expounded on this extraordinary mania. As the *Buffalo (NY) Morning Express* admitted on January 16, 1849: "This glittering, dazzling gold news has unsettled the minds of even the most cautious among us."

So it was that across the nation blacksmiths and farmers, lawyers and preachers, millwrights and gunsmiths determined to record their part in the great national adventure. For the first time hometown words would describe the wonders of the fabled West—the ocean of prairies, the herds of buffalo, the tribes of Indians, the snowy peaks of the Rocky Mountains—that were previously made known through the books of famous writers like Washington Irving and the official records of government explorers like John C. Fremont. And above this new awareness of the American continent there glittered the vision of California where fortunes of five thousand dollars, even fifteen thousand dollars, could be dug from that miraculous, auriferous soil.

Among those many thousands, Alonzo Delano of Ottawa,

Illinois, succumbed to what he described as "the astonishing accounts of the vast deposits of gold in California . . . I was suddenly seized with the fever of the mind for gold . . . and I commenced making arrangements for my departure" (14). Bidding farewell to his wife and two children, he joined a company of fifty men from the surrounding farms and villages and set forth for the frontier on April 5, 1849. From that date Delano persevered in recording each day's experiences and, too, his thoughts and emotions, as he and his companions struggled for five months to cross the wilderness they had previously seen on maps as the Great American Desert. Finally, on September 10, 1849, they reached California's "diggings."

From the first page the reader knows that Delano is no ordinary diarist. For example, consider his description of the emigrants crowded onto boats bound for St. Joseph via the Missouri River.

[S]ince the invasion of Rome by the Goths, such a deluge of mortals had not been witnessed, as was now pouring from the States to the various points of departure for the golden shores of California. Visions of sudden and immense wealth were dancing in the imaginations of these anxious seekers of fortunes, and I must confess that I was not entirely free from such dreams; and like our sage statesmen, cogitating upon the condition of the National Treasury, with the extinguishment of the National Debt . . . I wondered what I should do with all the money which must necessarily come into my pocket! (15)

From this taste of the author's self-conscious formality and erudition (at once pompous and charming), it is obvious that Delano expanded, polished, and otherwise "improved" his original diary entries for the purpose of creating a book (originally published as *Life on the Plains and among the Diggings; Being Scenes and Adventures of an Overland Journey to California* in 1854) to take advantage of the nation's interest in the dramatic westward migration to California and that state's notoriety as a society of shocking immorality. In all, more than seven hundred titles relating to the emigration to California from 1849 to 1853 (and many more titles dealing with later years) have been identified by bibliographers. Of these, Delano's has long been sought by collectors and heralded by historians as a classic in gold rush literature.

That distinction derives from his story being more ambitious in its scope—minuscule details to encompassing descriptions—than almost any other account of the overland journey. Delano maintained those qualities in his chapters describing his company's sufferings on Lassen's Cut-off, the route made famous in the fall of 1849 as a death-dealing detour into northern California rather than the expected shortcut into the Sacramento Valley.

From St. Joseph to Sacramento, Delano's account attends to every aspect of the five-month trek from cooking meals to burying comrades, dangerous Indians to exasperation with lazy campmates, beauty of western mountains to the stench of dead oxen. Of special value, each chapter opens with a summary listing of events, dangers, surprises, amusements, and sorrows recounted in that segment of the journey. For example: "Antelopes and wolves—poison water—Indian depredations—Night Travel—Arrival at Fort Hall—Oasis in the Desert."

Also setting apart Delano's "diary" from others, his did not end with his arrival in California. Most diarists, weary of their demanding task, gave up on reaching the mines and cities of El Dorado. In contrast, Delano continued his story but no longer in the form (indeed the pretense) of a daily diary. Rather his twelve California chapters (16 to 27) offer the reader a broadly reportorial narration that interweaves his own experiences and business enterprises (mining along the Yuba River) with expository reports on "the disposition and character of the Indians," (309) "the causes of failure in mining," (378) "the insecurity of life and property" (363). On this latter subject he wrote in each chapter about the increase in crime ("audacious murders"), leading to his lengthy reports in the Spring of 1851 about the work of the San Francisco Vigilance Committee which he characterized as a "political revolution."

These chapters make clear what has been increasingly evident from the first—that Delano was first a journalist and second a gold seeker. Better expressed, he used his gold-seeking adventures as the subject for his writings.

That fact requires a brief diversion to explain the writing style and perspective as well as the character of this journalist who gained some fame from his writings published in newspapers and books.

Before leaving his home in Illinois, Delano entered into an agreement with the proprietors of the local weekly newspaper, the *Free Trader*, to write a series of letters describing his overland journey and experiences in California. He made a similar commitment to a New Orleans newspaper, the *True Delta*. The thirty-six letters published in these newspapers between April 1849 and August 1852 were collected and published as *Alonzo Delano's California Correspondence* by the Sacramento Book Collectors Club in 1952. It's a wonderfully readable, richly informative book.

Delano also wrote a series of articles for the *San Francisco Daily Courier* during the years 1850–1852. These witty observations of gold rush times were collected and published in 1853 as Delano's first book, *Pen Knife Sketches; or, Chips of* [sic] *the Old Block*. This book reportedly sold sixteen thousand copies.

(The full story of Alonzo Delano as journalist, author, and gold seeker is told in Irving McKee's introduction to *California Correspondence* and in the magisterial bibliography *The California Gold Rush* by Gary Kurutz [San Francisco: Book Club of California, 1997]. According to Kurutz's bibliography *Life on the Plains and among the Diggings* went through several printings and sold nine thousand copies.)

In the last chapters of this book, Delano concluded his broadly informative assessment of California with an optimistic forecast, comparable to that of later promoters. "The mines can never be exhausted. . . . [H]undreds of years must elapse before the ground can be dug over; and, besides, the veins of quartz are so deep that a single mine may be worked for many years. . . . [I]f [California's] resources are properly developed, no State in the Union can present a greater amount of real wealth" (380–81).

Alonzo never gained much of that wealth, only a few hundred dollars in gold dust. He died in Grass Valley, California, in 1874, later to be judged as California's first man of letters and surely known to readers of this book as the ideal guide on the plains and among the diggings.

To Colonel E. B. Morgan.

WHETHER toiling through the deep sands of the barren desert, suffering from hunger and thirst; or weary and way-worn in climbing stupendous heights of the Siérra; whether surrounded by death and desolation on the Plains, or obtaining slight repose in the new cities of. the Pacific — the reminiscences of our happy, school-boy days, too often intrude on my memory, to permit me to forget my old and well-tried friend of early years. And now that the dangers are passed — when we can sit side by side in "the old arm chairs," and trundle the hoop, or throw the ball, in fancy, and laugh over our boyish follies — these recollections of *by-gones* only cement the kindly feeling, which is rarely " of this world."

It is only a slight testimonial of respect — indeed, were it an hundred fold greater, you would deserve it — but such as it is, my heart dedicates this little work to you.

THE AUTHOR.

CONTENTS.

CHAPTER I.

PAGE.

Unexpected era in life — Company formed at Dayton, Ohio — Departure to St. Joseph — On the Missouri — Brown — Boat Embassy — Crowded emigration — Death by cholera and burial of a young Virginian — Indian Territory — Safe arrival of cattle at St. Joseph — Death by cholera and burial of Harris — Chill and Fever — Harney's Landing — Ferry across the Missouri — Indian country — Timber land — Panorama Plains — Our seventeen wagons — Fifty Ottawa men — Great and Little Namaha.................................... 13

CHAPTER II.

Rolling prairie — An old pioneer — Strangers with mules and ponies — White men and Indian — Indian theft and deception — Prairie — Grass and water — Thunder shower at night — Mistake of the day — Spoiled bacon — Dividing ridge — The two Namahas — Broken country — Out of the way — Crossing the Great Namaha — Bridge built and crossed — Westward — Tributary of the Little Namaha — Severe thunder shower at night — Wyeth's Run — Hall's Ford — Unknown stream — Pioneer Green — Absentee — South-west course — Crossed the stream — Signs of Buffalo.......... 23

CHAPTER III.

PAGE.

Big Namaha — Lost run — The Big Blue — Dry weed fuel —
No water — Prairie dogs — Onion family — Table land — S.
S. Course — Road found — Nineteen days on Prairie — Companies of gold-seekers — Little Blue — Sand hills — Valley
of the Platte — Muddy Missouri — Fort Kearny — St. Joseph
road united — Colder atmosphere — Meeting old friends —
Captain Tutt — Indian company — Fort — Willow — Severe
rain storm... 42

CHAPTER IV.

A change for the better — Islands in the Platte — Indian robbery — South Bend company — Terrible storm and great loss
of cattle — Forks of the Platte — Buffalo — Meeting Friends
— Buffalo meat — Fording the river — Men lost — Washing
day — Serious results of a joke — Indian village and burying ground — Tindall's grave — Smith Creek — Court-House
Rock — Chimney Rock — The "post-office" — Unexpected
meeting — Emigrant trains — Picturesque valley — Scott's
Bluffs.. 55

CHAPTER V.

Laramie Peak — Laramie River — Fort Laramie — South Bend
company — Warm Springs — Cold Water Creek — Division
of the company — Horse Creek and Riola Bonta — Black
Hills — Crow Indians — Rock Ridge — A beautiful creek —
Alkaline district — Colonel Joseph Watkins — A sublime
Government — Poison water — Dead cattle — Ferry over the
North Platte... 75

CHAPTER VI.

Over the North Platte — Wagon on the current — Mule trains
— Sand-stone cone — Antelopes and wolves — Dry pond —
Saleratus — Poison water — encampment — immense number
of emigrants — The red Buttes — Sand Rock — Willow

PAGE.

Spring — Timely hospitality — Independence Rock — Sweet
Water River — Intense heat — Perpendicular rock — River
through the chasm — Devil's Gate — Shooting a desperado—
Myriads of crickets.................................... 90

CHAPTER VII.

Valley of the Sweet Water — Wind River — Toils of the emigrant — Rencounter threatened — Ice in the desert — Prairie dogs, antelope and mountain sheep — "All is not gold
that glitters" — Trading post — Fraudulent post-office — A
beautiful prospect — Ascent to the South Pass — Face of the
country — Great numbers of dead cattle — suffering of the
emigrants — An old settler — A man accidentally shot —
South Pass — Over the mountains — A last look homeward
Disbanding of trains.................................. 103

CHAPTER VIII.

Leaving South Pass — Little and Dry Sandy Rivers — Passage
by Sublett's cut-off — Hardships in the desert — Green River
— Re-union of old friends at the Ferry — Brutal murder —
Search for the criminal — Irregular jury trial — Indepen-
dence day — Unpleasant incidents — A welcome shade —
Bear River — Camp of Snake Indians — Rough traveling —
Face of the country — Mountain Indians and traders —
Game.. 118

CHAPTER IX.

Hunting Excursion — Mountain scenery — Bear River Valley
— Beer Springs—Mineral Springs—Visit to the craters of two
extinguished volcanoes — Lindley's misfortune — River Neuf
— Arrival at Fort Hall — Panack River — Trading with the
Indians — Mule train from Oregon — Valley of Raft River
— Large snake — The author gets lost — His suffering for
water — Return — Valley of Goose Creek................ 135

CHAPTER X.

PAGE.

Hot Spring Valley — Post-office — Destitute Emigrants — Chill
and fever — A party of Digger Indians — Anecdotes — The
great basin — Humboldt, or Mary's River — Wild fowl —
Appetite and provisions — News from the Platte — Sickness
and abandonment of Mr. Ware — Incidents by the way — Indian depredations — Mary's River — Night travel — More
trouble from the Indians — wolves — sleeping in the open
air... 154

CHAPTER XI.

Broken Surface of the country — Visit to Lieut. Thompson's
camp — Col. Kinkead — Bad news from the Sink — Pastimes
— Left the Humboldt River — Journey over the desert — Sufferings for want of grass and water — A mother's affection
for her child — The oasis in the desert — Hot springs....... 172

CHAPTER XII.

Hot springs — Applegate's route — Onward over the desert —
More Indian theft — In pursuit of the Indians — Distressing
reports from the desert — Quantities of dead cattle and horses — Remarkable curiosity — Cañon through the mountains
— Standing sentry — Travelers from Oregon — Lake of salt
water — Fresh beef.................................... 187

CHAPTER XIII.

The Siérra Neváda in sight — Dry bed of a lake — Excursion
to the mountains — Narrow escape from an Indian's arrow—
Mountain scenery — Crossing the mountain — Salt Lake —
Pitt River — A hill of magnesia — Mount Shasta — A noble
act of relief — Magazine Rock—Heroic fight with the Indians
— Adventure among the Indians........................ 201

CHAPTER XIV.

Leaving the valley of Pitt River — False alarm — Good forage
— Feather Creek — Timely hospitality from a brother Odd-

PAGE.

fellow — An under-ground river — Game — Cooking a beef
steak — Prospecting for gold — Venison — Effects of starvation — Deer Creek — Starting alone for the valley of the Sacramento — Incidents by the way — The valley in sight —
Sensations — Col. Davis' house — Lawson's Settlement — Prices of provisions — Emigrants............................... 217

CHAPTER XV.

Sufferings of the emigrants on the journey in the fall of 1849
and 1850 — Destitution — Cholera — Employments in the
mines — Narrative continued — Arrival in the valley — Broken contracts — Separation — In pursuit of supplies — Indians at the Ranches.................................... 234

CHAPTER XVI.

Arrival at Sutter's Fort — Plans for the future — Meet Captain
Greene and Doctor Angel — Friendly aid — Sacramento City
— Departure for the mines — Bear River — Cayotes — Yuba
River — Arrival at the mines — Sickness — Success in trade
— Return for more goods.............................. 249

CHAPTER XVII.

Hardships of the miners — Unexpected meeting with Colonel
Watkins — Kindness of Doctor Morse — Doctor Patrick —
Crossing the Yuba River — Sickness — Severe rains — Theft,
and its cause — Returning from the mines — Melancholy
death of Mr. Chipman................................. 258

CHAPTER XVIII.

Trouble with the Indians on the South Fork — Fate of Mr. Henderson on the North Fork of the Platte — His wife and children — Prospecting for gold — The result — Disappointed
hopes, and failures — Getting rid of the Indians — Mr. Turner — Melancholy incidents............................ 272

CHAPTER XIX.

PAGE.

Stolen cattle — Rapid growth of cities and villages — Speculation — Uncertainty of titles — Sacramento City — Its gambling houses — Refinement — Great flood — Crayon sketches — A speculation in town lots — The Indians............. 285

CHAPTER XX.

Influence over the Indians — Their character and habits — Bu-
rial rites — Affection for the dead — Their language — Food
— Selection of marriage partners — Government — Dress —
Their propensity to gamble............................. 295

CHAPTER XXI.

Disposition and character of the Indians — Their honesty —
Cruelty and injustice of the whites — Incidents — Their confidence — Number of wives — Anecdotes — Their final extermination 309

CHAPTER XXII.

Peter the hunter — At the battle of Waterloo — His adventures
— His daughters — Jim Beckwith — His daring act among
the Blackfeet, and escape — Southern Indians — Influence of
the Catholic missions — Change of quarters — Miners in
search of the Golden Lake — The result.................. 321

CHAPTER XXIII.

Departure for the Gold Lake country — Mexican muleteers,
and pack mules — A California lion — Arrival at Grass Valley — Settlers and gamblers — A quarrel — Loss of mules —
Sublime mountain scenery — Onion Valley — Difficult descent from the mountains — mules precipitated down the
steep banks — Arrival and settlement at Independence — Uncertainty of business operations at the mines — A storm —
Sudden departure of the miners — A losing business........ 334

CHAPTER XXIV.

PAGE.

Nelson's Creek — Independence bar — The climate — Mountain life — Struggles of the miners — their disappointments — Population — Mining life — Gambling and dissipation — Horrible murder — Robberies — Volcanic remains — Change of Location — New acquaintances — Departure for San Francisco.. 347

CHAPTER XXV.

Arrival at San Francisco — Admission of California as a State — Excitement and rejoicing of the citizens — State of the country — Indignation at the delays of Congress in admitting her into the Union — The need of laws — Previous good order of the inhabitants — Commencement of crime — Particular cases of crime — Insecurity of life and property — Indignation of the citizens — Bold robbery and apprehension of the criminals — Execution of Stuart and Wildred — Public sentiment — Immense meeting on the plaza — The Vigilance committee of San Francisco — Execution of Jenkins — Resolutions to establish the People's Court — Salutary effects, 356

CHAPTER XXVI.

Resources of California — Uncertainty of mining — Probable extent of the gold region — Where gold is usually found — Hints to persons prospecting — Talc beds — Auriferous quartz veins — Cause of failure in mining — Crushing the rock and separating it from the gold — The Chilian mill — Process of separation — The mines inexhaustible — Enterprise of the Miners.. 372

CHAPTER XXVII.

California — Her resources — Mineral wealth — Climate — Tillable land in the valleys — Richness of the soil — Productions — Water-power — Timber — Rapid increase of population — Health — Conclusion............................ 381

Life on the Plains.

---·---

CHAPTER I.

UNEXPECTED ERA IN LIFE — COMPANY FORMED AT DAYTON, OHIO — DEPARTURE TO ST. JOSEPH — ON THE MISSOURI — BROWN — BOAT EMBASSY — CROWDED EMIGRATION — DEATH BY CHOLERA AND BURIAL OF A YOUNG VIRGINIAN — INDIAN TERRITORY — SAFE ARRIVAL OF CATTLE AT ST. JOSEPH — DEATH BY CHOLERA AND BURIAL OF HARRIS — CHILL AND FEVER — HARNEY'S LANDING — FERRY ACROSS THE MISSOURI — INDIAN COUNTRY — TIMBER LAND — PANORAMA PLAINS — OUR SEVENTEEN WAGONS — FIFTY OTTAWA MEN — GREAT AND LITTLE NAMAHA.

NINETY days previous to the 5th of April, 1849, had any one told me that I should be a traveler upon the wild wastes between the Missouri river and the Pacific ocean, I should have looked upon it as an idle jest; but circumstances, which frequently govern the course of men in the journey of life, were brought to bear upon me; and on the day above named, I became a nomad denizen of the world, and a new and important era of my life began.

My constitution had suffered sad inroads by disease incident to western climate, and my physician frankly told me, that a change of residence and more bodily exertion was absolutely necessary to effect a radical change in my system—in fact, that my life depended upon such a change, and I finally concluded to adopt his advice. About this time, the astonishing accounts of the vast deposits of gold in California reached us, and besides the fever of the body, I was suddenly seized with the fever of mind for gold; and in hopes of receiving a speedy cure for the ills both of body and mind, I turned my attention "westward ho!" and immediately commenced making arrangements for my departure. A company had been formed at Dayton, a few miles above Ottawa, under the command of Captain Jesse Greene, for the purpose of crossing the plains, and I resolved to join it. Our general rendezvous was to be at St. Joseph, on the Missouri, from which we intended to take our departure. I had engaged men, purchased cattle and a wagon, and subsequently laid in my supplies for the trip, at St. Louis. My wagon I shipped by water to St. Joseph, and sent my cattle across the country about the middle of March, to meet me at the place of rendezvous, in April.

All things being in readiness, on the day first named, I bid adieu to my family and to Ottawa, and proceeded to St. Louis on the steamer Revolution, and there took passage for St. Joseph on the Embassy. The companions of my mess were Messrs. J. H. Fredenburg, Matthew Harris, and Eben Smith, from Ottawa—the two last I had engaged to take across the plains, on condition of their assistance during the journey, and half they should make for one year from the time we left home—a contract which was then common. We were joined on our trip up the river by a young man named Robert Brown, who was looking out for some opportunity of going to California, and who was proceeding to St. Joseph for this purpose.

There was a great crowd of adventurers on the Embassy. Nearly every State in the Union was represented. Every berth was full, and not only every settee and table occupied at night, but the cabin floor was covered by the sleeping emigrants. The decks were covered with wagons, mules, oxen, and mining implements, and the hold was filled with supplies. But this was the condition of every boat—for since the invasion of Rome by the Goths, such a deluge of mortals had not been witnessed, as was now pouring from the States to the various points of departure for the golden shores of California. Visions of sudden and immense wealth were dancing in the immaginations of these anxious seekers of fortunes, and I must confess that I was not entirely free from such dreams; and like our sage statesmen, cogitating upon the condition of the National Treasury, with the extinguishment of the National Debt, under the administration of General Jackson, I wondered what I should do with all the money which must necessarily come into my pocket! Our first day out was spent in these pleasing reflections, and the song and the jest went round with glee— while the toil, the dangers, and the hardships, yet to come, were not thought of, for they were not yet understood. But they were understood soon enough, *nous verrons.* On the second day, amid the gaieties of our motley crowd, a voice was heard, which at once checked the sound of mirth, and struck with alarm the stoutest heart—"the cholera is on board!" For a moment all voices were hushed—each looked in another's face in mute inquiry, expecting, perhaps, to see a victim in his neighbor. "The cholera? Gracious Heaven! How?—where? Who has got it?"—and from that moment anxiety prevailed— for who could tell that he might not become a victim? At length calmness gained the ascendency, and excitement passed away; but the subdued tones of those who had been the most gay, attested the interest which they felt in the melancholy announcement. A young gentleman, belonging to a company from Virginia, who had indulged in some imprudence in eating and drinking, while at St. Louis, was the subject of attack; and although every attention was rendered which skill and science could give, the symptoms grew worse, and he expired at ten o'clock on the morning after he was taken ill.

It was a melancholy spectacle, to see one who had left home with high hopes of success, so prematurely stricken down; and although he had no mother near him to soothe his last anguish, or weep over his distress, he was surrounded by friends who were ready and willing to yield any assistance to mitigate his pain. Indeed, there was not a man on board, whose heart did not yearn to do something for the sufferer. Preparations were made for his interment; and a little before sunset the boat was stopped, to give us, his companions, an opportunity to bury him.

It was in a gorge, between two lofty hills, where a spot was selected for his grave. A bright green sward spread over the gentle slope, and under a cluster of trees his grave was dug by strangers. A procession was formed by all the passengers, which, with a solemnity the occasion demanded, proceeded to the grave, where an intimate friend of the deceased read the Episcopal burial service, throughout which there was a drizzling rain, yet every hat was removed, in respect to the memory of a fellow passenger, and in reverence to God. How little can we foresee our own destiny! Instead of turning up the golden sands of the Sacramento, the spade of the adventurer was first used to bury the remains of a companion and friend.

A tedious passage of ten days brought us, on the 19th, to St. Joseph, where we learned that the Dayton company, which had preceded us, had left that day, with the intention of moving up the river to some other point for crossing into the Indian

Territory, where they would halt until the grass was sufficiently advanced to afford forage for our cattle, and which would give us ample time to overtake them before setting out from the land of civilization, on our arduous journey across the plains. I also heard that my cattle had arrived safely, and were waiting, under the charge of Henderson, about a day's journey in the country ; and I dispatched Smith to notify Henderson of our arrival, and to bring them in. Our goods and wagon were soon landed, and as every public house in town was crowded by emigrants to overflowing, (having a portable cooking stove,) we slept and messed in our wagon, in one of the back streets; and up to Sunday night, all were enjoying our usual health.

About four o'clock on Monday morning, we were awakened by groans, and cries of distress, from the outside of our wagon. " Who is that?—what is the matter?" I exclaimed, starting from a sound sleep. " Who is sick?"

" It must be Mr. Harris," said Brown, " for he is not in here." We sprang out, and indeed found poor Harris, writhing and agonized, under an attack of cholera. I immediately gave him a large dose of laudanum, the only palliative we had at hand, and dispatched a messenger for a physician. He was violently taken with the worst symptoms, but within an hour was undergoing regular treatment from a skillful physician. For about three hours he suffered intense pain, with vomiting, purging, cramps, and cold extremities, while a clammy sweat started from every pore. During the day we moved him to a more quiet and secluded spot, and his symptoms became more favorable. The evacuations and vomitings ceased, his limbs became warm, his eye brightened, and he thought, as we did, that he was better. He remained in this state about three hours, during which we continued our exertions in rubbing him, and

2

making the applications advised by the physician, when all looked upon him as out of danger. Suddenly, and without any warning, he began to gasp for breath, and in five minutes lay a corpse before us. We could scarcely credit our senses. He, who but the night before bid as fair to live as any one of us— he, who passed the good natured jest with us, in the fullness of health and strength, now lay extended, an inanimate mass of clay, "one of the things that were." Alas! it was too true, and our friend had "gone to that bourn, from which no traveler returns."

We laid him out on the ground decently, and as well as our slender means would allow, and Brown and myself lay near him that night, keeping a melancholy watch by the light of our camp fire, over the remains of our companion and friend. If an honest, well-meaning man ever lived, poor Harris was one and his simple habits, and virtuous inclinations, had endeared him to us all. We dug his grave ourselves, in the morning, and with no tolling bell to mark the sad requiem, we buried him in a cluster of trees, by the side of a beautiful rivulet.

My wagon-top had received some injury when getting it on board at St. Louis, and while repairing it, after the sad duty of burying Mr. Harris, Henderson and Smith arrived with the cattle, and by Wednesday morning we were ready to pursue our journey. Brown was installed in Harris' place, and under the direction of Mr. Fredenburg the party started off to follow the track of the Dayton company, while I remained to get letters, which might be forwarded to St. Joseph by the mail of the following day. I may say here that in this we were disappointed, for no letters came, and it was ten months before we received the first word from our friends at home. While I was at work repairing my wagon, the day was very warm, and being unaccustomed to labor, when night came, I went early to bed, at a house where I had obtained lodgings, exhausted by the fatigues of the last few days. Before I got to sleep, I felt strangely. Was there a change in the weather? I could not get warm. I piled on more clothes. I felt as if I was in an ice-house. Ugh! the cold chills were creeping along my back. I involuntarily drew up my knees, and put my head under the bed clothes, but to no purpose—I was shivering, freezing, and then so thirsty!—I wanted a stream of ice-water running down my throat. At length I began to grow warm, warmer; then hot, hotter, hottest. I felt like a mass of living fire—a perfect engine, without the steam and smoke. There seemed to be wood enough from some source, but I poured in water till I thought my boiler would burst, without allaying the raging thirst which consumed me. At last the fever ceased, and then, indeed, the steam burst in a condensed form through the pores of my burning skin, and my body was bathed in a copious perspiration, that left me as weak as any "sucking dove." I had had a visit from my old friends, chill and fever.

Thursday came, and I felt too ill to ride. I lay up to dry; but on Friday morning I went through another baptism of fire and water, the ceremony of which closed about noon. Determined to be with my friends if I was doomed to be sick, and as our medicines were in the wagon, I mounted the pony, Old Shabanay, which had been left for me, and although so weak that I could hardly keep my seat, I started. I soon found my strength increase in the fine air, and when I reached Savannah, a pretty town fourteen miles above St. Joseph, I felt quite well, though weak.

On Saturday morning, I made the chief part of my breakfast from blue pill, and started off in pursuit of my wagon, which I overtook in a ride of ten miles. Suspecting my illness, the company had driven slowly, in order to let me overtake them. On Sunday we reached English Grove, sixty-five miles above St. Joseph, where we learned that the Dayton company had resolved to cross the Missouri at a ferry just established, called Harney's Landing, and remain on the opposite bank until it was ascertained that there was sufficient grass for the cattle, and then take an obscure route, over which only one train had passed, about four years previous, and strike the St. Joseph and Platte road at a point which it was said would put us in advance of the St. Joseph and Independence trains, at least ten days.

Feeling that it was absolutely necessary for me to lay up and nurse myself, and as there was plenty of time to overtake the train, while the boys went on with the wagon, I made the acquaintance of Mr. Van Leuvin and family, to whom I am much indebted for the kindness which a sick man requires, and went resolutely into "drugs and medicines."

On the 2d day of May, feeling that I could "throw physic to the dogs," I took leave of my kind host, and again mounting Old Shab, I rode to the ferry, where I learned that the company had started that day, determined to go on as far as the grass would allow the cattle to be driven.

After dinner, dropping a few words to my friends by the last regular mail, I crossed the river, which is, perhaps, a third of a mile in width, and stood, for the first time, in the Indian country.

The camp of the company had been about a mile and a half below the ferry, on the bottom, but I found it vacated when I reached it, though the trail of their wagons was plainly to be seen, leading up the high bluff, which runs parallel with the river, and I turned my pony's head towards the Platte. Ascending a long hill, I found the land sparsely covered with timber, and much broken, as far as the eye could see among the trees; but the road marked by our train was on an easy ridge, which led beyond the broken ground into the interior.

The timber continued four or five miles, when it ceased, and the eye rested on a broad expanse of rolling prairie, till the heavens and earth seemed to meet, on one vast carpet of green. In vain did the eye endeavor to catch a glimpse of some farm-house, some cultivated field, some herd of cattle, cropping the luxuriant grass in the distance; yet no sign of civilization met the eye. All was still and lonely, and I had an overwhelming feeling of wonder and surprise at the vastness and silence of the panorama. It seemed as if the sight of an Indian would have given relief, but not one appeared, and on, on I rode, without seeing a sign of life, and with none but my own thoughts to commune with.

A little before night-fall, on rising a hill, I came suddenly in sight of the encampment of our company, consisting of seventeen wagons and fifty men, all of whom were from the neighborhood of Ottawa. They were encamped in a hollow, near a fine spring, and putting Old Shab to his best gait, in three minutes I stood among my friends, with a glorious appetite to partake of their savory supper of bacon, bread and coffee. They had made about fifteen miles. Soon after my arrival, all hands were summoned, by the blast of the bugle, for the purpose of adopting general rules for mutual safety in traveling and also to detail a guard for the night.

My own mess was now composed of Messrs. J. H. Fredenburg, Benjamin K. Thorne, Robert Brown, Hazel Henderson, John Morrell, Eben Smith, and myself. It was the intention of our company to keep the dividing ridge between the Great and Little Namaha, to a certain point which had been marked out, and then strike off to the St. Joseph road, which we had been assured we could reach in about eight days, and we relied much on following the trail of the train which had passed over the ground four years before, and which here was plainly perceptible.

Our guards being posted, we all turned into our tents, and fatigue and the novelty of our situation were soon forgotten in the arms of the god of sleep.

CHAPTER II.

ROLLING PRAIRIE — AN OLD PIONEER — STRANGERS WITH MULES AND PONIES — WHITE MEN AND INDIAN — INDIAN THEFT AND DECEPTION — PRAIRIE, GRASS AND WATER — THUNDER SHOWER AT NIGHT — MISTAKE OF THE DAY — SPOILED BACON — DIVIDING RIDGE — THE TWO NAMAHAS — BROKEN COUNTRY — OUT OF THE WAY — CROSSING THE GREAT NAMAHA — BRIDGE BUILT AND CROSSED — WESTWARD — TRIBUTARY OF THE LITTLE NAMAHA — SEVERE THUNDER SHOWER AT NIGHT — WYETH RUN — HALL'S FORD — UNKNOWN STREAM — PIONEER GREENE — ABSENTEE — SOUTH-W. COURSE — CROSSED THE STREAM — SIGNS OF BUFFALO.

MAY 3, 1849.

OUR company was well arranged and provided for the great journey before us. Every wagon was numbered, and our captain, with the concurrence of the members of the company, directed that each wagon should in turn take the lead for one day, and then, falling in the rear, give place to the succeeding number, and so on, alternately, till the whole seventeen advanced in turn. Every mess was provided with a portable light cooking stove, which, though not absolutely necessary, was often found convenient, on account of the scarcity of fuel; each man was well armed with a rifle, pistol, and knife, with an abundant supply of ammunition, and each mess had a good and substantial tent. Each wagon was drawn by from three to six yoke of good cattle; and it was agreed that they should be prudently driven, for we could well anticipate the helplessness of our condition, should our cattle give out on the plains, where they could not be duplicated. To prevent their being stolen by the Indians, or straying at night, a watch was set while they were feeding; and at dark they were driven in and tied to the wagons, where they were constantly under the supervision of the night guard; and it is owing to this watchfulness and care, that we lost none by Indians throughout the trip.

Before sun-rise the cattle were driven out to graze, and all hands were astir, and some engaged in that business of life, cooking breakfast. The wagons formed a circle, outside of which the tents were pitched, so that had thieves been disposed to get at our valuables, they would have been compelled to pass into the inner circle, under the eyes of the guard; and in case of an attack, the wagons would form a barricade. Anticipating a scarcity of fuel, the company, on leaving the timber of the Missouri, had thrown wood enough on the wagons to serve two days for cooking, and now before each one the smoke gracefully curled, in active preparation for wooding up the engine of life. Brown was installed cook, the other boys agreeing to perform his duty as night-watch. Henderson drove our cattle, and Smith made himself generally useful, in collecting fuel, pitching and striking the tent—in fact, all had their respective duties to perform. About nine o'clock the camp was broken up, the tents put into the wagons, the cattle driven in and yoked, and our second day on the plains commenced.

The country was rolling prairie; with the little Namaha on the right, four or five miles distant, and no timber in sight, except on the banks of the stream. Our route was traced mainly by marking the course of the hollows and little streams which diverged to the right or left, keeping such ridges as appeared to divide the waters which flowed into the Great or Little Nama-ha. Old Mr. Greene, the father of our worthy captain, from his experience in traversing the western prairies, acted as our chief pioneer, and he was rarely at fault, although, at times, it was extremely difficult to determine the true ridge, from the evenness of the ground and the windings of the hollows. About ten o'clock I had walked in advance of the train about a mile, and was a little behind Mr. Greene, who was accompanied by Mr. Fredenburg, on the pony, when suddenly two strangers came in sight upon an eminence, having three mules and ponies. On seeing us, they halted and gazed for a few moments, and then took a direction as if to cut off a circuitous bend, which our train was making, without approaching us. Messrs. Greene and Fredenburgh, desiring to make some inquiries, galloped across the plain and intercepted them.

These men told them that they belonged to a company of an hundred wagons, which had started out from Old Fort Kear-ny two weeks before, and had gone about forty miles on the plains, when the grass failed, and the company were compelled to stop, and that they were then returning to the settlements for some additional supplies. After getting some directions, the parties separated, each continuing their several routes.

About two hours afterwards we were met by two white men and an Indian, who were in pursuit of these men. It appeared that the two men belonged to no company of emigrants, and their story of the hundred wagons was a sheer fabrication. They had stolen their animals from an Illinois company, at Fort Kearny, and were making their escape. Their pursuers, sus-pecting the Indian to be accessory to the theft, forced him to go

B

with them in pursuit. At night the two men returned to our camp, having overtaken the thieves, who, on seeing that they were pursued, jumped from their animals, and made their escape in the timber on the bank of the creek. When they were running off, the Indian asked permission of his companions to mount a fine pony for the purpose of intercepting the rogues. One of them dismounting from his recovered animal, the Indian mounted, and set off in pursuit at a round gallop, and soon disappeared behind a hill. After waiting some time for his reappearance, they chanced to look in another direction, and saw the outline of the Indian, making off with their pony, a new saddle, and an overcoat which had remained on the saddle. It was now too late to think of overtaking the red runaway, and they had to submit to their loss with the best grace they could, cursing their own credulity, but giving the Indian credit for his ingenuity.

Our course through the day was a little north of west, over a beautiful prairie. The ground was generally ascending, with an abundance of grass and water, and our cattle looked well. As the sky portended rain, we encamped about four o'clock in the afternoon, and made preparations accordingly. Trenches were dug around the tents to allow the water to run off, and about night-fall the sky was overcast with black clouds. The wind blew a gale, and the thunder and lightning was terrific. Peal after peal rolled along, as if heaven's artillery were doing battle, and soon its flood-gates were opened upon us in a perfect deluge. I never saw it rain harder, yet we found our tents a perfect protection, and we slept on our buffalo-skin couches with as much composure, as if we had had a tiled roof over our heads. Distance sixteen miles.

MAY 4.

The rain made the roads heavy this morning, but we were moving at our usual hour, over a charming, undulating country, without a tree or shrub in sight only along the streams at a distance, and whose dark verdure along the Little Namaha, in a measure indicated our general course. Once we were at fault. The old trail had become obliterated, and we pursued what we thought was the dividing ridge, till we were suddenly brought up at a bluff which formed a point on the banks of the Little Namaha. Before the train came up, we sent messengers back to turn its direction, while I jumped on a mule, and followed a small tributary a mile and a half to its source, where I found the old trail, and the dividing ridge only a few rods wide. We encamped near the tributary, where there was good grass and excellent water, after a drive of fourteen miles, and were merry over our coarse fare, laughing at the mistake of the day.

MAY 5.

We found this morning on driving up our cattle, that one of Mr. Greene's oxen had become too sore to travel; he was therefore turned loose, and a cow yoked in his place, which proved to answer the purpose exceedingly well. The road was still heavy, and our train moved slowly, while the wind, which blew a gale every day, retarded our progress with our high canvas-covered wagons. It was found to be a fault in having the tops of our wagons too large, for the force of the wind against them made the labor much harder on our cattle, and we resolved to stop at the first convenient place and reduce their dimensions, as well as to overhaul our provisions. We discovered that we had been imposed upon in St. Louis in the purchase of our bacon, for it began to exhibit more signs of life than we had bargained for. It became necessary to scrape and smoke it, in order to get rid of its tendency to walk in insect form.

We were now about forty-five miles from our starting point, and had approached by the windings of our course, to within about a mile of the Great Namaha, on our left; and now the course of both streams was plainly visible from the ridge. We drove to the bank of the Great Namaha, and spent the most of the day in overhauling our meat, and in reducing our wagon covers to a proper size, which was found to be a decided improvement. We had been in bed but a short time after the labors of the day were brought to a close, when some drops of rain pattering on our tents, admonished us that our preparations for a storm were incomplete, and one of the boys turned out and dug a trench around the tent, so that when the storm came upon us, we were prepared, and kept perfectly dry.

Since leaving the Missouri, we had seen no game except a few plover, which were wild and shy, and although we had been traveling in the Ottoe country for five days, not a single Indian, save the one pursuing the horse thieves, had been seen.

Grass was now scanty, and fuel scarce, and our practice was, when in the vicinity of streams, to gather wood enough to last two or three days, and carry it with us. Distance five miles.

MAY 6.

On looking around this morning, it was found that Old Shab had served us a shabby trick, for from appearances he had got tired of prairie life, having amply satisfied his curiosity, and had taken the back track for the settlements.

Morrell set out in pursuit, and directly came up with him.

"Whoa! Shab—whoa!" said John, in his most kindly tone, and Shab did "whoa" till John's hand was within six inches of his head, when he wheeled like lightning, and kicking up his heels like a dancing master, ran off a few rods, stopped, and looked around with the most impertinent composure. Not discouraged by this example of coltology, Morrell approached cautiously, and began his wheedling "whoa" again. Again Shab allowed his friend to approach him, but as he extended his hand to grasp his mane, he dodged the question with the most diabolical impudence, leaving Morrell to bless his stars at his singular good fortune in overtaking stray ponies. In this delightful way did Old Shab lead him for miles, till they nearly reached the old camping ground, when, like a coy maiden, he suffered his resolute follower to put his arm around his neck, and bring him in, after a weary and vexatious chase. Distance ten miles.

MAY 7.

We were up early, and although the wind was high and disagreeable, we were in fine spirits, and our cattle looked and felt well. As I was still weak and unable to walk all day, I mounted the pony, and rode in company with our pioneer, Mr. Greene.

The country was beautiful, well watered, with timber as usual only along the margin of streams, with a deep rich soil, the land rolling without high or abrupt hills—and this is the general character of the country between the two Namahas.

In keeping the dividing ridge, we sometimes passed within half a mile of the Big Namaha, and then in half an hour might be at the head of the main tributaries of the Little Namaha, where the dividing ridge was only two or three rods wide, the water flowing to the right and left.   Being about two miles in advance of the train, with Morrell, we came up to the tributaries of the Greater Namaha, on our left, with the Little Namaha on our right, which we desired to head.   And there were so many points, and the ground so broken with circuitous ridges, that an hour was spent in exploring, and determining the right course.   In my ride I started up an elk and a large prairie wolf, the only game which we had yet seen except the shy plover, but they gave leg-bail, and as at that moment we were not prepared for a close interview we did not seek a more particular acquaintance.   The grass improved in quantity, and there was plenty of water, but no wood; though we had still enough of the latter on our wagons for the present demand. We encamped after a drive of seventeen miles.

MAY 8.

On ascending a hill this morning we found ourselves between the creeks, at a point where it was difficult to determine our road.

There was much difference of opinion upon the subject, and we were all equally wise and keen in looking through a mill stone.   Where the true ridge appeared to run, was directly out of our general course, yet there was another ridge in our general direction, and our captain decided to follow it.   Taking the spy glass in my hand, I walked about eight miles ahead, over a very broken country, until I reached the apex of a high hill, from which I distinctly saw that the streams united, and that we were between the forks.   I was weak and tired and sat down to rest, expecting the train to arrive soon, when they would discover the mistake.   My appetite, too, reminded me that there was an emptiness in my pocket cupboard, and the only luxury my larder contained was a vial of quinine—rather slim fare for a hungry man on the plains!

I waited awhile, and the train not making its appearance, I raised the glass to my eye, and discovered them five or six miles off, making a retrograde movement. They had discovered their error, and were retracing their steps, and as there was no other way, it was necessary that I should retrace mine, or go supperless to bed, which, in my condition, to say the least, was very inconvenient to the "creature comfort." I became very thirsty as well as hungry, but there was no water, and I gathered and ate handfulls of sorrel, which grew abundantly, but I found it but a sorry substitute for meat and drink. Weak and weary as I was, by the aid of quinine I toiled on, and just at nightfall came up to the train, now encamped on the ground which they had left in the morning, where I regaled myself on our camp luxuries of fried bacon and bread. I had made sixteen miles, "*over the left*," and learned a lesson to keep near the train, which I remembered for many weeks, though I again forgot it to my sorrow. During the morning some large animal was discovered, at too great a distance to make out what it was. Some of our men rode out and discovered that it was a fine sorrel horse, well shod, which probably had been stolen by the Indians from some train, or had strayed off, and was enjoying the luxury of prairie life, solitary and alone. They tried ineffectually to capture him, but he was too fleet, and too shy for his pursuers to place him in bondage. Distance gained, nothing.

MAY 9.

The country during the forenoon march was hilly and broken. We were desirous of reaching the head of the Big Namaha, as that would bring us upon the St. Joseph road, and we thought a day or two would certainly find us there. The soft ground of the unbeaten prairie compelled us to advance slowly. The trail which we attempted to follow, sometimes disappeared altogether, and we placed our main dependence on keeping the dividing ridge, which ran in one general course.

In the afternoon the country was less broken, and afforded many beautiful views. We were on a ridge with a broad valley on each side, and many little creeks making down into the Namahas, and their courses were marked by timber sparsely growing on their banks. All around the grass was green and luxuriant, and it seemed, as we ascended one rise after another, that each view was still more charming than the other. I did not wonder that the aborigines were attached to their delightful country, and had it been mine, I should have defended my possession against the encroachment of any lawless intruder.

We had contrived up to this time to procure wood enough for cooking purposes, but now it disappeared, and in place of it there was an abundance of rosin weed, which was an excellent substitute. This contained a resinous gum, which exuded under the leaves, and it burned freely. It seemed as if when we were about to be deprived of one essential comfort, Providence had substituted another for our good, and an armfull of these excellent stalks could be gathered in a few minutes.

Having gained sufficient strength, I reported myself accordingly, and for the first time was detailed as one of the night guard. At the appointed time I shouldered my rifle, and commenced my two hours tour of duty. The night was dark, though clear, and there was not even a bush to magnify into an Indian. But I found it a glorious opportunity to *think*, and as I

"Pac'd my lonely rounds,"

old reminiscences passed rapidly before me, so that my guard was by no means a work of labor. I reviewed the scenes of a somewhat eventful life, checkered with good and evil fortune, from boyhood, when, with my early and still loved friend, Ed. Morgan, I got into a glorious scrape, in throwing fire balls to frighten the girls of a boarding school; the parental lecture which followed; then of the love scenes of later years, during which I fooled one good looking girl, and pulled the wool over her eyes in such a way as to make her believe I was a handsome young scamp, and she took me for better or worse, and is now the mother of my children; then other friends came up, as in Richmond's dream, not to frighten, but to enkindle old feelings of endearment; in short, I was in a most glorious train of thought, when the sergeant of the guard shouted, in the stillness of the night, "relief turn out," and soon my retrospections were buried, like my head, between two as good blankets as ever covered a nomad specimen of humanity.

Alas! for poor human nature, California was many days journey distant, and I had ample time to indulge in day dreams and retrospections, before I "dragged my weary length along" in the valley of the Sacramento. Distance eighteen miles.

MAY 10.

The scenery continued much the same, with no important incident, and we drove about sixteen miles.

MAY 11.

We had a capital breakfast—a change from our ordinary fare. Occasionally, men's appetites grow aristocratic on the plains, and for once we felt disposed to indulge in this anti-plebeian taste.

B* 3

A raccoon had been killed on the previous day, and an ample share was divided with our mess. As the merit of fresh meat is not properly appreciated at home, where it is too common, owing no doubt to the ordinary way of preparing it, I beg leave to append a recipe for the best mode of preparing coons for the delicate taste of epicures. MEM. First catch your coon and kill him, skin him, and take out the entrails; cut off his head, which throw away; then if you have water to spare, wash the carcass clean, but if you have not, omit the washing. Parboil an hour to take out the strong musk, then roast it before the fire on a stick. While it is roasting, walk ten miles, fasting, to get an appetite, then tear it to pieces with your fingers, and it will relish admirably with a little salt and pepper, if you happen to have them. A tin cup of coffee without milk, taken with it, makes, under the circumstances, a feast fit for the gods.

During the day we saw antelopes for the first time, but they were extremely shy, and our hunters could not approach them near enough to get a shot. They played around at a distance, and frequently stopped to gaze at our train as it passed along, with evident wonder, as if to ask what strange race we were, and what the dickens we were doing on their stamping ground.

We crossed the Pawnee trails in the course of the day, but the lords of the soil still kept aloof. About noon we came to a tributary of the Great Namaha, which we crossed by building a bridge, and here we found the trail again, and the remains of a bridge which the emigrant train had built four years before. We were in momentary expectation of reaching the St. Joseph road, and every eye was strained in the distance to catch the first view of the throng, who, like ourselves, were bound upon a golden voyage, but still we saw it not. Distance seventeen miles.

MAY 12.

During the night it rained again, and we found the road heavy, but the day was cool, and our course was direct.

At noon we reached the Little Namaha, where it was necessary to build a bridge before we could cross. We found a beautiful encampment, decidedly the best which we had had, on the margin of the stream, with an abundance of luxuriant grass and wood, and which put us in admirable spirits. We had now arrived at the point when we supposed a few hours drive would bring us to the road, and we were congratulating ourselves upon soon meeting the face of civilized men and fellow travelers. There was a broad bottom covered with rich green, bounded by a hill miles in extent, and the stream was fringed by a luxuriant growth of trees. Antelopes were running about in all directions, and the river was covered with ducks, swimming lightly about, while the opposite side was variegated with dead and green patches of grass, which covered the swells of the back ground as far as we could see. The men went cheerily to work, and during the afternoon a good bridge was built, the steep banks dug down, and a good place for crossing was made. Peter Hoes and myself took our rifles and sauntered out a couple of miles, and after crossing ditches, forcing our way through bushes, and getting tired, returned to camp without getting a single shot, much to our chagrin. At night we had a grand illumination. The dry grass on the opposite bank was on fire for a long distance, and as occasionally a current of air swept along, the blaze in a huge semi-circle glared up through the darkness like a sea of fire, rolling along from place to place, as the dry grass became ignited, with a most grand and pleasing effect. B. K. Thorne proved to be the best marksman of our mess for the day, and returned from an excursion with several ducks. Distance eight miles.

MAY 13.

After breakfasting on our ducks in the most approved method of prairie cooking, we crossed our bridge without difficulty, doubling our teams to haul the wagons up the steep bank on the opposite side, and pursued our way through the same kind of country as on the preceding day.

The fable of the turkey that twisted his neck off in watching a man walking around his perch, came forcibly to mind, for our own necks were strained and twisted in trying to get a glimpse of the expected road. Yet no such catastrophe of falling heads occurred, although the long wished for object did not present itself to our view. Inquiries were made of each other, which none could answer—" How far is it to the road ?" Maps were consulted, but this route had never been laid down, and the perspective glass was in constant use, but all to no effect. At noon we came to another tributary of the Little Namaha, which we thought certainly was the last. Over this we made a bridge in a short time, and at night encamped where there was plenty of grass and water, but no wood.

Antelope and elk were seen in great numbers, and a regular hunting corps was organized, composed of six in number, but they were generally unsuccessful, and our supplies of fresh meat mostly continued to run at large in a whole skin. Captain Greene and Mr. Fredenburg went out a mile or two, and thought they discovered the timber of the Big Blue, but were probably mistaken. Distance eighteen miles.

MAY 14.

George Whitikins ! how it rained during the night. It seemed as if heaven's artillery was firing a salvo over our devoted heads, and every flash of lightning was instantly answered by a crashing sound of thunder. No harm was done, however, except preventing our heavy eye-lids from closing. We made a circuitous march to avoid crossing streams, and it appeared by the map that we had been traveling for the last three days nearly parallel with the road. We struck the old trail again in the course of the day, which we had lost; indeed, we had long given up all attempts to follow it, and relied chiefly on the compass, keeping the dividing ridge where we could. Old Mr. Greene and myself were in advance of·the train some three or four miles, when we came to what we supposed to be Wyeth's Run, a fine stream twice as large as the Namaha. The train stopped by a pond of water, and we returned, when a consultation was held, at which it was decided that the company should change its present course, and strike the St. Joseph road as soon as possible, not doubting that we must be within one day's drive of it, and for this purpose it became necessary to cross the stream. The country was higher, the ridges more level, and of greater breadth than they had been, but the hills were more abrupt and the hollows deeper than we had found before. Wild onions of an excellent flavor were growing in abundance, and we found in the low grounds wild potatoes and artichokes of small size, which were luxuries to us, and relished exceedingly well with our "hog and hominy" fare. Distance sixteen miles.

MAY 15.

Doctor Hall, in searching for his cattle which had strayed off, brought in a report that he had discovered a good ford through the stream, about a mile from our encampment, and before breakfast he rode down with Mr. Greene to reconnoitre. They found it excellent, and we named it Hall's Ford, in honor of its discoverer·, and it was duly consecrated by an involuntary baptism of Mr. Greene. The old gentleman rode in to sound the depth, when his saddle-girth gave way, and he slid, body and breeches, over the mule's head into the water; but as cold baths are recommended by physicians, he consoled himself upon the water-cure principle against future disease.

Notwithstanding the consecration, fate claimed a mite for her share from the old gentleman, for when the train was about to ford, he rode in to show the way, when the girth gave way a second time, and made a cold-water man again of him: then he claimed the honor of being the best marksman in the company, for without firing a shot he had got a brace of ducks—certainly two duckings in one morning. On ascending the opposite hill, we found a level prairie, over which we traveled in a west-south-west direction all day, and at night encamped by an unknown stream of considerable size, flowing through a broad and beautiful bottom, skirted by trees and shrubs, but there was no sign of the road.

In fact, we did not know where we were—we had no trail to follow; the maps of that portion of the country were necessarily imperfect, and our wanderings and windings resembled those of the children of Israel in the wilderness; and although we knew the road lay somewhere south of us, and by the map should have been at hand, we were often obliged to make long detours to avoid hills and streams. And we found so many of the latter not laid down, that we could not determine with precision, those which were marked on the map. Our indefatigable pioneer, old Mr. Greene, determined to search for the trail once more during the day, and while the train went on, he set out without guide or compass, depending upon his long experience in traveling over prairies, and his rifle for safety. In the mean time we reached our place of encampment, on what we supposed to be the main branch of Wyeth's Run. Three of our hunters, including Mr. Greene, had not returned, and as night approached we looked somewhat anxiously for them. A little before sun-set our captain took the flag and went on an eminence, which commanded an extensive view of the prairie, that he might serve as a beacon to our belated brethren. At length the old gentleman was seen about half a mile distant, and exchanged signals with the captain. Suddenly he changed his course, and dashed off across the plain as fast as his mule could carry him, and soon disappeared among the inequalities of the ground. The shades of night were closing in, and still he did not appear. At length darkness came on, the hunters returned without having seen him, and the whole thing seemed to be involved in a mystery which we could not explain. A party went upon the hill, and after kindling a large beacon fire, discharged vollies from their rifles for a long time, and then a torch was prepared, which was left standing. But all was in vain. Time slowly wore on, the roll was called, guard set, and no one lay down that night upon his hard bed, without an anxious feeling for the safety of our brave old pioneer. Distance sixteen miles.

MAY 16.

The morning came in gloomily ; the sky, though calm, was shrouded in clouds, and anxiety on account of Mr. Greene brought every man to his feet at the earliest dawn. A voluteer party of six men started out in search of him, resolved to spare no exertion in ascertaining his fate, and to find him, if within the range of possibility. Another party, under the direction of our noble captain and Mr. Snelling, our wagon master, set to work on the bridge, over which we were to cross the stream, but

gloom generally pervaded our camp, and a party was left on
the look-out from the hill for our old pioneer.   About eleven
o'clock a shout arose from those on the look-out, and the old gentleman made his appearance over a knoll.   The word was passed,
" He's coming," " He's coming ! "   All rushed from their labors
to welcome him, and a treble round was fired as a *fue de joie*
for his safe return.   It seems that upon approaching our camp
in the evening, he recognized his son, the captain, but at the
same time an antelope started up near him, and he thought it
a capital chance to have a shot, and although he had eaten
nothing since early in the morning, with the hardihood of a
true western hunter, he started off in pursuit.   The foolish
animal, instead of quietly waiting to have his skin bored with
a bullet, led him a chase of two or three miles, and succeeded
in getting away, and he lost the direction to our camp.   With
perfect composure he took the saddle from his mule, and
wrapping himself in his blanket, lay down, with no music but
the howling of wolves to lull him to sleep.   The rising sun
showed him his true direction, when he mounted and rode into
camp, much to our relief.   Upon his coming in, a second party
was sent out after those who were in search of him, and it was
not until night that our company was all re-united, to talk over
the " mistakes of a night," and laugh off the effect which the
strange course of events had produced upon us.

The uncertainty of our position gave all a feeling of anxiety
on the subject, and our orderly sergeant, John Traverse, volunteered, with Morrell, to go out and explore the country in
the direction of the road.   They walked in a southerly direction about fourteen miles, and returned at night, without making
any discoveries as to our locality, and brought the unwelcome
intelligence that they had not found the road.   Ridge after

ridge was passed, creek after creek was forded, without success, until the declining sun admonished them to return; but it was still resolved to continue our west-south-west course.

Some of our men were successful in catching fish, and we were enabled to add another luxury to our meagre fare. Distance nothing.

MAY 17.

The bridge being completed, we left our excellent campground, crossed the stream, and passed over a charming bottom of more than two miles in width, before we reached the high table-land of the prairie on the south. Although our anxiety to reach the road was great, we were in good spirits and not daunted, for fifty able bodied men, well armed and provided with the substantial comforts of life, were not to be easily discouraged. Wild onions grew in abundance on the bottom. They were about the size of a hickorynut, and covered with a kind of close net-work, which is stripped off like a husk, leaving the onion clear and bright, and equal in flavor to any I ever ate. Signs of buffalo began to appear, and we passed several skeletons which were bleaching on the plain, but we saw none alive of the family with the "r'al hump, tail, horns and all." We were strongly impressed with the idea that this was a glorious country for the mastodon and all sorts of mammoths to curvet in, as there was plenty of room, and I made the following memoranda: "If we see signs of any before we reach the road, which is quite likely, I'll make a note of it in my journal." The water was execrable. Distance fifteen miles.

CHAPTER III.

BIG NAMAHA — LOST RUN — THE BIG BLUE — DRY WEED FUEL — NO WATER — PRAIRIE DOGS — ONION FAMILY — TABLE LAND — S. S. COURSE — ROAD FOUND — NINETEEN DAYS ON PRAIRIE — COMPANIES OF GOLD SEEKERS — LITTLE BLUE — SAND HILLS — VALLEY OF THE PLATTE — MUDDY MISSOURI — FORT KEARNY — ST. JOSEPH ROAD UNITED — COLDER ATMOSPHERE — MEETING OLD FRIENDS — CAPTAIN TUTT — INDIAN COMPANY — THE FORT — WILLOW — SEVERE RAIN STORM.

SINCE leaving the Missouri we have seen scarcely any rock. Occasionally, where the bluff was worn by the water, gravel appeared, and near the head of the Big Namaha a few granite boulders appeared scattered around, and still higher on the Little Namaha their strata of limestone schist appeared. When we forded Lost Run, probably a tributary of Wyeth's, the bottom of the stream was a dark limestone shade, and this was the only appearance of rock up to this point, perhaps two hundred miles from the Missouri. For days not a gravel stone was seen in the deep, rich soil of the prairie, and instead of the fine gravel beds of our eastern brooks, here we found nothing but quick-sand or mud. The water of the streams was softer even than rain water, though very palatable, yet we were frequently compelled to resort to holes in the hollows, and in sloughs, for this indispensable article, when at a distance from streams. The soil is a rich black mould, well suited for wheat, hemp, and cereal grains, but the scarcity of timber and stone is a great impediment to its immediate settlement. There was no indication of coal within the scope of my observation, but twice in the Namaha country I observed appearances of iron.

We found the country during this day's drive very level, and a little after noon we reached a plain, where there was not a tree or shrub, nor a sign of life except our own train, as far as the eye could extend. The glare of the sun upon the distant plain resembled the waves of a sea, and there were appearances of islands and groves, from the effect of the mirage.

Towards the hour for our noon halt, we passed the height of table land which turned the waters in the direction of the Big Blue, and we began almost imperceptibly to descend. The grass was dry and scanty, there was no water in sight, not even a slough, and the soil was thin and light—decidedly the poorest which we had seen since leaving the Missouri. Badger holes were numerous, and occasionally our hunters brought an animal of that species in, which we found quite palatable. As we were about making up our minds to pass the night without water and grass for our cattle, while ascending a slight elevation a broad meadow, two or three miles in extent, lay before us, in which was a fine pond. Captain Greene had advanced about a mile beyond this, and reported another smaller meadow and pond, and being anxious to get as far as we could, we drove on to it. For the last few days the rosin-weed had disappeared, and our fuel was dry weeds and buffalo excrement, which served us quite well to boil our coffee and fry our bacon. We had been able to keep a direct course through the day, from the nature of the country, and made a good drive of eighteen miles.

MAY 19.

The country resembled that of the previous day, with no water except occasionally in sloughs; and as we looked over the broad expanse of prairie, till earth and sky seemed to blend, we could not repress a feeling of loneliness.   We passed during the day a large town of prairie-dogs, but its inhabitants, having notice of our approach, did not vouchsafe their presence to welcome us, and we gained no information with regard to their peculiar manners and customs.   The little hillocks which marked their abodes stood arranged in regular order, with streets about twenty feet wide, crossing at right angles.   Notwithstanding we had no fuel but such as has been previously mentioned, and that scarce, our appetites were so keen that we could have devoured our bacon—aye, perhaps a young prairie-dog, without the usual process of cooking; and had an elephant made his appearance, we might have been able to have masticated one of his tushes by way of dessert.   We observed a rich pink flower blooming from bunches of a bright green color, from which many of our men formed nosegays, for its fragrant odor.   After a while some of them had the curiosity to taste this rare plant, and found it to be nothing more or less than wild cives, of an excellent quality, when in a moment, the nosegays were thrown aside, and a supply of this member of the onion family gathered for our evening meal.

Upon halting at night a foot-race excitement was got up, and many trials of speed were made among the younger portion of our company, but the long legs of Kent Thorne ran off with the palm.   Distance to-day, sixteen miles.

MAY 20.

Our road, like that of yesterday, was over broad table-land,

and we were able to keep a direct south-south-west course. But where the *dickens* was the St. Joseph road ? Where were we ?—and where had we been ? We had now been out nineteen days upon the wilderness. Our object in taking this new route had been to save time, and of getting in advance of other trains ; and the question naturally arose, Had we succeeded ? Had we gained anything by our erratic course ? For the last three days we were enabled, from the nature of the country, to make a direct line towards the road. When traveling between the Namahas, we supposed that we were within five or six miles of the road, and since then we had made an actual southing of more than fifty miles without reaching it ; and as far as we could see, and frequently our hunters were out four or five miles from the train, there was no indication of it. Anxiously we drove on, with " hope deferred," wishing that the next knoll would bring the long wished for object to our vision. This feeling was shared by all, when, about four o'clock, our captain, who had rode ahead four or five miles, was seen riding towards us at full speed, swinging his hat joyfully, when a shout was raised, " The road is found ; the road is found !" and a three times three was given, and our loud huzzas testified the joy of us poor Israelites, who had so long been lost on the prairie wilderness.

We encamped on a fine bottom near a pretty creek, a mile from the road, and a camp of emigrants was reported below us, to which Henderson repaired, and learned that a large number of wagons were ahead, and that we were only an hundred and fifty miles from St. Joseph. From the latter place we had been actually traveling twenty-four days, nineteen of which were upon the prairie, to reach this point ; while the trains that had come by the road, direct, had come through without difficulty in eleven days. This was gaining time and getting ahead with a vengeance! But we hoped that this error would not be again repeated—a hope which eventually was found illusive, and which led to hardships and suffering, notwithstanding our present experience in deviating from well known and beaten tracks. Distance sixteen miles.

MAY 21.

Our desire to be upon the road induced us to be stirring early, and we were moving as soon as our cattle had eaten their fill, when a drive of a mile placed us upon the great thoroughfare of the gold seekers.

For miles, to the extent of vision, an animated mass of beings broke upon our view. Long trains of wagons with their white covers were moving slowly along, a multitude of horsemen were prancing on the road, companies of men were traveling on foot, and although the scene was not a gorgeous one, yet the display of banners from many wagons, and the multitude of armed men, looked as if a mighty army was on its march; and in a few moments we took our station in the line, a component part of the motley throng of gold seekers, who were leaving home and friends far behind, to encounter the peril of mountain and plain.

To us it gave great relief, after being so long in uncertainty, and although we were strangers, yet there was a fellow-feeling in having one pursuit in common, and we drove merrily along, giving and receiving accounts of our various adventures since leaving Missouri.

About noon we reached the point of the Little Blue, where we were to strike across the plain to the Platte, a distance of twenty three miles, and ordinarily without water, but we received accounts as we were about filling our water casks, that the late rains had filled the sloughs so that it was unnecessary to carry water with us. We also ascertained that for the last three days we had been traveling across a portion of this identical dry plain, and had it not been for the rains, we must have suffered greatly, and ten days later, we must have been deprived of water on that route. We took the precaution to throw wood on our wagons, and at night encamped where there was plenty of grass and water. Distance eighteen miles.

MAY 22.

A little before noon we saw the grass-covered sand hills which bounded the valley of the Platte, and we were some hours in *ascending* the gentle slope to them. It appeared to me that from the time we left the Little Blue, we were gradually ascending, so that the Platte seemed really to flow through higher ground than the tributaries of the Kanzas; and that should a canal be cut from the Platte, it would descend to the Blue through a series of locks. As we rose to the apex of the last hill, the broad valley of the Platte lay before us, as level as a floor, and the great artery of the Missouri, with its turbid, muddy waters, a mile in width, divided by Grand Island, came in sight. Here, too, was a scene of active life. Here the road from old Fort Kearny united with the St. Joseph road, and for the whole distance in view, up and down the river, before and behind us, long trains were in motion or encamped on the grassy bottom, and we could scarcely realize that we were in an Indian country, from the scene of civilized life before us, and this was all caused by the magic talisman of gold. What will be the end? Who can foresee our future destiny?

On leaving the Blue and approaching the Platte, we felt a

great change in the atmosphere. From being warm, it became so cold that overcoats were necessary for comfort. I felt the premonitory symptoms of fever creeping over me, and was compelled to get into the wagon, being too weak to walk, and it became apparent that a thorough course of medicine was necessary to break my predisposition to bilious disease. The chill, however, passed off. When we arrived at the point of the hill above the valley, I observed a train coming in from the Kearny road, which I thought I recognized. Drawing nearer, I felt certain that it was a company from South Bend, Indiana, led by my friend Captain C. M. Tutt, with whom I had parted a month before at St. Joseph.

Our own train stopping for a noon halt, I mounted the pony and rode over to them, when I found it really was that company, and that by a singular coincidence, we had thus met at a distance of more than three hundred miles from where we last parted. Dear reader, if you would duly appreciate the pleasure of meeting old friends, just make a trip on the plains, and you will understand our joy at seeing old and familiar faces again. They had left St. Joseph and crossed the Missouri at Fort Kearny, some thirty miles above Harney's, the route we at first intended to take, where they had quietly lain for twelve days, and then had reached this point by a well-beaten road in eleven days, while we were boxing the compass, and wearying our legs on the prairie for nearly a month, in doubt and anxiety as to our position. By Captain Tutt we learned the probable cause why we had seen no Indians in our transit thus far. The Pawnees and Sioux were at war, and kept close to their towns and strong holds. On the evening of the 19th, a band of eighty Sioux warriors visited his camp. They were all mounted and approached at full speed, each armed with a gun, bows and arrows, lance, tomakawk and shield. Not knowing what their intentions were, he went alone towards them and motioned them back. They were coming up abreast, when they instantly dismounted and sat down on the ground in a line, and the chief beckoned Captain Tutt to approach, and on his doing so, he arose, took him by the hand, which was followed by every warrior in succession, in token of friendship. They informed him that the Pawnees had been up during the winter into their territory, and had stolen several ponies, and that they were seeking vengeance and reprisals, and exhibited five or six scalps as a proof of their prowess. They made anxious inquiries for a Pawnee whom they had wounded, but who had escaped. This wounded Pawnee, who was badly shot, four bullets passing through the lower part of his body, actually came to Captain Tutt's company two days before, and they rendered him every assistance in their power, but his pursuers were too close to allow him to remain.

He was subsequently driven to seek refuge in the wagon of another emigrant, who concealed him till his enemies passed, although they came up to the very wagon where he lay to make inquiries.

After getting the privilege of cooking their buffalo meat at Captain Tutt's camp fires, and begging a little bread, they peaceably departed. Being too ill to remain long, I returned to my wagon to lay down, and at night we encamped on the bank of the river, about eight miles below Fort Childs, now called Fort Kearny, after a drive of twenty miles.

MAY 23.

On leaving this morning I felt very ill, and finding the symptoms of fever increasing, I called physic back from "the dogs"

C   4 and luxuriated on a large dose of calomel, and when we reached the Fort, was too sick to get up. The Fort was nothing but a cluster of adobe, low, one-story buildings, sufficient for two companies of soldiers, who were stationed there as a check upon the Indians, but preparations were making to erect a horse-power saw mill, as well as to enclose the barracks within a wall. It was situated on the right bank of the river, half a mile from the water, and not upon the island as I had supposed.

A day or two previous to our arrival, an emigrant was tried here for shooting one of his comrades. He was taking his family to California, and when a few miles beyond the fort, a man offered a gross insult to his wife. In a country where there was no law—where redress could not be had by a legal process—he determined to protect his own honor, and raising his rifle, shot the scoundrel down. His companions took him back to the Fort, (with his consent,) where an investigation into the circumstances was made, and he was honorably acquitted. The banks of the Platte are high sand hills, scantily covered with grass, and present many fanciful shaped cones and broken ridges, which I can compare with nothing else in form than huge drifted snow heaps. The valley through which the river flows is flat—four or five miles wide; and the scenery, though pretty, is neither grand nor imposing. There was no wood except on the island, which at this time was difficult of access, and our fuel was chiefly small willows and buffalo excrement— the latter being very plenty. We saw the bones of many buffaloes, but up to this time we saw none alive. Distance eighteen miles.

MAY 24.

The weather was still very cold and uncomfortable. I felt

better, and was able to sit up a little, and hoped soon to be out again. The morning was rainy, but at the hour of starting it held up. The wind blew a gale, and about four o'clock it began to rain again, and we encamped. Our tents were pitched on low ground; deep ditches were dug around, and we thought ourselves secure from the storm. But the rain came constantly in torrents; the spray beat into our tents as it never had done before, so that we had but a poor protection from the wet, while the cold, chilling wind blew a hurricane without, and promised us no very comfortable night. We contrived to get a poor supper with buffalo chips, and at the usual hour stretched ourselves upon our hard beds. I was still weak, and too ill to sit up long at a time, for the fever was still coursing through my veins, and the prospect of speedy recovery, under the present circumstances, was far from encouraging. Near midnight I awoke from a feverish sleep, and although I had my boots on, my feet felt damp. Drawing them up to get them in a dry place, it seemed as if they rested in one still more wet. I awoke Smith, who was sleeping by my side, and told him the water was coming into our bed. " Humph ! " said he, turning over with a yawn, " my feet have been in water half an hour; keep dry if you can." " Well, that is very consolatory," said I; " but the wind has sprung the tent pins, and it will blow down." " N-no—I guess not," was his reply—and soon he began his nasal music again, at the rate of nine knots an hour.

The rain poured, the wind still blew a hurricane, and a corner of the tent was flapping " like mad." It was a worse night than that on which Tam O'Shanter outran the witches, and it did seem as if " Wee Cutty Sark" was cutting higher antics than usual. King Lear, in the height of his madness, would have been troubled to have got his mouth open to vent his spleen on such a night.

To add to the pleasure of the scene, the wind had veered around, and blew directly into the tent through the opening, so that now the rain was driving in upon us. Yet, amid all this uproar without, and the "moving of the waters" within, my messmates continued to sleep, as if they lay on beds of down. At length Brown awoke, and finding his feet in water, sung out,

"Boys—boys; something's wrong!" No reply was made, save the deep breathings of the weary sleepers. "Wake up! It's a fact, boys, there's something wrong. John, Kent, Fred!— don't you hear?" Kent finally got his eyes open, and on starting up, found one corner of the tent flapping in the gale. Several of the pins were out, and the poles leaning on one side most indecorously for a cold-water tent. Kent's cries aroused Fred, who, rubbing his eyes, crawled out of his wet bed to reconnoitre.

"It is a fact," he rolled out with emphasis; "John, Hazel!— why don't you turn out? Brown, Smith—what do you all lay there for? The tent is coming down. Get up, or you'll be drowned."

Thus exorcised, they awoke, and thus a cry was raised: "My boots—where are my boots? Who has got my boots?" But in the Egyptian darkness of the night, and the confusion of our mess, hunting boots was a *bootless* job. Hazel went out barefoot to endeavor to fasten the pins. Morrel stood by with his usual vocabulary of expletives; and Smith still lay in his soaking blankets, laughing with all his might, determined to risk the falling of the tent rather than "bide the pelting of the pitiless storm."

"There goes my hat!" roared Hazel, above the voice of the wind. "Whew! but I'm getting a baptism now."

"Go it while you're young, Hazel," grinned Smith.

"Down with the pins!" shouted Brown; "Don't cut the cords with the axe."

"The ground is too soft to hold the pins," echoed Hazel, as one pin after another came out, after being repeatedly driven, and the flapping of the tent increased. "The only way is to take to the wagons, boys;" and all but Hazel and myself made quick tracks for the friendly shelter of their covers. As for me, I lay half stunned, half crazed by the uproar and my illness, and cared not what became of me. Seeing that I did not stir, Hazel inquired, "Come, are you not going to the wagon?—the rest are all gone."

"No," I replied; "I think I will stay here, I'm well enough off, and feel quite comfortable."

"What! in the rain? The tent is almost down, and will fall very soon—you'll die here."

"I don't care," I responded, impatiently; and at that moment I felt that I did not care."

"Smith!" shouted the honest Norwegian, "is the wagon open? Hold the cover up—Delano is coming;" and suiting the action to the word, he lifted and carried me through the storm, to the wagon. I could not help laughing at his earnestness, and I yielded with a good grace. We went through the deluge to the wagon, and ensconced ourselves on boxes and bales, in the best manner we could with our wet blankets. Towards morning the flood-gates of heaven closed, and the rain ceased, but we were much like the mouse between the cat and the dog; "we could be happy with neither," for it was now very cold. Our teeth chattered as if it had been mid-winter; our limbs shook, and the long, dismal night wore wearily away.

When morning at length dawned, the boys crawled from their sorry nests, unrefreshed, but glad to be released from "durance vile," to stretch their stiffened limbs, and breathe the morning air. Poor Fred's lamentation, though different from Rachel's, was quite as heartfelt. "O my wife! what would she think of rats, could she see me now?—drowned rats, I mean. I am half dead!—I've seen enough of the world. California can't afford a better burrying place. Here you can sink deep enough without digging! Halloo! Delano—what's your opinion?"

"Humph!" I grunted, from my locomotive roost,—"*non gustibus disputandum.*"

CHAPTER IV.

A CHANGE FOR THE BETTER — ISLANDS IN THE PLATTE — INDIAN ROBBERY — SOUTH BEND COMPANY — TERRIBLE STORM AND GREAT LOSS OF CATTLE — FORKS OF THE PLATTE — BUFFALO — MEETING FRIENDS — BUFFALO MEAT — FORDING THE RIVER — MEN LOST — WASHING DAY — SERIOUS RESULTS OF A JOKE — INDIAN VILLAGE AND BURYING GROUND — TINDALL'S GRAVE — SMITH CREEK — COURT-HOUSE ROCK — CHIMNEY ROCK — THE "POST OFFICE" — UNEXPECTED MEETING — EMIGRANT TRAINS — A PICTURESQUE VALLEY — SCOTT'S BLUFFS.

MAY 25.

On crawling out from our sorry nests, we found a realizing sympathy from our wandering countrymen composing our train. There was scarcely a tent but what deviated from its upright character, and nearly the whole of our party had been compelled to seek refuge in the wagons.

The day opened cold, raw and windy, and the drive was extremely disagreeable. I was shut up in my wagon, suffering intensely from pain, thirst, and feverish excitement, and at night I had recourse to my usual comforters, blue-pill and oil. At evening the wind went down, and the sun showed his glorious face once more, like an old but long absent friend, above the blanket-clouds, and promised a fair day on the morrow. Distance, fourteen miles.

MAY 26.

The morrow came, and although there was a heavy frost, the

sun came out according to promise. The day, for a wonder, was calm, and the genial atmosphere, together with the effect of the apothecary shop in my bowels, made me feel that disease was subdued.

During the day we passed a poor fellow who had fallen from his wagon, which passed over him, breaking his leg in two places. Doctor Gillespie, of Captain Tutt's company, kindly set it, and the unfortunate man once more turned his face homeward—a long and dubious journey for one in his condition. Distance, sixteen miles.

MAY 27.

The day, like the one previous, was unexpectedly calm and pleasant—being the only two days of the kind in succession which we had had since leaving the Missouri. There were many wood covered islands in the Platte, and occasionally a few trees grew on the margin of the river. The banks, which bounded the bottom, were high and broken, and presented many fanciful shapes of cones and nebulæ. During the day, two men belonging to one of the accompanying trains, were out hunting, four or five miles from the river, and being a little separated, one of them encountered a band of Pawnee Indians, who advanced in a friendly manner, and after shaking hands with him, gave him to understand that he had no particular use for his arms and accoutrements on their hunting ground, and that they would take charge of them until he passed that way again. In short, they robbed him of everything, and he was forced to return to his wagon perfectly naked. His companion, who witnessed the interesting ceremony from behind a knoll, took to his heels, and saved his own clothes. Our own hunters came in without meeting either good or bad luck, having killed nothing, and were enabled to keep their shirts on their backs—frequently two weeks at a time, without washing. Distance, eighteen miles.

MAY 28.

The grass which we found last night was poor, and our cattle refused to drink the muddy water of the river ; in consequence of which they looked thin and hollow. We therefore encamped early, where there was good forage, and they made up amply what they had lost. My own health improved rapidly, and I began to feel like myself, though weak.

We had traveled for several days near the South Bend company, which gave me the pleasure of being with old acquaintances, with whom we frequently interchanged friendly greetings. Distance, about eighteen miles.

MAY 29.

We made only a short drive, and in order to recruit our cattle, we encamped about a mile and a half below the forks of the Platte, where the concomitants of a good camp were abundant. The scenery along the river varied but little, maintaining a general character of sameness. During the night, a terrible storm arose—much worse than any we had previously experienced. Although our tent did not blow down, being pitched on firm ground, the water beat in, and sleep was impossible. Distance, six miles.

MAY 30.

Morning dawned gloomily enough. It seemed as if a water spout was discharging its floods upon us. Our rain storms at home were only gentle showers compared with this. The wind blew a hurricane, and our cattle, when grazing, kept moving off,

C*

apparently in hopes of getting away from the storm, and it was absolutely necessary to keep driving them back almost constantly to prevent them from straying off. Finding it impossible to keep them together, and as they could not eat, from the fury of the storm, we drove them in, where they stood all day under the lee of the wagons, tied to the wheels,—this being the only way that we could keep them. In this dreadful storm hundreds of cattle were lost, and some trains were almost ruined; some lost half, while others had only one or two yoke left; and for several days after, we met many persons who were searching for their cattle, unable to proceed. No situation can be more deplorable than that of being left upon a broad prairie, hundreds of miles from aid, without the means of locomotion. We found families, with women and helpless children, in this sad condition, and yet we were without means to give them relief. We had only saved our own cattle by tying them up, for it was impossible for oxen to stand still under such peltings. Many were found twenty-five or thirty miles off the road, while others were lost entirely, having strayed beyond the reach of the owners, or were stolen by the Indians. It took us till nearly noon to cook our breakfasts. Our stoves were put into our tents, and the covers of boxes, or stray pieces of wood in the wagons, were used to start a fire, and then buffalo chips were heaped upon the stoves until they got dry enough to burn, and in this way we contrived to do our cooking. The comforts of home crowded on our memories, and many a sigh was given for those we had left behind. In addition to our other miseries, some of the cattle became foot-sore and lame. In some trains they had to be left, being too lame to proceed; while in others, rough boots were made, and fastened over the foot in such a way as to keep the dirt and sand from the foot, which was smeared with tar and grease. McClasky, McNeil, and Rood, in our train, had each of them one that was lame, but they contrived to get them along, by taking them out of the yoke, and wrapping up their feet. It continued to rain without cessation through the day, and we turned into our damp beds with a feeling of cheerlessness, though not dispirited. Distance, nothing.

MAY 31.

A cold wind blew this morning, the sky was overcast with clouds, and the gloom and air of November, rather than the genial warmth of spring, hung over us. We left our encampment about eight o'clock, and drove slowly all day. We constantly met groups of men, inquiring for lost cattle, and our own train was carefully scanned, to see if some missing ox had not been replaced by theirs. Among the unfortunate ones, one company, having an hundred head, lost seventy; another, out of eighteen, lost nine; and we passed two wagons with families, who had only three oxen tied to the wheels. It was a kind of *terra firma* shipwreck, with the lamentable fact, that the numerous craft sailing by were unable to afford the sufferers any relief. We passed the forks of the Platte, and continued our route up the south branch about ten miles to a ford, but hearing that there was a better ford still farther up, we continued on, leaving the South Bend company, who concluded to cross here, which they did without difficulty.

We saw buffaloes for the first time in considerable numbers, on the opposite side of the fork, and were much amused in seeing the emigrants, who had crossed, dashing in upon them in gallant style. One was shot in our sight. Not only was the chase exciting, but witnessing it was extremely so; and as the herd dashed off, we could scarcely repress a desire to be after them; but this was impossible, for a broad and dangerous stream was between us.

I had now gained strength enough to walk a little, and being half a mile in advance of my train, I was overtaken by a mule wagon at the top of a hill, which contained Messrs. G. C. Mer rifield, and A. M. Wing—old friends from Indiana—and whom I had not seen for some months. Meeting thus under peculiar circumstances, afforded us much pleasure, and getting into their wagon, we passed an hour or two in that agreeable manner, which none but travelers in a wild region, far from home and friends, can appreciate.

We were pained to see that many cattle were becoming lame, and that many showed evidences of being hard driven. In the great desire to get ahead, and the foolish rivalry of passing other trains, no rest was given to the cattle. Men placed themselves in jeopardy of becoming helpless, by imprudence, even at this early stage of the journey, where no human aid could be rendered; and were I to make the trip again, I would make it a point to stop every seventh day, where it was practicable, if from no scruples of conscience, certainly from dictates of humanity; and I do not hesitate to declare, that by doing so there would be a saving of time in the end, for both man and beast would more than make up the time so lost, by renewed vigor from rest. We daily saw many cattle giving out from want of rest, and imprudence in driving them beyond their strength, and when they reached the barren plains beyond the Rocky Mountains, many were unable to drag the wagons, even after the loads had been reduced, by throwing away all but barely enough provisions to sustain life to the end of the journey. Distance, fourteen miles.

JUNE 1.

We met many men during the day who were searching for cattle lost during the great storm, and who were helpless until they were recovered. We now had an abundance of buffalo meat, which, after being so long confined to salt provisions, was a luxury. The meat is coarser grained than that of domestic beef, and not so well flavored, but we devoured it with avidity, and many paid the forfeit of their imprudence by a diarrhœa which followed. Towards night we reached the ford, and encamped, after a drive of about fifteen miles.

JUNE 2.

The river is about half a mile wide, with a brisk current, and an uneven bottom of quicksand. The only way a passage could be made was to double teams, and then keep in constant motion, for on stopping the wagon would sink in the sand, and in time entirely disappear. One wagon, to which was hitched unruly or frightened cattle, began to sink, and was only drawn out by hastily hitching on an additional force of well-trained cattle. The deepest place which we found, by taking the course marked out by riding a horse in, only reached to our wagon beds, and by noon we had all crossed without accident. The north bank of the South Fork, which bounded the bottom, perhaps half a mile wide, was high and broken land, and our course was northerly, to the North Fork of the Platte, about eight miles distant. On passing to the ridge between the two forks, we found a broken country, without a tree or shrub, as far as the eye could reach, and there was nothing inviting in its appearance.

On crossing the South Fork, we fell in company with a young man from Janesville, Wisconsin, whose company had

lost thirty head of cattle in the great storm.   He was fortunate
enough to find them all about twenty-five miles south of the
road.   During his search he met a man mounted on a fine
horse, who had been looking for lost cattle, but being unsuccessful, was then on his return to his camp, as he supposed.
The young man, (Mr. Jenks,) told him that he was pursuing an
opposite direction to the road, and endeavored to set him right,
but he as confidently asserted that he was right, and that Jenks
was wrong.   After arguing the point in vain with each other,
they parted, and Jenks reached the road at night, while the unfortunate horseman was never heard of afterwards, having probably either starved to death, or been killed by the Indians.
From the same cause, a man and boy belonging to a Missouri
train got lost.   The boy, after wandering three days without
food, reached the road in a famished state, but the man was
never heard of, and probably perished.

We heard of numerous similar instances, and many an anxious
heart at home will have occasion to remember and deplore the
great storm on the Platte.   Buffaloes were very numerous, and
the novelty of seeing them began to wear off.   Towards night
we descended to the bottom land of the North Platte, where
we found luxuriant grass, and fine ponds of water, with dry
willows for fuel, and we resolved to lay over one day to rest,
after a drive of eight miles.

JUNE 3.

We took advantage of our leisure in airing our clothes and
provisions, and in making all necessary repairs.   Another important matter occupied the consideration, not only of our own
train, but of many companies encamped near us.   Loading our
wagons too heavily with cumbrous and weighty articles, and

with unnecessary supplies of provisions, had been a general fault, and the cattle began to exhibit signs of fatigue. We resolved, therefore, to part with everything which was not absolutely necessary, and to shorten the dimension of our wagons so that they would run easier. To sell superfluous articles was quite impossible, though I was fortunate enough to find a market for fifty pounds of coffee. Every emigrant was abundantly supplied, and we were compelled to throw away a quantity of iron, steel, trunks, valises, old clothes, and boots, of little value; and I may observe here that we subsequently found the road lined with cast-off articles, piles of bacon, flour, wagons, groceries, clothing, and various other articles, which had been left, and the waste and destruction of property was enormous. In this the selfish nature of man was plainly exhibited. In many instances the property thus left was rendered useless. We afterwards found sugar on which turpentine had been poured, flour in which salt and dirt had been thrown, and wagons broken to pieces, or partially burned, clothes torn to pieces, so that they could not be worn, and a wanton waste made of valuable property, simply because the owners could not use it themselves, and were determined that nobody else should. There were occasionally honorable exceptions. The wagons were left unharmed by the road side; the bacon, flour, and sugar were nicely heaped up, with a card, directed to any one who stood in need, to use freely in welcome. On leaving home, we were under the impression that corn meal would not keep on the plains without first being kiln-dried; that butter-crackers and flour would not keep well, and that our bread-stuffs must necessarily be in the shape of hard bread. This we found was a false impression, and that a little care in airing occasionally would preserve meal, flour, hams, and indeed anything, as well as in a store room at home. This overhauling was necessary only in the humid atmosphere of the Platte, and in crossing the South Pass of the Rocky Mountains. Even this care was not absolutely required,—and, under this mistaken impression, we had deprived ourselves of many comforts. Instead of suffering on the plains, the trip can be made, by taking the proper precautions, with comparative comfort and safety.

Up to this time I had had a sufficient supply of clean linen; but rather than have dirty clothes accumulate, I resolved to try my hand at washing. A number of us took our dirty shirts, and going to a pond near by, commenced our laundry manipulations, for the first time in our lives. It was no trouble to throw our clothes into the pond, and rubbing in soap was not much; but when it came to standing bent over half a day, rubbing the clothes in our hands, trying to get out the stains— heigho! "a change came o'er the spirit of our dreams," and we thought of our wives and sweet-hearts at home, and wondered that we were ever dissatisfied with their impatience on a washing day. Had they been present, we should heartily have asked their pardon, and allowed them to scold to their heart's content. I verily believe our clothes looked worse for the washing than they did before we began, and my poor knuckles—oh! they were sore for a month afterwards.

Our estimates were, that sixteen hundred pounds weight on a light wagon, was enough for three yoke of strong cattle to start with from home, and I became afterwards convinced that it was full weight enough.

At night two other trains from Illinois encamped near us, in one of which I recognized Mr. Lindley and family, from La Salle, with whom I had expected to travel before leaving home, but had been prevented by unforseen circumstances. We spent an agreeable hour together, when I returned to my camp and turned in. Distance, nothing.

JUNE 4.

Our cattle felt the benefit of rest, the day was pleasant, and we set out early, in good spirits. Our road lay along the bottom of the North Platte, with precipitous hills of oolite rock on our left, while the opposite bank corresponded with that on our side, without a tree or shrub to hide the nakedness of the ground, or relieve the eye from its barrenness. Two hours traveling brought us to a few stunted ash and cedar trees, with a small cluster of bushes struggling to grow from the rocks.

Towards noon I called at an encampment of Missourians, who were lying over to rest, and to attend the necessary duty of airing clothes and provisions, where I found several intelligent and accomplished gentlemen. A serious accident had occurred in their camp the previous night. After the guard had been set, a reckless young scamp, fourteen or fifteen years old, was desirous of perpetrating a joke on the sentry. During the middle watch he stole out unperceived, and throwing a white blanket over his head, cautiously approached the guard, who discovered and hailed him repeatedly, but to which he made no reply. The sentinel naturally supposed him, in the darkness of the night, to be an Indian, whose object was plunder, and receiving no answer to his hail, he raised his rifle and discharged it at the intruder, and wounded him severely, though not dangerously, as it happened, in the arm and side. This satisfied the young gentleman that he was walking on dangerous ground, and roaring lustily for aid, was borne to the camp, convinced that such practical jokes were attended with more danger than fun.

About noon we were obliged for the first time to leave the

level bottom of the river, as a high bluff extended its point to the water, and compelled us to make a detour of three or four miles, to pass across it. The wind blew severely, and on reaching the top of the hill a multitude of hats were flying faster than the legs of their owners, and the pastime of running after them was not much enjoyed by the tired pedestrians. We descended into a deep and narrow ravine, named Ash Hollow, so called from being covered with a stunted growth of ash trees. The rocks on each side were high and perpendicular, with a sandy bottom, through which a little brooklet meandered, made from springs—the first that we had met with since reaching the Platte, and which entered the river below the ravine perhaps half a mile. Sheltered from the wind by the high banks, the ravine was warmed by the sun, and the cool shade of the trees, as well as the clear water, was delightfully refreshing. On coming to the river bottom at the mouth of the ravine, we discovered a small village of Sioux Indians. Their lodges were made of tanned buffalo skins, of conical form, well calculated to resist the action of the weather. Both men and women were better formed than any Indians I had ever seen. The men were tall, and graceful in their movements, and some of the squaws were quite pretty, and dressed in tanned buffalo skins, highly ornamented with beads, while many of the men wore barely a blanket around their waists, and one or two of them were quite naked. On our approach, one of the Indians, who was armed with an old sword, made us some kind of a speech, and invited us into a lodge, where he motioned us to be seated. Several squaws were engaged in making moccasins, for which they found ready purchasers among the emigrants. Almost the first request made to us was for whiskey, for which I verily believe they would have sold their children—showing conclusively that temperance societies were not yet well organized on the Platte. Of course we had no fire-water for them, and we left them lamentably sober, and encamped about a mile above them, where several came out to beg bread, whiskey, and shirts.

During the evening two young men came to our camp on mules, who had turned their faces homeward without supplies. They said that they were from Indianapolis, Indiana; that their mules had given out, and that they had determined to return, depending on the charity of the emigrants for their subsistence, which no doubt was fully and freely accorded to them. We availed ourselves of the opportunity to send letters to our friends, to be mailed at St. Joseph; but these were never received. If they were mailed they were lost by the burning of the mail steamer at St. Louis, as we learned a year afterwards; and it was many months before any intelligence of us reached home. Distance, fifteen miles.

JUNE 5.

The day was excessively warm, the road sandy, and the cattle labored hard. The bluff began to assume a more interesting appearance. The high and precipitous oolite rocks, based upon clay, which appeared to be hardening into rock, with deep ravines often breaking the regularity of the layers, apparently water-worn, which to one accustomed to mountains and high broken hills, might not be particularly interesting, but to those who are used only to the level prairies and plains of the Western States, were looked upon with curiosity and interest. I now for the first time, was able to walk all day, but at night I found myself completely exhausted, proving that my full strength had not returned. Distance, twelve miles.

JUNE 6.

The grass where we encamped the preceding night was poor, and our cattle looked hollow, but the day was cool, and a shower during the night had packed the sand, so that the traveling was much easier than it had been the day before. About ten o'clock we came to good grass, when we unyoked the cattle and allowed them to graze. During the afternoon we passed a Sioux burying ground, if I may be allowed to use an Irishism. In a hackberry tree, elevated about twenty feet from the ground, a kind of rack was made of broken tent poles, and the body, (for there was but one,) was placed upon it, wrapped in his blanket, and a tanned buffalo skin, with his tin cup, moccasins, and various things which he had used in life, were placed upon his body, for his use in the land of spirits. We gazed upon these remains of humanity, without disturbing any of the arrangements; but I afterwards learned that some Goths from Missouri wantonly cut the limbs away, and let the body fall, which no doubt produced the same impression upon the Indians that it would have done on themselves, had some traveler dug up the body of one of their own friends, and left it exposed to the maw of wolves and birds of prey.

A short distance from our place of encampment, I observed a newly made grave, upon a green knoll, and in examining the wooden head board, I found it to be the last resting place of George W. Tindal, a young man from Tecumseh, Michigan, who had died of consumption. I became acquainted with him on our passage from St. Louis to St. Joseph, and was much pleased with his intelligence and amiable manners. Poor fellow, it was hard to die so far from home, and friends; and a sick bed on the plains is a desolate place, even when every attention is bestowed that the slender means of travelers can afford.

Our hunters were very successful, and our camp was abundantly supplied with fresh meat, though it produced diarrhœa in many instances. Distance, fifteen miles.

JUNE 7.

During this as well as the previous day, we passed many low places, which appeared to be saturated with alkaline particles, and in holes and wells dug by emigrants the water resembled in color and taste the lye of ashes, but was totally unfit for use, and our cattle would not drink it. As there had been several showers previous to our arrival, it was probably much weaker than it otherwise would have been. The rain thus favored us by reducing the strength of the alkali in the soil, and preventing its deleterious effect upon the feet of the cattle, which are very liable to become foot-sore in traveling here. We approached Court-house Rock during the day, over a broad bottom perhaps fifteen miles wide, crossing in the meantime Smith's Creek, the most beautiful stream which we had found since leaving the Missouri. It flowed from the hills over a clear sandy bed, and the water was cool and delicious to our parched mouths, after drinking so long the water of sloughs, or that of the muddy, insipid Platte.

The atmosphere in this region is of remarkable clearness, for which cause we were unable to estimate distances with any precision. Court-house Rock appeared only about two miles off, when in reality it was ten or twelve. Some of our men set out to walk to it, but as they approached it appeared to recede, and after walking a couple of hours, some returned, while those who finally reached it did not return till nearly nine o'clock at night, having walked steadily for about ten hours. It stood upon a little ridge above the bottom—was of a circular form, with an elevation on the top much like a flattened dome, and at the distance at which we stood, it resembled a huge building. It was really about two hundred feet high, although from the road it appeared only about fifty. Near it, on the east end, was another blunt pointed rock, not quite as high, which was not particularly remarkable, but which is embraced in the same view. Both of these stand isolated on the plain, although a few miles west are bare bluff ridges of the same kind of rock— a soft sand and clay, intermixed with lime, easily cut with a knife—all probably of volcanic origin; and this is the general character of the rock in this region. When within a few miles of Court-house Rock, we came to a ledge called the Post-office, over which we passed. It was full of water-worn fissures, and in one cavity we saw a number of letters deposited, for individuals who were behind, and in the rock was cut in capitals, "Post-office." The usual mode of giving intelligence to friends behind, is to write on a bleached buffalo skull, or shoulder-blade. Thousands of these novel communications lay upon the plain, and we frequently got intelligence in this way from acquaintances who preceded us. When we got beyond the buffalo region, it was customary to write on paper, and slip it into an upright stick, split at the end.

About noon we came in sight of Chimney Rock, looming up in the distance like a lofty tower in some town, and we did not tire in gazing at it. It was about twenty-five miles from us, and continued in sight until we reached it on the following day.

We encamped where there was good grass and water, after a drive of eighteen miles.

JUNE 8.

We traveled all day in sight of Chimney Rock, occasionally

over low wet places, containing alkaline earth in great quantities, and so strong that the ground in some places was whitened with it like a frost. At night we reached a point opposite to, and about three miles from Chimney Rock, where we found the concomitants of a good camp in abundance. The rock much resembled the chimney of a glass-house furnace. A large cone-like base, perhaps an hundred and fifty feet in diameter, occupied two thirds of its height, and from thence the chimney ran up, gradually growing smaller to the top. The height of the whole is said to be two hundred and fifty feet above the level of the river, from which it is between three and four miles distant. It is a great curiosity, and I much regretted that I had not strength enough to visit it. I think it is decaying from the action of the elements, and it is quite likely that the chimney will be broken off in time, leaving nothing but its cone to gratify the curiosity of the future traveler. The hills in the vicinity present a fanciful appearance—sometimes like giant walls, of massive gray rock, and again like antiquated buildings of olden time.

During the day we met many old acquaintances, among whom I was gratified to meet Doctor M. B. Angle, from Michigan. The meeting was as agreeable as unexpected, for neither of us knew that the other was a California adventurer until we met, far from kindred and friends.

It was curious to see the quaint names and devices on some of the wagons: the "Lone Star," would be seen rising over a hill; the "Live Hoosier" rolled along; the "Wild Yankee," the "Rough and Ready," the "Enterprise," the "Dowdle Family," were moving with slow and steady pace, with a "right smart sprinkle" of "Elephants," "Buffaloes," and "Gold Hunters," painted on the canvass of the wagons, together with many other quite amusing devices. Around the camp-fires at night, the sound of a violin, clarionet, banjo, tambourine, or bugle would frequently be heard, merrily chasing off the weariness and toil of the travelers, who sometimes "tripped the light fantastic toe" with as much hilarity and glee, as if they had been in a luxurious ball-room at home. But when morning came, and the day's work commenced, too frequently ill-humor began; and the vilest oaths, the most profane language, and frequent quarrels and feuds, took the place of good humor, which not unfrequently required all the patience that a quiet man is possessed of to endure.

I was much amused at the remark of a young Missourian, with whom I fell in company one day. In speaking of the ill-nature which so frequently presented itself, he replied; " Yes, if a man has a mean streak about him half an inch long, I'll be bound if it wont come out on the plains."

The Dowdle Family were a company of gentlemen from South Bend, Indiana, with whom I was personally acquainted, and we met here for the first time on the plains. Captain Greene and myself went to their encampment, and passed an hour of the evening very agreeably. Distance, twenty miles.

JUNE 9.

The wind blew cold and unpleasant as we left our pretty encampment this morning for Scott's Bluffs, a few miles beyond. The bare hills and water-worn rocks on our left began to assume many fantastic shapes, and after raising a gentle elevation, a most extraordinary sight presented itself to our view. A basin-shaped valley, bounded by high rocky hills, lay before us, perhaps twelve miles in length, by six or eight broad. The perpendicular sides of the mountains presented the appearance of castles, forts, towers, verandas, and chimneys, with a blending of Asiatic and European architecture, and it required an effort to believe that we were not in the vicinity of some ancient and deserted town. It seemed as if the wand of a magician had passed over a city, and like that in the Arabian Nights, had converted all living things into stone. Here you saw the minarets of a castle; there, the loop-holes of bastions of a fort; again, the frescoes of a huge temple; then, the doors, windows, chimneys, and columns of immense buildings appeared in view, with all the soleum grandeur of an ancient yet deserted city, while at other points Chinese temples, dilapidated by time, broken chimney rocks in miniature, made it appear as if by some supernatural cause we had been dropped in the suburbs of a mighty city. For miles around the basin this view extended, and we looked across the barren plain at the display of Almighty power, with wonder and astonishment. These, however, lost their interest, on approaching them, and like the fabled castles of the middle ages, dwindled down to bare, shapeless, water-worn rocks. Yet days might be spent agreeably in examining them, and I regretted that our want of time and my own enfeebled health should prevent my inspecting them more thoroughly. They were composed of volcanic matter, like that of Court-house and Chimney Rocks, marl, sand, clay, and gravel—a kind of volcanic conglomerate, which yielded to the action of the elements, by which they were worn, in the lapse of ages, to their present fantastic forms. Every year, probably, wears them more, and time slowly changes their shapes, and it is not improbable, that at some former period, even Court-house and Chimney Rocks were portions of hills which have decayed. At the western extremity of the basin a violent rain storm overtook us, and we hastily pitched our tents. Near us were a

D

large number of dead cedars, which served for fuel; but it was a matter of inquiry where they came from, for there were no trees of their size in the vicinity, and I could form no other conclusion than that they had been washed there by some mighty flood, which had caused the river to overflow its banks, and which must have inundated the whole valley of the Platte.

The grass and water were poor, the evening was wet, cold, and cheerless, and moodily eating our suppers, we turned into our hard beds in a sorry humor, which the interesting scenery around us could not dispel. Drive, sixteen miles.

JUNE 10.

The morning opened calm, and the bright sun restored our good humor, and we made a long drive over a barren, uninteresting country, having scarcely any grass, and no good water, for the want of which we suffered. Since we crossed Smith's Run, on the 7th, we have had no good water; the little which we found was muddy and full of impurities, and unpleasant to the taste. We encamped at night by the side of a muddy pond hole, and were compelled to drink it, or have none. Distance, twenty miles.

JUNE 11.

The country was still uninteresting, with but little which would conduce to our comfort. A large buffalo bull was feeding about a quarter of a mile from the road as we drove along, when being frightened, strangely enough, he started and ran towards us, passing only a short distance in front of our train; but before the boys could get their rifles from the wagons, he had got out of their reach. A good camp, after a drive of sixteen miles.

CHAPTER V.

LARAMIE PEAK — LARAMIE RIVER — FORT LARAMIE — SOUTH BEND COMPAN-
IONS — WARM SPRINGS — COLD WATER CREEK — DIVISION OF THE COM-
PANY — HORSE CREEK AND RIOLA BONTA — BLACK HILLS — CROW INDIANS
— ROCK RIDGE — A BEAUTIFUL CREEK — ALKALINE DISTRICT — COLONEL
JOSEPH WATKINS — A SUBLIME GOVERNMENT — POISON WATER — DEAD
CATTLE — FERRY OVER THE NORTH PLATTE.

JUNE 12.

WE were now approaching Fort Laramie. The country
became more broken, though by no means difficult, yet we
began to feel wearied with our incessant journeying. There was
a sameness in our daily routine of life, and after being so long
confined to meagre prairie fare, the "flesh pots of Egypt" would
occasionally intrude upon our memories, and a sigh for our
cupboards at home involuntarily burst forth; still, all was resolution, and no one thought of backing out from the undertaking we had commenced. Thus far we had gone without accident, and if our clothes were soiled, and our beards unshaven,
we had the consolation of thinking that no one could boast over
another on account of good looks. About ten o'clock in the
morning we were upon a ridge, when suddenly we got a view
of the snow-capped head of Laramie Peak, fifty or sixty miles
distant, and became aware that we were approaching a spur of
the Rocky Mountains. A drive of seven miles from our encampment brought us to Laramie River, where we found a

multitude of teams, waiting their turn to cross a swift and not safe current. It became necessary to raise our wagon boxes about six inches, in order to prevent the water flowing in and wetting our provisions. We here found Captain Tutt's company and the Dowdle family, who had got ahead of us, waiting their turn to cross. The passage was made in safety, although I lost two pails which were hooked to my wagon. Fort Laramie is simply a trading post, standing about a mile above the ford, and is a square enclosure of adobe walls, one side of which forms the walls of the buildings. The entrance into the court is through a gate of sufficient strength to resist the Indians, but would be of little account if besieged by a regular army. Its neat, white-washed walls presented a welcome sight to us, after being so long from anything like a civilized building, and the motly crowd of emigrants, with their array of wagons, cattle, horses, and mules, gave a pleasant appearance of life and animation.

Around the fort were many wagons, which had been sold or abandoned by emigrants. A strong, heavy wagon could be bought for from five to fifteen dollars. In ordinary seasons the company were able to keep some small supplies for emigrants, but such was the rush now, that scarcely anything could be obtained, even at the most exorbitant prices. Here was a deposit for letters to be sent to the States, and thousands left letters for their friends, to be deposited by a messenger in some post-office beyond the Missouri, on which the writers paid twenty-five cents. Although many of our company placed letters in the keeping of the ostensible agent, not a single letter ever reached its destination. We afterwards found such agencies among the traders on the road, and paid several quarters and halves for their delivery, yet none ever went through, and we were compelled to believe that it was a deliberate fraud, perpetrated on the emigrants. Fort Laramie stands in a valley, on Laramie River, surrounded by high, broken land, and in the distance are seen spurs of the Black Hills, which are offshoots of the Rocky Mountains. A mile below the ford the river empties into the Platte, and at this point the road from Council Bluffs unites with that from St. Joseph and Independence. We made but a short stay at the fort, and drove about a mile, when we overtook the Dowdle and South Bend companies, at their noon halt by the road side, and after weeks of weary traveling, it was extremely pleasant to meet so many old friends and acquaintances, so far from home, in a wild, Indian country. In South Bend they were a well-dressed, clean-shaved and good-looking set of men, with civilized notions of good order and propriety ; but now they belonged to the great unwashed and unshaved family of mankind,who spurned "Day & Martin's blacking," and rose soap, as of no account; while their uncombed locks, their ragged unmentionables, their sun-burnt faces, made them look as if a party of loafers had congregated tagether, to exhibit their contempt of civilized fashions. And, alas! my old, greasy, buckskin coat and *outre* appearance proclaimed that I was an anmial of the same species. Yet, as rough and weather-beaten as we were, our meeting was of the most cordial kind, and hilarity and good feeling animated us all. On joining them, I was offered a piece of pie and cheese. Ye gods! Pie — veritable dried apple pie, which Charlie Lewis made with his own hands! — and although his own mother might have turned up her nose at it, to us, who had literally fed on the " salt " of the pork barrel for weeks, with pilot bread for a dessert, it was a perfect luxury.

My stay with them was brief, for our train went on, and I

was compelled to follow, though with the hope of often traveling in their company. We took a road over a high hill on the west, and about ten miles west of Fort Laramie we saw the first outcrops of sandstone and limestone which we had observed since leaving the Missouri. There we encamped, without water. To get this for cooking purposes, Henderson took a pail and went a mile and a half to a luke-warm spring. Showers were falling on the hills all around us, and the night closed in wet and uncomfortable, and we retired to our couches ill at ease and dispirited. Drive, seventeen miles.

JUNE 13.

The morning dawned somewhat more propitious, and the day was calm and clear. Mr. Fredenburgh had symptoms of ague and fever. A few days before reaching Fort Laramie, Smith had taken cold in one leg during a noon halt, by laying on the damp ground in a hot sun, and it had now become swollen, and so painful that he could not walk, and he suffered much. There was no way left for him but to get into the wagon, thus increasing the weight of the load at least an hundred and fifty pounds. I was now able to walk most of the day, though riding occasionally when the ground was favorable, and I exerted myself to give him a chance to ride — a measure for which I afterwards received little thanks at his hands. About a mile and a half from our encampment — perhaps half a mile north-east from the road — we came to the warm spring, gushing out from a limestone hill, and the most of our thirsty cattle drank the water from buckets, though many would not touch it as it ran aff from the fountain.

Our course lay through a narrow gorge nearly all day. Towards noon we came to a beautiful creek of pure, cold water, and we followed it several miles up a wooded bottom, crossing it twice — our cattle fording it. It was a perfect God-send to them, and it truly found much favor with ourselves. At night, however, we were miles beyond it, and encamped where there was but little wood, and no grass or water, and concluded that here we should be obliged to pass the night, like travelers on a desert, destitute of the choicest blessings of heaven. We had not even a drop of water left in our canteens, to wash down our hard bread. While we were gloomily submitting to our fate, with tongues already parched for want of moisture, a cry was heard on the hill above, " Water, water! Water is found!" Captain Greene had gone over the hill about a quarter of a mile, and made the discovery of a small spring, and the announcement completely changed the complexion of things in our camp. In a moment, stoves were taken down, fires lighted, and men with buckets on their arms were seen going swiftly over the hill; there was a rattling of dishes, and active preparations for cooking going on, and instead of going supperless and *tealess* to bed, our evening meal passed off as usual.

After supper a consultation was held, at which it was resolved to divide our company, on account of procuring forage more readily, for we often found places where a small number of cattle could be supplied, while there was scarcely enough for so many together. This proposition was generally acceded to; however, among so many men it would be strange if any course should not be opposed by some. The wisdom of the measure, however, was afterwards abundantly proved, for we certainly got along with much less difficulty. Captain Greene continued in command of eleven wagons and twenty-nine men, and Mr. Fredenburg was elected to direct the movements of the remaining six wagons and twenty-one men I fell in with the lot of the latter, and though I submitted with the best grace I could, I parted from Captain Greene with regret, for his modest, unassuming manner, and his sterling good sense had made me much attached to him.   John Traverse was selected for our wagon-master, and as everything disorderly was at the moment voted a bore, the rest of us resolved ourselves into a company of orderly privates — a condition which was not fully sustained by all throughout the journey.   Drive, fifteen miles.

JUNE 14 & 15.

But little occurred during these two days which possessed sufficient interest for a journal.   The scenery continued much the same, and on the 14th we encamped on a pleasant bottom, well supplied with the concomitants of a good camp, after a drive of fourteen miles.

On the 15th we crossed Horse Creek and the Riola Bonta— two beautiful streams of clear water, with pebbly bottoms. We had been in advance of the South Bend trains, but they passed us to-day.   We came upon a tract of red ochre earth, which extended several miles, and it was so highly colored that it stained our clothes, while the road in the distance appeared like a stripe of red paint from the high points.

At about eleven o'clock, after a gradual ascent nearly all the morning, we came to the ridge of the Black Hills, which we were to cross, and follow on the west side for several days. From this height we commanded an extensive view of the country, which was much broken and nearly destitute of timber; and the earth, particularly the broken bluffs, were highly discolored with red, ocherish earth.   The Black Hills were a lofty mountain ridge, bristling with gray rock, and sharp, pointed fir trees, and seemed to be a mighty wall, elevated as a

boundary line between hostile countries. In fact, we had passed the Sioux nation, and had entered the territory of the Crow
Indians. Between these two people there is a marked difference, which we observed to increase in the various tribes as we
journeyed on towards the Pacific Ocean. The Sioux are a tall
and handsome race; the Crows are much darker, and not so
tall, nor well formed generally. They seem to be a connecting
link between the Asiatic and the Atlantic tribes.

As we passed over the spur of the Black Hills, and descended to the western side, we came into a kind of valley, through
which flowed a creek of clear water, and a short distance before we reachad it, we came to a plat of white pumice-stone,
which abundantly proved the country to be volcanic, if other
proof was wanting. This pumice was white, and easily broken
by a stone, and one could well fancy it the centre of a huge
caldron, boiling and bubbling, from the effect of vast, internal
fires. Along the margin of the creek stunted trees beautified
the scene, but around it all was barren, bleak and desolate.
It is the opinion of many that this is the crater of an extinguished volcano; but whether it be so or not, (and it is quite different from any I have ever seen,) it is quite probable that at
some former period there has been an irruption of fire.

Smith's leg was very painful, and he suffered extremely from
every jolt of the wagon, and we had but slender means for making him comfortable. Captain Greene's company, (which I
shall designate as the Dayton company,) passed us to-day.
Ours took the name of the Ottawa company. At night we encamped on a grassy plat, surrounded by high hills, but affording no water; nevertheless we had secured enough in our kegs
to answer the purpose of cooking. Drive, sixteen miles.

D*   6

JUNE 16.

How many beautiful creeks, and limpid streams of pure, cold water have I passed at home with scarcely a notice, while the deep shade of some pretty grove has often passed unheeded. How men change with circumstances! In passing through this desert country, over the barren hills, a clear, running stream is hailed with delight, and long remembered for the relief it gives the thirsty traveler; while a small cluster of stunted ash and willow bushes, charily scattered about on the banks of a brook, is a perfect oasis, for its cooling shade in the glaring, summer sun. We found one such during the sultry day, and it made an impression on our memories never to be forgotten. Our road was not as hilly as that of yesterday, but the scenery of the Black Hills, at whose base we were traveling, was peculiar and romantic. A high, narrow, rocky ridge was on our left, many hundred feet high, which stood like some nondescript monster, bristling at our approach; while peculiar lesser hills in various forms, attested the force of volcanic action. Near our camp a perfect cone of fine-grained sandstone had been thrown up sixty or eighty feet high, which almost looked as if it had been formed by the hand of man, so regular and perfect was its shape. The stone was of a beautiful kind — some of it much like the Missouri oil stone, and our men picked up some fine pocket whet-stones, which gave a delicate edge to their knives. We encamped near this singular cone, the soil around being highly colored with ochre, but affording little grass and poor water. It became necessary to lay over a day, to give our weary cattle rest, and indeed we needed it for ourselves; and as we were now but about six miles from the North Platte, we felt sure that upon its level bottoms we should find plenty of grass and wood, while its turbid stream would furnish us with good water. We determined, therefore, to lay up on reaching the river, and retired with this pleasing anticipation in view. Drive, sixteen miles.

JUNE 17.

"*We know not what a day may bring forth.*" We had been toiling five days, over rugged roads, scantily supplied with grass and good water, so essential to our comfort, yet feeling a certainty that on reaching the Platte these would be abundantly supplied. We accordingly took an early start, so that we could reach the destined point in good season, to lay by and rest. The day was sultry; yet, weary as we were, we drove on with spirit, passing Fourche Boise, a beautiful creek, where we refreshed our parched mouths, and then hurried on over the hills to the valley of the Platte, some two or three miles beyond. On descending the hill to the bottom, instead of the good grass and promised rest, we found a barren soil that bore only weeds, which our cattle could not eat, and a sandy road which doomed us to another day of toil and disappointment. There was no help for it, and we were compelled to go on all day, with the naked Black Hills peering down upon us, like goblins, laughing at our way-worn wretchedness, and apparently deriding our search for gold, in the language of Macbeth's witches:

> "Double, double, toil and trouble,
> Fire burn and caldron bubble."

Pshaw! If our caldron is full we'll upset it, and begin anew: so drive on, Hazel. Ho! for California.

We came to another alkaline district on reaching the bottoms of the Platte, much stronger and in greater quantities than we had previously found. The soil from the bluffs to the river was filled with this efflorescence, and the whole country was barren and worthless for agricultural purposes.

It is difficult to judge of the character of men on the road by external appearances. A Mexican hat, a beard of twenty days' growth, an outer covering soiled with dirt and dust, a shirt which may have seen water in its youth, will disguise any one so that he may look like a ferocious brigand, while at the same time his heart may be overflowing with the "milk of human kindness." During my morning walk, before reaching the Platte, I overtook an elderly man, who, judging from his appearance, had seen some life on the plains, and whose outward habiliments were more likely to proclaim him a well-digger than a gentleman and a scholar. With the ease with which travelers on the plains become acquainted, we commenced conversation with little ceremony, and instead of his being a plain country pumpkin that I had at first set him down for, I found him to be a scientific man, a gentleman of education and research, and assuredly a most agreeable traveling companion, despite his California costume. Colonel Joseph S. Watkins, now from Missouri, but lately from Memphis, Tennessee, had been a large contractor in the Navy Yard at Norfolk, Virginia, and previous to removal to Tennessee, had been a member of the Virginia Legislature for twenty-one years, and at one period of his public career had wielded a great influence in the politics of his native State. He had been actively engaged in business during an eventful life, and his connection with some of the most distinguished men of our country, gave him a fund of anecdote; and I scarcely knew which most to admire, his decided talents, or his prominent philanthropic goodness of heart, which he exhibited throughout our conversation. He gave me an amusing account of his setting out from Missouri, with a company from Tennessee. They were seventy strong, having a republican and military form of government, a constitution and by-laws, a president and vice-president, a legislature, three judges, and court of appeals, nine sergeants, as well as other officers, who, by their laws, were to be exempted from the performance of camp duty by virtue of their dignified stations — leaving it for the plebeians and common soldiers to do the drudgery of camp duty, and of standing guard at night. All this read very well on paper, and quite to the satisfaction of those who were to be exempt from labor, but reduced to practice, it was not strange that it produced murmuring, which ripened into actual rebellion. Thinking it smacked too much of favoritism and aristocracy, the Colonel petitioned the legislature for an amendment of the constitution, which, after much discussion, was decided to be out of order, as it was not presented in due form by an honorable member of that august body; and no member was found willing to present a petition which compromised his own privilege. This led to an open rupture, and the Colonel withdrew, after holding up the folly of their course to view, followed by thirteen wagons, and which finally ended in the dissolution of the government of the traveling republic, whose legitimate business it was to guard against the thieving Indians. Thus this sublime government fell to pieces by the weight of its own machinery and exclusive privileges. I laughed till my eyes run over at the Colonel's ludicrous description.

We learned that there was a ferry across the Platte about twelve miles above our place of encampment, which we had to cross, and that there were hundreds of teams waiting their turns, and that several days must elapse before ours would come. In addition to this agreeable news, we were told that the grass in that vicinity was exhausted, and that many cattle were dying for want of food.

A hard drive during the day, over a sandy road, brought us to a point where there was but little grass ; and much fatigued, we encamped, near nightfall, after a drive of eighteen miles.

JUNE 18.

There were no fords on the North Platte, and crossing was effected by means of ferries of a somewhat primitive character, and it was desirable to ascertain something relative to the means and chances for getting to the opposite bank. It was decided, by a consultation the previous evening, that Mr. Fredenburg and myself should ride on this morning, and find out how the transit was to be made.

Accordingly, after hastily swallowing a cup of coffee, Mr. Fedenburg on old Shab, and I on McNeil's mule — a second edition of a double-geared saw-mill — set out about sunrise for the ferry, about twelve miles higher up. The road resembled that of the previous day, except it was rather more broken, and the valley of the North Platte became more undulating. A few miles from our encampment, on descending a hill to some low meadow-land, near the margin of the river, we observed a notice posted up on a board by the road side, which read as follows : "Look at this — look at this ! The water here is poison, and we have lost six of our cattle. Do not let your cattle drink on this bottom." The water was so abundantly charged with carbonate of soda, that cattle soon died in consequence of drinking it. I may as well observe here, that from this time until we left the Humboldt, or Mary's River, many weeks afterwards, we were obliged to use great precaution in allowing the cattle to drink; and never, before we had ascertained the character of the water. Many times we had to drive long distances to find good water, and frequently to guard our cattle at night to keep them from drinking. It was almost certain death to them, unless a remedy was immediately applied. This was either vinegar, or bacon, or both, forced down their throats, which seemed to neutralize the alkali in their stomachs. Saliva would flow freely from their mouths; they soon began to swell, and grow weak and trembling, and would fall to the ground, and in a few moments expire. Nothing but the utmost vigilance saved our cattle; for, after being driven all day, in a hot sun, it was almost impossible to keep them from this deleterious water, on being turned loose at night. We often found good and poor water near together, and it was to direct them to the pure water that demanded our care. The grass which grew on the alkaline soil could readily be distinguished by its lighter green color; but this did not appear to injure them.

Within about three miles of the ferry, we observed a company of men building a raft on the river bank, half a mile from the road; and, riding down, we ascertained that we could have the use of it after they had ferried their own train, with two or three others. This might detain us a day, and it was judged expedient for me to ride on to the ferry, to see what chance there was there of gaining time; and I therefore rode forward, while Mr. Fredenburg remained, to stop our train when it should come, until I reported. On arriving at the ferry I found about two hundred and fifty wagons, among which were Captain Tutt's and the Dowdle family, from South Bend, waiting their turn to cross, while the number was augmenting by constant arrivals every moment. About four miles still farther up was another ferry, established by the Mormons. I learned that there was quite as many, perhaps more emigrants, to cross at that point than here, so that our turn would not come for several days; and I judged that our quickest way would be to try the raft below. I found that at least forty head of cattle were lying dead near the ferry, from the effects of drinking alkaline water and want of food, the grass being nearly consumed, as had been reported.

The mode of ferrying was by lashing three small canoes together, which were sufficiently buoyant to sustain the weight of an empty wagon. A rope long enough to reach across the river was fastened to each end, and a number of men on each side pulled it back and forth, the strong current making it slow and laborious work. Each company furnished its own ropes, and performed all the labor, and for the use of the canoes paid five dollars each wagon. The proprietor of the ferry was from New Orleans, and a melancholy incident will appear in its proper place with regard to him, which occurred soon after we crossed the river. When he reached this point, thinking it a speculation, he resolved to stop and establish a ferry for a time — sending his family on, with the intention of overtaking them. He was coining money in the operation. While I was there, a man was drowned by falling out of the canoe, being swept down by the swift current. The cattle, horses, and mules, were swum over to the opposite bank, and very few accidents occurred to them, though occasionally one was drowned by being carried to where the bank was too steep to get out.

I rode back to the raft, and found our train just arrived, and all hands making preparations for crossing. A rope was attached to each end of the raft, in the same manner as to the canoes, and it was found capable of sustaining the weight of a loaded wagon, while thirty or forty men on each side pulled it back and forth quite expeditiously, and with perfect safety. The work went briskly on for awhile. By some mismanagement, however, one of the ropes was broken before our turn came, after crossing thirteen wagons ; and all attempts to get the line across again that night, proved abortive. Our train was thus compelled to remain on the south bank till morning. This detention was scarcely a loss; for notwithstanding the labor of ferrying was severe to us, our cattle had the benefit of rest, although the grass was poor and scanty. Distance nine miles.

CHAPTER VI.

OVER THE NORTH PLATTE — WAGON ON THE CURRENT — MULE TRAINS — SAND-STONE CONE — ANTELOPES AND WOLVES — DRY POND — SALERATUS — POISON WATER — ENCAMPMENT — IMMENSE NUMBER OF EMIGRANTS — THE RED BUTTES — SAND ROCK — WILLOW SPRING — TIMELY HOSPITAL-ITY — INDEPENDENCE ROCK — SWEET WATER RIVER — INTENSE HEAT — PERPENDICULAR ROCK — RIVER THROUGH THE CHASM — DEVIL'S GATE — SHOOTING A DESPERADO — MYRIADS OF CRICKETS.

JUNE 19.

There were many trains congregated here, and the number increased hourly — it having been understood that means of crossing existed, poor as it was. As there was but one raft, and the line was not yet replaced, considerable delay was occasioned. Many men showed much hardihood in swimming the strong current, in their endeavors to carry the line across; and it appeared that the success of the previous day was more the effect of good luck in this respect than a want of energy. All trials this morning were abortive, when Brown, of our mess, mounted a strong horse, and at length succeeded by great effort in carrying the rope to the opposite shore, and by noon it was again ready. It was stretched to an island, from which to the main shore was a ford that could be passed without much difficulty. The crossing proceeded well; but a little after noon the wind blew a gale, and the wagon covers acted as sails.

The raft being confined by the rope, frequently dipped so much that the wagons were in danger of sliding off into the stream. Seeing this, I removed the cover from my wagon, as did many others, and they were ferried over in perfect safety. One man, from New Jersey, neglected this, in spite of the remonstrances of his friends, and when in the middle of the river, the wind against his wagon cover acted like a lever, raising one side of the raft till the wagon slid off into the water. It floated down about half a mile, when a sharp turn in the river brought it to the bank. Two wheels were secured, out of which he rigged a cart, and saved a portion of his provisions — though in a damaged state, not utterly ruined. He had to deplore his carelessness, without much sympathy from those around.

The supreme selfishness of men was exhibited in a palpable manner here. Our men worked very hard yesterday, in helping two mule trains across the river, on their assurance that they would reciprocate this morning, by assisting us. No sooner were they across, than like the lying fox in the fable — who, at the bottom of the well, persuaded the foolish goat to come down, that he might climb out on his horns — they hitched up their teams and drove off, leaving us chagrinned at their faithlessness, and vexed at our credulity. Instead of following their example, our men toiled on to aid those who assisted us, and it was not till night-fall that we all met on the main shore, where our tents were pitched. Our cattle swam across safely to the island, and on the main shore we found a plat of grass — better than we had seen for many days.

Another company, who had been unable to cross, got their cattle over, and among them, two fine cows, which they desired to have milked; when our wagon master, John Traverse, volunteered to perform the agreeable duty. Stripping off his clothes, he prepared to wade to the island, where the cows were feeding, observing, "We'll go it to-night, boys! Let us have a rousing dish of mush and milk, and a feast fit for the gods once in our lives." Our men had not yet all come in, and we determined to give them an agreeable surprise. While Traverse was gone, I put a large kettle of water over the fire, and made mush enough for half of the company. There was plenty of dry wood, and as the evening was chilly, we built a roaring fire, and when the boys came in wet and hungry, we sat down with tin cups, pail covers, basins, and everything that would hold milk; and a more luscious feast I never enjoyed. The pail was full of milk — the kettle full of mush — the boys full of fun, notwithstanding their hard labor — and with full stomachs, we closed the labors of the day.

All around, the country bore evidences of volcanic action — Trap rock, in the dark mountain which was frowning over us on the south; cones of burnt sand-stone, scattered about — some as they appeared to have been originally formed, others worn into fantastic shapes by rain and the action of the elements — and knolls covered with black, burnt gravel. There were several immense cones, which appeared as if their tops had been smoothly and evenly cut off, or had been built as watch-towers by ante-diluvian giants; while from the Black Hills to the skirt of the River bottom, were two ridges, which resemble immense even embankments, for railroads or canals, so perfect were they in form. The soil was barren, with scarcely any grass. The vegetation was wild sage bushes and prickly pear — the latter inconvenient on account of its thorns, for man or beast. The sage is a scraggy shrub, generally from two to four feet high, with a stem from one to three or four inches in diameter, though in a few instances I have seen it in particular situations, ten feet high, with a trunk twelve inches in diameter; though this is unusual. It has a leaf which resembles in smell and taste that of the plant cultivated in our gardens, but is much stronger and more bitter. It grows in barren, sandy ground, and burns freely, and for many hundred miles, is almost the only fuel which the traveler finds. Without it he would be compelled to dispense with fire on the vast wastes beyond the western prairies, and on the sand plains beyond the Platte. Distance, one mile.

JUNE 20.

The grass had been excellent, and our cattle had enjoyed the benefit of rest, although we had been hard at work. They traveled finely this morning. Our road lay along the bottom for four miles, when we were compelled to diverge to the right on account of a mountain, which approached near the river a little beyond the ferry above us. While the train kept the road in the valley, I went out to the hills, and kept along in a line parallel to the road. I found deep chasms of vitrified rock, and it was often laborious traveling. I found little to repay me for my toil, except frightening a herd of antelopes, and putting a pack of wolves to flight. A short distance before I came to the road, I discovered a plat, or dry pond, white with an incrustation of carbonate of soda, or saleratus, several inches thick. It was several acres in extent, and probably a thousand wagon loads could have been gathered. We frequently used it in making bread, and it answered quite as well as that which had been manufactured and brought with us; indeed, it seemed to be quite as fine. The utmost vigilance was required to keep our cattle from it, whenever we halted for the purpose of letting them graze. The whole of this sandy region seemed to be filled with it. It exudes from the hill sides and the bank of the river; and the water along the margin of the river in places tastes of it. Good water was scarce, and we found it only at intervals in springs, at the distance of eight or ten miles. Leaving the river by ascending a long hill, we found the country barren and worthless; even the wild sage was knarled and scrubby, and could scarcely gain a foothold.

The Black Hills were still in view on the south, occasionally showing white spots of snow in hollows, and sparsely covered with pines. Diverging from the river to cross the hill, it was a late noon halt before we again reached it, after a fatiguing drive of perhaps eight miles, through deep sand, under a burning sun. About four o'clock, passing the Mormon ferry, where we saw the valley dotted with the white covered emigrant wagons, we reached the point where we were to leave the Platte for the Sweet Water River — a distance of forty-five miles; and ascending a hill nearly a mile in length, we gazed for the last time on the mountain walls of the Black Hills, as they stretched away toward the Rocky Mountains, and the sterile and arid soil which bordered the stream. We found an encampment beyond the ridge, about two miles from the river, near two large ponds of poison water; and to supply ourselves and cattle with drink, we were obliged to follow a lateral valley to the river. Grass scanty and poor. Distance, sixteen miles.

JUNE 21.

Leaving our encampment early, we drove over a barren, undulating country, and reached the Red Buttes about noon. We found a small creek flowing through a narrow valley, where there had been good grass, but which had been mostly consumed by the trains which preceded us. Although I speak particularly of our own train, and of the events which came under my own eye, the reader should bear in mind that there were probably twenty thousand people on the road west of the Missouri, and that our train did not travel for an hour without seeing many others, and hundreds of men. For days we would travel in company with other trains, which would stop to rest, when we would pass them; and then perhaps we would lay up, and they pass us. Sometimes we would meet again after many days, and others, perhaps, never. As near as we could ascertain, there were about a thousand wagons before us, and probably four or five thousand behind us.

The Red Buttes are three isolated mountains, south of us, between the road and the Platte, large portions of which are of bare rock of a bright red color, showing the effect of volcanic fires in producing an ochre tint. They are singular and interesting in their appearance. The country around was a desert, with water only at long intervals, without grass, and not a tree to afford shade from the burning rays of the sun on the sandy soil; and not only ourselves, but our cattle, suffered much from thirst during the day. About four o'clock, we came to a singular outcrop of sand rock, standing up in perpendicular strata like a huge wall of more than a mile in length, and so perfect in its arrangement, that it seemed to be the work of art rather than an accidental formation. Under one portion of this, as well as in the bank of a little run of brackish water, I discovered bituminous coal of an excellent quality.

We were compelled to drive between twenty-five and thirty miles, in order to get grass and water; and it was after dark before we reached a little, narrow brook, where we could slake our thirst. It being three miles farther to Willow Spring, before we could find grass, and our fatigue so great, we concluded to unyoke our cattle here for the night. Several trains, like ourselves, had been hurrying over this desert; and although we were the first to arrive, in fifteen minutes there were fifty tents or more around us, and their camp-fires of sage bushes glared up in the darkness, and made it look like the encampment of an army. All were anxious to reach the Sweet Water, where, we were told, travelers' comforts existed in profusion; and we longed to taste an element which we felt must be refreshing, after drinking the nauseating waters of the muddy Platte. Wearied with our long march, we slept soundly, after a drive of at least twenty-five miles.

JUNE 22.

At the earliest dawn, the hungry cattle were yoked, and we followed a narrow, ascending valley about three miles, till we came to a beautiful spring, from which flowed a pretty brook, fringed with willows, named Willow Spring. The soil, irrigated by the water, bore excellent grass, and we halted to refresh our cattle, and to get breakfast for ourselves. After a halt of a couple of hours, we drove perhaps two miles to the top of the ascent, when, through the pure air of this barren region, we obtained a charming view of mountain scenery. Looking across an undulating plain, the Sweet River Mountains appeared to be only six or eight miles distant; but it was after noon the following day before we reached them — probably a distance of thirty miles. In the distance was a pond of water, more than a mile in circumference, which we afterwards found to be highly alkaline, and totally unfit for use. The river, although between us and the mountains, could not be seen. After driving about fifteen miles, the train reached a creek, the waters of which, though poor, could be used, and we stopped for a noon halt. Supposing the company would come on, after eating a slice of raw bacon and a biscuit of hard bread, I walked on through the burning sand, the day being intensely hot. I was eager to reach the river to obtain a draught of good water; and it was not until I was on an elevation, about three miles ahead, that I discovered they had not moved, and that they evidently intended to remain through the day. The labor of retracing my steps, fatiguing as the road was, I could not think of; and I had about concluded to trust luck for a bed and supper, when I fell in company with a Mr. Marks, a young gentleman belonging to a company from Hennepin, Illinois, under the command of Captain Ham, who had ridden back a couple of miles to find a horse-shoe, so valuable was such an article here. He kindly invited me to go on to the river and share a bed with him in their tent, which I embraced with much pleasure. We overtook the Hennepin train after proceeding a few miles, it being near sunset before we reached the river. There was not a tree or shrub to mark its course, and although it flowed through a plain, the inequalities of the ground prevented our seeing it until we were almost upon its bank. It is perhaps eighty feet broad, fordable at this season at almost any point, and its waters, though not entirely clear, were so much purer and sweeter than those of the turbid, muddy, and insipid Platte, that it richly deserves its name. My first impulse was to take a long, deep draught of its refreshing water, and then to bathe my aching feet. The train encamped in a depression on its bank, and in a short time the tents were pitched; camp-fires were burning brightly; supper was prepared, and with a glorious appetite, I sat down to a rich feast of antelope steak, and enjoyed, with a double zest, a good meal, through their kind

E　　　　　　　　　　　　7

hospitality. Dear reader, if you are an Epicure, for heaven's sake, walk to California across the plains, and you will learn to enjoy with a zest you know not, the luxury of a good meal.

Near our encampment, and immediately at the ford, stood Independence Rock, a huge boulder of naked granite, forty or fifty rods long, and perhaps eighty feet high. It stands isolated upon the plain, about six miles from the mountains on the right, and three from those on the left. It is not difficult of access on its southern point, and may be ascended in many places on the east. In a deep crevice on the south, is a spring of ice-cold water — a perfect luxury to the thirsty emigrant. Hundreds of names are painted on its south wall, and among them I observed some dated 1836. Fatigued as I was, a hyena might have tugged at my toes without awaking me, for I had paddled through the sun and sand twenty-two miles.

JUNE 23.

I parted from my Hennepin friends with regret, and while they moved on, I waited for our own train to come up. As they had about ten miles to drive, I made an excursion to the mountain range on the left, which appeared to be only a mile distant. I walked fast one hour before I reached the base, and instead of finding the ground level, as it appeared to be from Independence Rock, it was gullied and broken. From the principal range, a spur extended in a point to within half a mile of Independence Rock, and gradually wore down to a moderately elevated point on the plain. I ascended this at the base of the mountain. It was, I should think, two hundred feet high — a bare pile of rocks, with deep chasms and crevices; and although the ridge seemed to be level from the valley below, when I reached the top, I found it so difficult to get along over the scraggy rocks, and deep chasms — it being necessary to leap the latter, or descend and climb out — that I was glad to go to the bottom and take the more even surface of the ground below. Our train came up and crossed the river just as I reached the end of the point, and made a halt for noon.

After our dainty feast of raw bacon and hard bread, we drove on about five miles to a gap in the mountains, over a deep sandy road. This gap is a narrow pass, which seems to have been caused by a separation of a point of the Sweet Water Mountains, where it unites with the Platte range. Passing through the gap, as through a huge gateway, a fine valley is opened to the view, with the Sweet Water meandering through, with bright green grass bordering its banks. On the right, as far as the eye could extend, a wall of gray granite rock, nearly perpendicular, ranged along, and on the south the rugged peaks of the Platte glittered with snow, and made us cast many a wishful glance at it, bringing forcibly to mind the deliciousness of an ice lemonade in the scorching sun which was pouring down upon us, the rays of which were rendered more intense by the reflection of the hot sand.

About fifty rods below the mouth of the gap, a curiosity indeed presented itself. The river has apparently broken through the mountain, and passes through a chasm of perpendicular rock, probably over three hundred feet high. It was evidently done by volcanic force, for the blackened, burnt rocks which lay around, and a dyke of black trap rock which had been forced up in the granite on the right wall, showed that it had been subjected to intense heat. The river flowed through this singular chasm nearly a quarter of a mile, quite through the mountain, when it again entered the valley which we had just left. At the base of the wall we found the remains of a mountain sheep, or ibex, which had probably been driven off from the top by the wolves; but his strong horns and stiff neck were not staunch enough to protect his life against such a force. Sam Patch himself, the prince of jumpers, would hardly have ventured his carcass in mid air from this wall. There were large quantities of yellow mica in the stream, and as it was determined to turn everything into gold that was possible, some of our boys insisted that this was ore, but an application of nitric acid instantly dispelled the pleasing hallucination, and proved that Sweet Water valley was not the valley of the Sacramento. Large masses of saleratus, several inches thick, and very pure, were found on the plain around, and it is not necessary for the emigrant to lay in a supply of this useful article any farther than to this point.

The singular chasm which the Sweet Water passes through, has not inaptly acquired the *soubriquet* of Devil's Gate, and it did seem as if his Satanic majesty had been cutting queer antics in this wild region. We encamped about a mile above this entrance, where we found excellent grass, and all the concomitants of a good camp. "Honor to whom honor is due."

The evening previous to our arrival at Devil's Gate, a man was shot under peculiar circumstances. An emigrant named Williams, from Plymouth, Marshall county, Indiana, had taken a stranger into his employ at St. Joseph, who was anxious to get to California. It proved, after they got beyond the limits of law and order, that this man was a perfect desperado, and, as he afterwards acknowledged, was traveling under an assumed name. Some difficulty occurred between him and Mr. Williams, on account of the latter reproaching him for being remiss in his duty, when he threatened to take Mr. Williams' life, and it was regarded at the time as an idle threat; but subsepuently

it appeared that he was determined to put his threat into execution, and Williams, from the advice of his friends, kept out
of the way as much as possible, and at night slept either out of
the camp, or where his enemy could not commit the deed. The
man, whose name I have forgotten, continued his threats in
such a manner, and sought so palpably to carry them into
effect, that Williams, who was a quiet and peaceable man,
came to the conclusion that there was no safety for himself but
to anticipate his antagonist. At this time, the man was detailed as one of the night-guard, and Williams was to relieve
him. The hour of relief came, when, on approaching Williams,
the latter took his pistol and shot him down. The man lived
two days, and confessed that it was his intention to have killed
Williams, and that he should have done so, if he had had an opportunity. In the morning, Williams went to several trains
and offered to give himself up for trial, but upon a just representation of the facts by his company, he was honorably ac-
quited, on the ground of self-defence, where a judicial investigation could not be had. Distance, seven miles.

JUNE 24.

We continued in our camp until noon, and then moved on
eight miles, to a point where we should leave the river for ten
miles before we came to it again, and as there was neither grass
nor water in the interval, we deemed it advisable to lay over till
morning. There had been no rain since the 12th, and the cloud
of dust was intolerable. But the scenery was interesting. The
naked granite wall on our right, without a green thing to hide
its bare sides, and the high mountains on the left, presenting a
variety of undulating forms, kept our eyes upon them in won
der, and made us almost forget our weariness. As soon as the

road turned from the river bottom, toward the more elevated plain, we came in contact with the sage; and here, too, were myriads of crickets, which were crushed by the wheels of our wagon as we passed along, the sight of which produced a feeling of nausea.   Distance, eight miles.

CHAPTER VII.

VALLEY OF THE SWEET WATER — WIND RIVER — TOILS OF THE EMIGRANT —
RENCOUNTER THREATENED — ICE IN THE DESERT — PRAIRIE DOGS, ANTE-
LOPE AND MOUNTAIN SHEEP — "ALL IS NOT GOLD THAT GLITTERS" — TRA-
DING POST—FRAUDULENT POST-OFFICE—A BEAUTIFUL PROSPECT—ASCENT TO
THE SOUTH PASS — FACE OF THE COUNTRY — GREAT NUMBERS OF DEAD CAT-
TLE — SUFFERING OF THE EMIGRANTS — AN OLD SETTLER — A MAN ACCI-
DENTALLY SHOT — SOUTH PASS — OVER THE MOUNTAINS — A LAST LOOK
HOMEWARD — DISBANDING OF TRAINS.

JUNE 25.

OUR road still lay along the peculiar and interesting valley
of the Sweet Water; but at this point we left the river, and
for ten miles there was neither grass nor water, and the deep
sand and dust made the traveling extremely laborious. Long
trains of wagons and of animated life, as usual, varied the wild
scenery; and had it not been for excessive weariness of long
travel, we should have enjoyed it with infinite zest.

It is not, on the whole, surprising that the ill tempers of men
should be called forth, and be exhibited in their worst features,
in a journey of this kind. It almost daily happened, that when
the day's journey was performed, we were tired enough to sink
to rest without attempting to do more; but the moment the
place of encampment was reached, much labor remained to be
done. Our tents were to be pitched, our cattle driven out to
graze, and a guard set to prevent their straying, or drinking
poison water — wood and water must be procured, for which

we were often obliged to go a mile or more; and then a fire to be built of buffalo excrement, or sage, or both; our suppers to cook, the dishes to wash; and then, a portion of our mess, in regular turn, to spend part of the night watching around the camp, to prevent the inroads of Indians, — all this added to our weariness, it was impossible that words or actions should always flow in the same even and smooth tenor. Bickerings and ill-humor would frequently break out in all the trains, and sometimes lead to unhappy consequences. Still, I may safely say that there was perhaps as little among our own men, with two or three exceptions, as in any train; and on the whole we got along passably well, with the thousand and one petty annoyances to which we were subjected.

During our drive in the early part of the day, on gaining a slight elevation, we obtained a view of the lofty Wind River Mountains, covered with snow, at an apparent distance of thirty or forty miles. They are much higher than those of the Sweet Water, and present a magnificent appearance. On the north side of the road stood a bare, isolated rock of granite, sloping like a roof, which, though not as large as Independence Rock, was something of a curiosity, from its immense size. In the bare granite range on the right was a mountain rock many miles distant, which resembled a castle with a dome, and it looked like the strong-hold of some feudal baron of olden time; but as we passed on, it soon changed its appearance to a shapeless, broken mass of granite. At night we again reached the river, where a new road had been made through a singularly gloomy gorge in the northern mountains, through which the river flowed. It was reported to be the best road, although it was necessary to ford the river four times; but it was said that by this route we should avoid a heavy sand road, and we therefore thought we would take it. The grass, though not abundant, was passably good. Distance, fifteen miles.

JUNE 26.

We crossed the river at the first ford, and entered the rocky gorge through which the river flowed, and proceeded about a mile to the second ford. A narrow pathway had been cut in the bank, capable of admitting but one wagon at a time, and the ford was so deep that every wagon box had to be raised about six inches from its bed to prevent the water from flowing in. The ford was crooked and bad, and a large number of teams were in advance of us, which would detain us till noon before our turn would come to cross. Under the circumstances we judged it best to return and take the old road, which was described as being sandy and hard. We accordingly faced about, and on reaching the road and leaving the river, we found about four miles of sand road, but the rest of the way was good, and the distance was no greater. We gained time, for on reaching the point where the two roads united, at a distance of eight miles, we found ourselves meeting trains which had been a day ahead of us, and they represented that the road by the gorge was not good, and that the river had to be crossed four times by deep and bad fords, which delayed them. The day was excessively warm, the dust deep, and the cloud which arose from the passing trains rendered traveling extremely unpleasant.

There was no water for eight miles, and while the sun was pouring his burning rays down upon us, we observed showers on the mountains to the south. A peak, apparently about four miles distant, was white with snow ; and some of our boys in their ignorance insisted that it was a ledge of white rock. On the spur of the moment, when we halted for noon, I volunteered
E*

to go and bring some into camp. By the consent or rather request of young Thorn, who had an interest in the pony, I mounted old Shab and started off. As I started, Morrell, who also claimed an interest in the pony, but as it afterwards proved, only held a sort of *quasi* possession, ordered me to dismount. This proceeded only from ill-feeling towards me, from an imaginary insult which he asserted I had given him at home, long before I knew him, and for which he vented his spite in a continued series of insulting acts and bitter language, better becoming a billingsgate felon than a man of sense, when I was sick and helpless on the plains. I refused to obey, having the consent of an actual owner and worthy man, when he seized his rifle, and with the impulse of a maniac, began to approach me, raving like a madman. I was armed with a revolver and a double-barreled gun, and had he made an assault, I should most surely have shot him down, unless he had been beforehand — a course in which I afterwards found I should have been upheld by the company — for his abuse had been so glaring that he had rendered himself disgusting to every one, and all wondered that my patience had held out so long. But he stopped in his mad career, returned to his wagon, and I slowly and deliberately rode off, thankful that, notwithstanding his constant provocation, I had not shed his blood.

About two miles from the road the plain began to be broken, and on reaching the mountain I followed up a gulf, which was thickly lined by dwarf firs and underbrush, through which a little brook ran, when I was suddenly brought to a stand by a high, perpendicular wall of rock, with snow many hundred feet above me. I got a shot at a herd of antelopes, but was too poor a marksman to kill one, and set out on my return. I had gone but a short distance when I was overtaken by a heavy hail storm, and was completely drenched. Shivering with cold, and wet to the skin, I went on towards the road in the direction of the train, when I came to a fine brook of sufficient capacity to turn a mill. This I followed down to within a mile of the road, where it sank into the earth and disappeared in the sand. I learned, on reaching the train, that there had been no rain in the road, and that they had seen no brook, or a sign of water, but that the day had been intensely hot, and the road dry and sandy.

I followed the train and overtook it about four o'clock in the afternoon, on the borders of a morass, perhaps a mile in length by half a mile in breadth. Some of the boys, thinking that water could be easily obtained, took a spade, and going out on the wild grass, commenced digging. About a foot from the surface, instead of water, they struck a beautiful layer of ice, five or six inches in thickness. Many trains were passing at the time, and all stopped and supplied themselves with the clear, cooling element, and buckets were brought into use to supply ourselves with frozen water for our supplies. This natural ice-house is not only a great curiosity in itself, but from it peculiar situation, in this dry, barren, sandy plain, is justly entitled to be called the diamond of the desert. To the unsophisticated this may look like a traveler's tale, but it is easily explained upon natural principles. We were now at an elevation of about six thousand feet. The morass was either a pond, or a combination of springs, covered with turf or swamp grass; and at this high altitude the temperature of winter is very severe, converting the water of the morass to solid ice. Although the sun of summer is intensely hot in those mountain valleys, the turf and grass intercept the intensity of its rays, and prevent the dissolution of the ice, on the principle of our domestic ice-houses; thus a kind Providence affords a necessary and indispensable comfort to the exhausted traveler in these dry and barren regions.

We were now on a plain, sixteen miles distance to water. The sage here attained a great growth, being as high as my head, and the trunk frequently six inches in diameter. I observed a new species of prairie dog, or it may be, a connecting link between the prairie dog and ground squirrel. They are about the size of the latter, with much the shape of the former, and burrow under the sage bushes, to which they fly on the least alarm. We found them so numerous at some of our encampments, that we could knock them over with sticks, and the boys amused themselves in killing them with pistols. They were very fat and oily, but, on being parboiled and roasted, were quite good. Many days afterwards, when traveling down Bear River, I saw a man who was traveling to California on foot and alone, who lived upon them entirely, except what the charity of the emigrants afforded him. His manner of killing them was to shoot them with arrows from a bow which he carried, as he walked along. Antelope were plenty, and droves of mountain sheep, or ibex, were upon the hills. We made about six miles on the sixteen mile stretch, when we encamped, with none but alkaline water, and scarcely any grass, and it required all our care to keep our cattle from straying in search of food, and to prevent them from drinking the fatal water. Drive, eighteen miles.

JUNE 27.

As our cattle were suffering for want of forage, and our own supply of ice-water was exhausted, we left our encampment at daybreak, in order to reach the river as early as possible, and,

passing over the sandy plain, which varied but little in its character from that of the preceding day, we gained the river about
ten o'clock, where we found the concomitants of a good camp.
Our wagon-master, Traverse, was one of the best marksmen
in the company, and during our morning transit he made an
excursion on the plain with his rifle, and brought in two young
antelopes, and while our hungry cattle were turned loose to pick
up their own rations, we regaled ourselves on antelope steak
and Jews' abomination (bacon.)

After a three hours' halt we pursued our way up the valley,
over the point of a long hill, crossing the river three times during the afternoon. The fords were easy, as the river now was
little more than a fine creek. The road was excellent; the
mountain wall less marked; and for the first time in many
days we found an encampment where there was an abundance
of fuel, water and grass. There was a large quantity of yellow
mica in the sands of the streams, and in all of its affluants, and
some of our men could hardly relinquish the idea of its being
gold; but, alas! the application of nitric acid dispelled their
pleasant dreams, and proved that California was, in the language
of Khorner, "Not yet — not yet!" Distance, nineteen miles.

JUNE 28.

We had encamped near a temporary trading-post of a hardy
pioneer. Half a dozen cloth and buffalo-shin tents stood near
each other; two or three wagons, belonging to the chief, and
his handful of goods were in a tent by themselves. Being invited into the grand lodge, I was surprised to find a fine carpet
spread on the ground, a comfortable camp bed, several chairs,
among which was a nice cushioned rocking chair, several vol-
umes of standard books, and last though not least, a rather

pretty and well dressed American woman, with an easy, pleasant address — the companion of the gentlemanly proprietor of the post. Of course my old, soiled, buckskin coat and weather-beaten hat had to bow before the majesty of female influence, and I felt a blush of shame mantling my cheek as I thought of my squalid appearance. In the company were several Spanish woman, of mixed breeds, and attaches, with most villainous looks, and it seemed strange that a woman of her apparent character, could be content to pass her life in such a wild country, and among such an uncouth set of companions. But as there is "no accounting for taste," I am not disposed to moralize on the subject, and let it pass.

A sign stood near the road, labeled "Post-Office," with a notice that one of the company was about leaving for the States, and would carry letters, &c., &c. — "price, half a dollar." Many a half dollar was left, but those letters which our company left for their friends never reached them, and it was only a pleasant ruse to gull travelers, and "raise the wind."

Upon ascending a hill of nearly two miles in length, a fine view presented itself to our vision. On our right, twenty or thirty miles distant, the Wind River Mountains, extending from beyond the South Pass into Oregon, were mingling their snow-white crests with a rich drapery of clouds. On our left, and partly behind us, as the road momentarily changed our direction, lay the granite cliffs of the Sweet Water, fading away in the dim distance, while east of north, a broad undulating plain spread out for many miles, with occasional buttes or solitary hills, rising from its surface. Before us lay the hills which still marked the course of the valley of the Sweet Water, while on the elevated plains were piles of rock and stones, thrown up by volcanic force, which looked, at a distance, as if they had been gathered by the hand of man. Occasionally, in the hollows, heaps of snow glittered in the sunlight, and as we gathered it we found it most refreshingly cool, while perspiring in the sultry heat of the day. The ascent to the South Pass of the Rocky Mountains is so gradual that we perceive no difference in the road; and had we not been assured by mathematical demonstration that such was the fact, we could scarcely have believed that we had been ascending since leaving the Missouri. The rarification of the air, which now began to be apparent in our short breathings, on going over hills, was often attributed by those unacquainted with the true cause, to some unaccountable failure of strength.

The face of the whole country from the Black Hills to the South Pass is peculiar and interesting. High table elevations, with flat sufaces; solitary conical mountains, with flattened tops; spurs, like huge embankments for rail-roads or canals, running at angles from the main ranges, may here be seen. Red earth-column buttes seem to rise from the plain — the granite hills often assuming fantastic shapes which cannot be described, with here and there barren sage plains, and ponds of carbonate of soda. These are the general characteristics which mark this strange portion of the world. Antelope and buffalo are very numerous; and lizards and crickets, crawling in vast numbers over the burning sands, are the principal varieties of insect life which the traveler sees. The Indians are warlike and treacherous, and the solitary traveler may think himself well off, if, after being robbed, he escapes with his life.

We passed many dead cattle during the last ten days. Their death was generally attributed to weariness and bad water, but my impression is that there existed another cause, which was generally overlooked, and that was the rarification of the air.

On driving up long and steep hills, we became almost breath-less. The cause was suggested to our company, and we often stopped to give our cattle a chance to breathe. Many did not use this precaution, and cattle and mules sometimes dropped down in the harness, exhausted. We saw more dead cattle the first day after crossing the Pass than at any other time, until we reached the Great Desert. This, with hard labor and scanty food, must have been the cause.

An express rider passed to-day, who told us that there was an immense throng behind, and that at least a thousand wagons were detained at the South Platte, on account of a sudden rise of the river, which prevented fording. He informed us that there was a vast amount of sickness and suffering among them ; the grass was consumed, and many of the cattle had perished for want of food. To us their prospect seemed cheer-less enough, for a great part of the way along the North Fork, and up to our present advance, the grass barely afforded suste-nance to the trains already passed, and we were sometimes compelled to pass two miles out of the road to find forage. None would be left when they came along. We crossed two or three ledges of rocks, cropping out from the top of high and steep hills, which made the labor for our cattle exceedingly hard.

A singular accident, of a serious nature, occurred to-day in a Pittsburgh company, at their noon halt. A young man belong-ing to their train was standing by a wagon, tieing his horse to a wheel. A loaded musket lay on a knoll at a little distance, and a horse was feeding near it. The horse passed over it, when his halter caught in the lock, and discharged the musket, the whole charge taking effect in the young man's knee, inflicting a dangerous wound, and it was found necessary to amputate the limb to save his life.

Passing three fine creeks during the afternoon, we encamped on the river bottom for the last time, about two miles from the road, and then drove the cattle a mile below, where they found good grazing. Our encampment was in a large community of the species of prairie dogs I have mentioned, and they were running about like rats, and many were killed by the men, in endeavoring to escape to their holes. Distance, twenty miles.

JUNE 29.

As early as we could, consistently, we left our encampment for the ford, at which we were to bid adieu to the Sweet Water, and launch into the region beyond the Rocky Mountains. Near the ford, which was two miles below our camp, we found a cluster of lodges, which belonged to one of a singular class of men, who leave the comforts of civilized life, and bury themselves in the wild, inhospitable regions of the far west. At first I mistook him for an Indian, from his dress, his long black locks, and his swarthy, weather-beaten complexion. He was a man apparently thirty-five or forty years of age, with a pleasing countenance, and mild blue eyes, whom I found to be well educated — far above the humble sphere of life to which he had consigned himself. He was surrounded by three or four squaws and a number of children, who seemed to look upon him as the grand head of the family, in the relative position of husband and father. He readily entered into conversation, and told me that he had lived that life for eighteen years, without once having been to the States, depending upon chance for supplies.

"And do you never think of returning? Do not old thoughts of home and friends intrude upon your memory, and awaken old feelings of endearment?"

" O yes," he replied, rather sadly, " very often. Once, about

8

five years ago, I determined to return, and made my arrange
ments, but after all, I could not make up my mind to leave;
and when I think of it now, and almost determine to go once
more, I look at my responsibilities, (and he glanced around at
his wives and his young brood of half-breeds,) and I give it up.
You see I have cares; and then I am so accustomed to this mode
of life, that I am unfitted for social intercourse in refined society.
True, I think I will go some time, but I may never do it. Who
would protect my children in danger, if I was absent?"

Nature clings to its offspring, irrespective of color, thought I,
and bidding him farewell, I followed the train. Crossing the
river, we ascended a steep hill from the bottom land, and then
found a good and almost level road to the South Pass — only
about eight miles distant.

A herd of about thirty buffaloes were bounding off over the
plain as we rose the hill, frightened at the sight of so many
enemies. These, and one other which we saw the day after we
went through the Pass, were the only ones which we saw during
the remainder of our journey.

There are no particular land-marks to distinguish the scenery
on the east side of the Pass from that of the valley, through
which we had come. The ascent is so gradual that the culminating point is a matter of doubt with the thousands who
have crossed it, and I can only give my own impressions. Half
a mile before we reach the highest rounded knoll, according to
my ideas of the highest point, are two small conical hills, which
stand near each other, on the same plain, perhaps twenty rods
asunder, between which the road passes. Here Bryant and
Fremont fix the culminating point. I cannot agree with them,
for from this a slight ascent brings the traveler to the termi-
nus of the plain, over which you pass a slight convexity, and

begin to descend towards a second curvative of an equal height. From the second curvative, the descent is regular and certain, and on commencing this, the hills are not large on either side, but approach so near that, like a small, water-worn gulley, there is barely sufficient room left for a good wagon road betwen them. The declination on the west side is more rapid than on the eastern, but not difficult; and this narrow road continues about a mile and a half, when we get a view of the first water which flows into the Pacific Ocean. This is called Pacific Spring, and is in boggy ground on the right, where there are also sulphur springs. The water is clear, and of icy coldness, and a little brook here takes its rise, and flows to the west. As we proceed down, the valley expands, and the hills on the left immediately bounding the Pass, are perhaps two or three hundred feet high, (by estimation) — no worse than those on which roads are laid out in some States at home. On the north, you look across a broken, mountain plain, to the Wind River range of mountains, apparently twenty or thirty miles distant. The South Pass proper is about two miles long, after which we come to a large basin, perhaps four miles across, with a rim of the peculiar table hills and ridges, easy of ascent, which seems to be the commencement of a series of basins and valleys, though often interrupted by mountain streams and hills extending quite to the Siérra Neváda, of a character peculiar to themselves, and differing much from those east of the South Pass.

From the culminating point, the view is not as grand as at many places along the Sweet Water Mountains, for these mountains, though here much diminished in size, hinder any extended view in that direction. The point has an altitude of between seven and eight thousand feet, and the rarification of the air is so great that it is necessary to stop frequently to get breath on ascending the hills in the vicinity.

We arrived at Pacific Spring a little after noon. Being told that our next day's drive would be twenty miles, without water, we stopped where there were tolerable grass and good water. The Hennepin company had arrived just before us, and the Dayton company were encamped but a short distance below, and we made and received visits to our mutual satisfaction.

We were now in Oregon — the ridge of the Rocky Mountains being its eastern boundary — and fifteen hundred miles from our homes. We had toiled steadily in our weary journey for two months, and were but little more than half way to our point of destination ; and although thus far, no serious mishap had befallen us, no one could tell what trials awaited us. My own health had vastly improved, and I endured the labors of our daily routine, and the absence of comforts, much better than I could have apprehended. One object of my journey was successfully accomplished, and I was in better health than I had been for years. Would the other grand desideratum be also accomplished, and my labor meet its reward? Time alone could tell. In a musing mood, I ascended a high hill opposite our camp, to take a parting look at the Atlantic waters, which flowed towards all I held most dear on earth. Old reminiscences were crowding on my memory. As I turned my eye eastward, home, wife and children, rushed to my mind with uncontrolled feeling, and in the full yearnings of my heart, I involuntarily stretched out my arms as if I would clasp them to my bosom ; but no answering look of affection, no fond embrace met me in return, as I was wont to see at home, but in its place there lay extended before me barren reaches of table land, the bare hills, and desert plains of the Sweet Water, while long trains of wagons, with their white covers, were turning the last curve of the dividing ridge, their way-worn occupants bid ding a long, perhaps a last adieu to eastern associations, to mingle in new scenes on the Pacific coast. Sad, but not dispirited, I descended the hill, and sought the dubious comfort of our weather-beaten tent, where memory kept busy till fatigue closed my eyes in slumber.

On leaving the Missouri, nearly every train was an organized company, with general regulations for mutual safety, and with a captain chosen by themselves, as a nominal head. On reaching the South Pass, we found that the great majority had either divided, or broken up entirely, making independent and helter-skelter marches towards California. Some had divided from policy, because they were too large, and on account of the difficulty of procuring grass in one place for so many cattle, while others, disgusted by the overbearing propensities of some men, would not endure it, and others still, from mutual ill-feelings and disagreements among themselves. Small parties of twenty men got along decidedly the best; and three men to a mess, or wagon, is sufficient for safety as well as harmony. Distance, ten miles.

CHAPTER VIII.

LEAVING SOUTH PASS — LITTLE AND DRY SANDY RIVERS — PASSAGE BY SUB-
LETT'S CUT-OFF — HARDSHIPS IN THE DESERT — GREEN RIVER — RE-UNION
OF OLD FRIENDS AT THE FERRY — BRUTAL MURDER — SEARCH FOR THE
CRIMINAL — IRREGULAR JURY TRIAL — INDEPENDENCE DAY — UNPLEASANT
INCIDENTS — A WELCOME SHADE — BEAR RIVER — CAMP OF SNAKE IN-
DIANS — ROUGH TRAVELING — FACE OF THE COUNTRY — MOUNTAIN INDIANS
AND TRADERS — GAME.

JUNE 30.

WE had a toilsome day before us of twenty miles, to the
Little Sandy, one of the waters of the Green River, or Rio
Colorado, and this distance was to be passed before water or
forage could be obtained.   On emerging from the Narrows of
the Pass, we observed for the first time, at a great distance, the
Rocky Mountains, towering to the skies in lofty grandeur, with
their snow-white peaks blending with the blue sky, and on the
right the Wind River chain presented a bleak, broken and
cheerless appearance.   Before us lay the basin, bounded by its
tables of nebulæ, and through it meandered the brooklet which
took its rise from Pacific Spring.   By an easy ascent, after
passing across the level plain, we gained the rim of the basin,
and before us lay another, differing but little from the first.   I
ascended one of nature's watch-towers, and found the top covered with pebbles and scoria, which bore the appearance of having

been in fire. The flat surface might have contained two acres, and the inclination of the sides was perhaps at an angle of for-ty-five degrees. Fourteen miles brought us to the Dry Sandy — not inaptly named, for it was the dry bed of a creek where salt and unpleasant water could anywhere be found at a depth of six or eight inches below the sand. Once in every mile, at least, we saw the carcass of a dead ox, having closed his career of patient toil in this land of desolation in the service of his gold-seeking master, to become the prey of ravenous wolves, or food for croaking ravens, which covered his dead body, screaming at our approach. Six miles beyond Dry Sandy, where even the everlasting sage is scanty and of dwarfish growth, is Little San-dy — a fine creek of pure and sweet water. The road through the day was good, and we reached our place of encampment a little before sunset, but found grass and wood scarce. Game, which before had been plenty, now entirely disappeared, as if the Mountain Pass was a barrier to that portion of animal life necessary to the wants of man. On arriving at the creek, men and animals rushed to the water to quench their raging thirst, after which the latter were diven off a mile, where they picked up enough to satisfy the cravings of appetite, and we had re-course to the simple larder of our wagon. Drive, twenty miles.

JULY 1.

On getting our cattle together this morning, I found that one of my best oxen was sick. We felt sure that it was not the effect of bad water, and concluded that it was more from hard labor in the rarified atmosphere than the effect of disease. There was a cow in the company, owned by Messrs. Wilson and Hall, and I purchased Wilson's interest, and with the consent of Doctor Hall, put her in the yoke, and drove my ox before the train. She was worth nothing except to bear up the end of the yoke, but our loads by this time were much lighter, and the other cattle could draw it, so she answered a temporary purpose. After crossing the creek and proceeding a mile and a half, we came to where the road forks — the one to the left leading to Salt Lake and Fort Bridge, the other more direct to Fort Hall, by what is known as Greenwood's or Sublett's cut-off. The former was about seventy miles further, and had been the traveled road until the other route was discovered the previous year. The latter was by a desert route, without grass or water, (as our guide books informed us,) thirty miles to Green River; but which we found by actual measurement by road-ometers to be fifty-four miles from Big Sandy, which was six miles from Little Sandy. We decided to take the cut off, and drove on over an arid plain to Big Sandy. As this was the last water, it is customary to start about four o'clock in the afternoon on the dreaded desert, and by driving continuously night and day, make the distance in about twenty-four hours. This was our course. We found good grass at Big Sandy, and here we again threw away all superfluous articles. All our kegs were brought into requisition for water, and I had an india-rubber bag, which I took to the stream to fill, but just as I was pouring in the last bucket full, the bag burst, and it was rendered wholly useless. The desert over which we were to pass was an arid plain, without a drop of water, or a blade of grass, the soil being of soft, dry, ashy consistence. The dust was an impalpable powder, and the dense clouds which arose almost produced suffocation. Happily for us, one hour before we started a fine shower came on, which laid the dust for thirty miles, though in some places the mud was sticky and bad.

At four o'clock we set out. The rain had cooled the sultry atmosphere, and the night was comfortable and pleasant. I had walked six miles during the day, and now I was to try my bottom on one of the most severe attempts I had ever made. Slow, but steadily, we walked on. The night closed in upon hundreds of wagons, and the road was lined by horsemen and pedestrians, and lucky was he who had the good fortune to have the shadow of a mule to ride. All walked who could, in order to make their loads as light as possible, to save their cattle ; and as the night wore heavily on, all sounds of mirth or of loud profanity ceased, and the creaking of wheels and the howling of wolves alone were heard. It was with difficulty I could keep awake. Tired as I was, and as the small hours approached, my weary limbs frequently gave way under me, and I fell headlong to the ground. This aroused me for a time, and I kept plodding on, driving, with the assistance of Brown, my poor ox, who needed rest perhaps even more than we. Smith was still in the wagon, suffering from his swollen leg, which pained him excessively, and the care of him had been severe to us; but we still attended assiduously to his comfort. With an intense desire to make our load light, by the order of Henderson, he nearly emptied a bag of corn meal in the road as we drove along ; a measure which was afterwards regretted, when our provisions failed, and even Henderson would have been glad of a corn cake, which he affected to despise.

JULY 2.

At day-break we were a little more than half way across the desert, where we stopped for an hour, to give our cattle rest, and a drop of water from our kegs, and then set out again. The morning air somewhat revived me, and I managed to crawl

F

along.   For about ten miles before reaching the river, the country became broken, and we passed several hard hills.   There
had been no rain here; consequently the dust was ankle deep.
The wind blew a gale, and the impalpable powder filled our
eyes and nostrils, and our faces, hair, and clothes looked as if
we had been rolling in a heap of dry ashes.   Even respiration
was difficult.   Completely exhausted, when within about five
miles of the river, I crawled into the wagon, and lay helpless
as a child.   This was my birth-day, and it was the hardest one
of all my life, for without sleeping I had walked fifty-five miles.
It was five o'clock in the afternoon when we reached the river,
all of us exhausted, when, instead of finding grass for our cattle, there was nothing growing on the broad, barren bottom
but a weed which they could not eat, and the nearest grass was
nearly four miles from our camp, over a high hill, accessible
only at two points, through deep ravines.   It was impossible,
in our exhausted state, to drive the cattle out, and they were
left to roam, ar take care of themselves, till daylight; and after
getting our tents erected, we fell upon our blankets, and were
lost in utter unconsciousness till morning.   Distance, in two
days, sixty miles.

JULY 3.

When morning dawned, our first care was to drive our cattle
over the hills, where there was grass; and then, after dispatch-
ing our breakfast, to ascertain the chances for crossing the river.

The ferry was nearly two miles below our stopping place,
and I went down to make inquiries.   The whole plain was
covered with tents, wagons and men, and there were also a detachment of troops, on their way to Oregon, under the command of Major Simonton, who were stopping a few days to

rest, and recruit the strength of their animals. On inquiry, I found that a register was kept by the ferryman, of the applicants, and each had to be served in turn. This, though fair, consigned us to two or three days delay; yet, as there was no help for it, I gave the name of our company, and then took a view of the premises.

There was a small but good scow, capable of carrying two wagons at once with safety, and to which oars were attached. The river was one hundred yards broad, with a very rapid current; and when the boat reached the shore, it was towed up by a long line and a strong force, to the place of departure. The landing on the west side could be made by rowing, allowing for the velocity of the current. The river rose in the Wind River Mountains, and the melting snows made it of icy coldness, and sweet to the taste. The only timber was a few cottonwood trees, and willow bushes growing sparsely on the margin. The whole bottom was sand, in which stunted sage, greasewood and weeds struggled to grow. The hills on the eastern boundary of the bottom were perpendicular rocks, of the same formation as at Scott's Bluffs; and like them presented a fanciful appearance, resembling architecture in some places, though not to a very great extent. On the north and west, at a great distance, were high mountains, capped with snow; and from the hill above, the barren plain could be traced to the extent of vision, bearing nothing but stunted sage and greasewood bushes.

In looking about the camps, I found Captain Tutt and my South Bend friends, who had arrived before us, and who were then crossing the river. They had got along thus far well, no accident having happened to them. Among others, I met for the scond time on the plains, my old friend, Doctor M. B. Angel, formerly from Niles, Michigan — a generous, open-hearted and benevolent gentleman. With the enterprising spirit for which he is remarkable, he, in company with two others, was building a ferry-boat, with the intention of remaining here a couple of weeks, and then go down the river to the Salt Lake road, and visit the Mormon City, which he subsequently did. I saw him no more till I strangely met him in Sacramento City, when he rendered me an essential service in my utmost need.

Soon after my arrival, the whole encampment was thrown into great excitement by a cruel and fiendish murder, which was committed on the west bank. A reckless villain, named Brown, requested a young man who acted as cook in his mess, to get him a piece of soap. The young man was at the moment bending over the fire, engaged in preparing the meal, and replied by telling him to get it himself, as he was busy. Without further provocation, as it appeared, the wretch raised his knife and stabbed him in the back, killing the young man almost instantly. The murderer fled. A meeting of emigrants was called, and General Allen, from Lewis county, Missouri, was called to the chair, when the atrocious deed was set forth, and it was determined by a series of resolutions to arrest the villain, give him a fair trial, and if found guilty, to execute him on the spot. Major Simonton seconded the views of the emigrants, in order to protect them against similar assassinations. In addition to a dozen athletic volunteers, who stood forth at the call, he detailed a file of soldiers to assist in the capture of the murderer. Several murders had been committed on the road, and all felt the necessity of doing something to protect themselves, where there was no other law but brute force. The party set out in pursuit of Brown, and I lounged around among the different camps till afternoon, when our train came up, and established an encampment on the river bank among the crowd, from which we experienced much courtesy.

JULY 4.

On reaching the mountains at Fort Laramie, I felt the bracing air acting favorably upon my health, and from that day I had been growing strong, and supposed that my predisposition to disease was wholly conquered; but as the sun arose over the eastern mountains this morning, certain unmistakable signs warned me that "the end had not yet come." The cold chills which were dancing along my back, gave me an inkling how my fourth of July was to be spent. Dear reader, may you be spared such a celebration of our glorious anniversary as I was doomed to endure. My old enemy nailed me to my bed, and kept me there, rioting in fever and chill, till after high noon. It was four o'clock in the afternoon before I was well enough to crawl out, and gather the news of the camp.

The volunteers had returned, without being successful in capturing Brown, but they had overtaken Williams, who had killed the rascal at the Devil's Gate, and thinking that some example of justice was necessary, they intimated that his presence was required to stand trial before a Green River jury, and he willingly returned; but his companions, dreading delay, would not accompany him. Upon his return it was resolved to try him. As his witnesses would not come, he feared a true representation of facts would not come out, and he employed B. F. Washington, Esq., a young lawyer from Virginia, to defend him. Had he known it, there were witnesses enough in the crowd to have justified him, but as he did not, he was disposed to take advantage of any technicality, and therefore employed counsel.

A court of inquiry was organized; General Allen elected chief justice, assisted by Major Simonton, who, with many of his officers, and a large crowd of emigrants, was present. A jury was empanneled, and court opened under a fine clump of willows. There, in that primitive court-house, on the bank of Green River, the first court was held in this God-forsaken land, for the trial of a man accused of the highest crime. At the commencement, as much order reigned as in any lawful tribunal of the States. But it was the 4th of July, and the officers and lawyers had been celebrating it to the full, and a spirit other than that of '76 was apparent.

Mr. Washington, counsel for the defendant, arose, and in a somewhat lengthy and occasionally flighty speech, denied the right of the court to act in the case at all. This, as a matter of law, was true enough, but his remark touched the pride of the old commandant, who gave a short, pithy and *spirited* contradiction to some of the learned counsel's remarks. This elicited a *spirited* reply, until, spiritually speaking, the spirits of the speakers ceased to flow in the tranquil spirit of the commencement, and the spirit of contention waxed so fierce, that some of the officer's spirits led them to take up in Washington's defence. From taking up words, they finally proceeded to take up stools and other belligerent attitudes. Blows, in short, began to be exchanged, the cause of which would have puzzled a " *Philadelphia lawyer* " to determine, when the emigrants interfered to prevent a further ebullition of patriotic feeling, and words were recalled, hands shaken, a general amnesty proclaimed, and this spirited exhibition of law, patriotism " *vi et armis,*" was consigned to the " vasty deep." Order and good feeling " once more reigned in Denmark." Williams, in the meantime, seeing that his affair had merged into something wholly irrelevant, with a sort of tacit consent, withdrew, for his innocence was generally understood, and no attempt was made to detain him.   The sheriff did not even adjourn the court, and it may be in session to this day, for aught I know.

JULY 5.

An old ox was offered for sale to-day by one of the emigrants, and though I knew he was nearly worn down, yet my friend McNeil thought he might do to hold up the yoke better than my cow, and as I thought he would give my sick ox a still better chance to recruit, I paid ten dollars and called him my own. He was driven out to graze with the other cattle, but on getting them together the following morning, the old ox was *non est inventus*, and I was assured by Henderson and Morrell that he had gone where neither goad, load, nor wagon-train would worry him more ; in short, like Uncle Ned, he " had gone where all good oxen go ;" and for some days I was the butt of my companions for my unfortunate speculation in beef.   However, it appeared afterwards that instead of being dead, Henderson would not take the trouble to drive him up, but left him on the mountains, without caring whether I made or lost by the operation.

JULY 6.

Ferrying had continued night and day since our arrival, and a little before daylight our turn came, and the passage was safely effected in about an hour.   Although the water was of icy coldness, our cattle swam over without difficulty, and we were ready to start from the opposite shore a little before noon. We had to drive through a slough before we reached terra firma, when, in the hands of Brown, my cattle became a little unruly, and suddenly drew the wagon to a deep place.   The water came into the box and wet all my clothes, *unstarching* all my fine shirts, playing the deuce with my wardrobe; and doing considerable damage to sundry articles. For the next two days I was improving every moment of our noon halt to dry my goods and chattels. The nights were very cold, the ice forming in our buckets half an inch thick. This was generally succeeded by a sultry and oppressive heat during the day. Smith was relieved of his sufferings by having his leg lanced, and from this time he rapidly recovered.

Leaving the river we drove down a sandy bottom, and then ascended a narrow ridge on the right, just wide enough for a good road, from which we had a view of the bottom and river which we had just left, and the broad bottom of a beautiful creek on the left, along which the road ran. To attain this by following the ridge, we made a half retrograde movement of three miles, to get the distance of one in a straight line. On reaching the creek bottom we found good grass, and for two days we had the comforts of forage, water and wood, and a level road.

On the 7th we left the creek, and from this to Bear River, which we reached on the 9th, the road passed over a broken country, with many difficult and bare hills. In the hollows we generally found excellent grass, but no game except mountain sheep, which were numerous on the hills. In some places we found ripe strawberries, but they were sour and unpleasant; we also found flax growing abundantly, and occasionally wild oats. From the hills, on both sides, we could see mountains covered with snow, rising to the clouds in sublime grandeur.

We passed a mountaineer's encampment during the morning, from whom we gained much information of the route to Fort Hall. He told us, too, that usually the valleys were filled with snow, and that he resided with his wives and children beyond the Rocky Mountains, on the east, where there was no snow, and where the grass was green all winter. He had a drove of horses, and had picked up many cattle which had been left by emigrants, and they were now in good condition.

Fremont, in speaking of the old route, says "that between Green and Bear Rivers grass is scanty." On this route we found it good and abundant, and were it not for the fifty-four mile desert of Sublett's cut-off, I should recommend this route to future travelers. The mountaineer told us, however, that the season was unusual, and that there were more and later rains than he had ever known, and more grass; that usually there was but little grass on the hill sides, which were now covered. The road leads through valleys, wherever practicable, in the general direction, but sometimes we found long and steep hills to ascend and descend, and during the afternoon we made the ascent from a valley, the worst I ever saw a wagon driven over. It was up a narrow ridge, with almost perpendicular sides, and had a wagon broke loose, it would have been dashed to atoms in a moment. We got over safely, however, and on the top we found a mountain plain, gradually descending, and' an encampment. Over a bank on the left, was a morass covered with cotton-woods, and where there was good grass and pure water.

JULY 8.

Leaving our good camp in excellent spirits, with a good road and strangely interesting country before us, we drove about four miles, when we came to a singular novelty, near the top of a mountain, easy of access. This was nothing less than a beautiful grove of fir trees, standing thickly together — a kind

F*   9

of wooded island in the desert, about half a mile in extent.
The road passed directly through it, and our emotions were of
the most pleasing kind, in once more getting beneath its cooling
shade. It was the first grove of timber which we had passed
through since leaving the Missouri, having seen none but the
scattered trees which grew immediately on the banks of streams.
For more than two months we had been traveling, exposed to
the fervid heat of the sun, or the cold and stormy blasts along
the Platte, without a leaf to offer protection, and now the deep
green foliage, the stillness which reigned unbroken, except the
hollow sound of a woodpecker upon some decayed trunk, the
dead trees which lay prostrate on the ground, brought forcibly
to mind the wood-covered land which we had left; and thought
and tongues were busy in reviewing the comforts and pleasures
of that happy and favored land. Leaving with reluctance this
mountain paradise, we drove on against a cold wind, which afterwards increased to a gale, and found an encampment among
the sage bushes — a long day's drive from the valley of the
Bear.

JULY 9.

About noon we reached the top of the last high hill of this
broken country, and looked down upon the rolling, bottom-land
through which Bear River was winding its crooked course, and
thinking it only three or four miles, I walked forward alone to
the river. The road ran through a kind of rolling, lateral valley, without vegetation, between the mountains and river, and
it was not till nearly sundown that I reached the bottom, a mile
from the river, and it became dark before the train got up, after
a fatiguing day's drive. The grass was excellent, and in the
dusk of evening we discovered no deleterious water. After

stationing our night watch, we turned into our blankets. Dis
tance from Green River, sixty-five miles.

JULY 10.

On driving up our cattle this morning, they exhibited the
appearance of having drunk alkaline water, and those who drove
them reported the ground white in places with the efflorescence.
The usual remedy was applied at once, after which we drove
on till noon. As they appeared weak, we resolved to lay
over.

About a mile below our mountain camp we crossed a fine
mountain stream of fresh water, where several lodges of Snake
Indians were encamped. They were very friendly, particularly
the females, who showed no signs of fear, laughing and chatter-
ing with us as if we were old acquaintances. One of the best
looking women took quite a fancy to Brown, and made him
propositions, which rendered him the laughing stock of the company for the hour ; but he modestly declined the honor. These
Snakes are of small stature ; the men ill looking and diminu-
tive, who, in speaking to us, scarcely raised their eyes from the
ground. In this particular they exhibited a strong contrast to
the women, bringing forcibly to mind the musty adage of " the
gray mare is the better horse." We saw a marked difference
between these Indians and those east of the Rocky Mountains.
The Ottoes, the Pawnees and Sioux are a fine looking race of
people, often handsome and well formed, warlike and bold.
The Crows are not so well formed, are nearly as dark skinned
as the lighther shade of negroes, broad shouldered, and rather
stout built, yet possessing courage, and it is said much honor.
The Asiatic features begin now to appear, which seem to become more apparent in the tribes as we approach the Pacific,

till they resemble the islanders of the South Sea, though generally of a darker skin. I speak of those I saw. We passed through a beautiful valley about five miles beyond, when, coming to a good encampment ground, we gave our cattle another dose of bacon, and, turning them out, took a substantial dose ourselves, but for quite another purpose. Distance, six miles.

JULY 11.

Our cattle were perfectly recovered from their potations of soda, and we pursued our journey along the beautiful valley of the Bear at an early hour. Henderson gave up the team a short time for the purpose of hunting, and going into the mountains, had the good fortune to kill a mountain sheep. As it was too heavy for him to carry, he gave it in charge of two men belonging to a mule train, who promised to bring it on, for which they were to receive one-half. On Henderson's report, when overtaking us, we congratulated ourselves at the prospect of having a good meal of wild mutton at our noon halt. Noon came, and with it came not the mule train ; and after waiting to the last moment, we were compelled to resort to our bacon, grumbling the while at the bad faith of our neighbors, wishing that every mouthful they ate of it might choke them. In a drive of ten miles over a delightful, grassy plain, we reached Thomas' Fork, a mountain affluent of the Bear, about fifty feet wide, which we crossed without much trouble. The bank was steep, and one wagon upset as it was drawn up, but without damage. Here Bear River was walled by mountains for about ten miles, and this spur we had to cross. The country was romantic and interesting, though hard for our cattle. The descent from one hill to another was often precipitous. After going down one long, steep descent, and winding for a mile or more through a narrow ravine, we came to a beautiful valley, through which flowed one of those fine, clear, mountain brooks peculiar to this region. Ascending another long hill, we passed through another crooked and rocky gorge, and by a long ascent of perhaps three miles, we once more gained a view of the river and valley below, from an elevation of more than a thousand feet, from which the descent was very steep, and somewhat difficult. The view of the valley with its green grass along the river bottom revived our spirits, and we drove on with the satisfaction of knowing that comfortable quarters awaited us. In the valleys we found strawberries, but they were sour and insipid, and upon the hills we found flax and wild oats growing thriftily. On descending the hill, the road lay over a barren soil without water, till we reached the river at a point about three miles distant, where we encamped near a village of Indians, who exhibited the most friendly feelings towards us. Distance, twenty miles.

JULY 12.

In the morning we visited the village, where we found traders, who had established a post there. The Indians had a large number of ponies, and we made attempts to trade; but the traders interfered, and we could effect nothing. We were told that during a hard winter they ate their horses, as we do cattle; and we found, some weeks afterwards, that the mountain Indians were not particular in their choice of food, for they esteemed the steak of a lean horse quite as much as that of a fat ox. We found them very expert in throwing the lasso. Their mode of catching a horse was by throwing the lasso over his head. Our route during the day was along the level bottom of the rvier, and while our train moved slowly on, I took my rifle and went to the mountains, in search of game. Deer and antelope made their appearance again, but I could not get near enough for a shot, and my only reward was a badger, which I did not think worth bringing into camp. Distance, eighteen miles.

CHAPTER IX.

HUNTING EXCURSION — MOUNTAIN SCENERY — BEAR RIVER VALLEY — BEER
SPRINGS — MINERAL SPRINGS — VISIT TO THE CRATERS OF TWO EXTIN-
GUISHED VOLCANOES — LINDLEY'S MISFORTUNE — RIVER NEUF — ARRIVAL
AT FORT HALL — PANACK RIVER — TRADING WITH THE INDIANS — MULE
TRAIN FROM OREGON — VALLEY OF RAFT RIVER — LARGE SNAKE — THE
AUTHOR GETS LOST — HIS SUFFERING FOR WATER — RETURN — VALLEY
OF GOOSE CREEK.

JULY 13.

Not satisfied with my ill luck in hunting the previous day, in company with McNeil, a right good fellow of our train, I made another excursion to the mountains. From the purity of the air, the distance to the base of the hills did not appear to be more than half a mile, but we walked steadily for more than an hour before we reached it. Following a gorge, which was lined with a thick growth of bushes, we were assailed by such a cloud of mosquitoes, we were obliged to cover our faces with our handkerchiefs, which they frequently covered so completely that we could not see without brushing them off. The moment we stopped the blood thirsty insects covered us worse than the flies did the fox in the fable; and had we not fought with bushes and hands, a coroner's jury might have rendered a verdict on our bodies — "bled to death by mosquitoes." At length we came to a point which we could ascend, when we resolved to climb to the summit and take a view of the country.

The ascent was a toilsome one, for we could not go more than ten rods without stopping to breathe. After clambering over rocks and threading narrow ridges, we finally sat down, exhausted, on the top, fifteen hundred feet above the valley, and the scenery richly rewarded us for our trouble. Along this green valley the river wound its serpentine course like a thread. At the south, a lake several miles in circumference laved the foot of the high mountains like a gem, (as it was,) in these solitudes, while behind us, as far as we could see, were broken ridges, valleys, and ravines, sparsely covered with fir and cedars. As we sat upon the bank of snow, the four seasons lay before us. Winter, with its snow, was under us; a few feet farther down, the mountain plants were just starting from the ground; and next the flowers and strawberries were in bloom; while at the foot the growth of summer was parched to autumn dryness, and withered under the fervid sun. The valley of the Bear River may be briefly described. It varies from two to four miles in width, with a rich soil. The mountains rise abruptly from its sides; the hills are generally covered with bunch grass, and sometimes fir and cedar trees appear on the sides near their summits, and aspen are occasionally seen, giving a cheerful relief to the dull monotony of nakedness, which this region of country universally presents. On approaching Beer Springs, the mountains are white with carbonate of lime, the surface resembling slacked lime, but a few inches within it has the appearance of lime just burnt.

After admiring the charming view till satisfied, we descended to the valley through another wooded ravine, committing a second slaughter of thousands when we reached *mosquitodom* below; and overtook the train after noon, with a glorious appetite.

At night we reached the first Beer Springs, two conical mounds, twenty feet high, with a base of more than a hundred feet in diameter, which was formed by the deposite of lime from the water. These are rather more than half a mile north of the road, and near them is a fine brook, lined with cedars, which runs into the river a mile or two below. These springs are one of the greatest luxuries on the whole route. They are highly charged with carbonic acid gas, and are as delicious as they are refreshing. They are equal to any soda water in the world, and though good without any additional concomitants, with lemon-syrup, or sugar, they are delicious. Two miles below are a dozen more, near the brink of the river, some of which are even stronger than the upper ones. On the opposit bank of the river are numerous cones, formed by the deposite from springs, but the incrustation has completely prevented the water from flowing. A spring is on the right bank, near the Soda Springs, through which volumns of gas are discharged with a loud noise, resembling the ejection of steam from a boiler, and is, in consequence, called Steamboat Spring. The follow-is an analysis of the water, according to Fremont:

Carbonate of lime, - - -	92.55
Carbonate of magnesia, - - -	42
Oxide of iron, - - - -	1.05
Silicia, alumina, water and loss, - -	5.98
	100.

The surrounding country is barren mountains, romantic and peculiar, abounding with evidences of volcanic action. With the abundance of traveler's comforts which existed, and the way-worn and weary condition in which we were, we felt a strong desire to linger a week amid the curiosities of this place;

but our great anxiety to reach the end of our journey, induced us to spend only the night, after a drive of sixteen miles.

JULY 14.

About three miles below the Soda Springs the river makes a short turn to the south, around a high, perpendicular cliff of black trap-rock, as it seeks its way to its mysterious resorvoir of Salt Lake. Here we took leave of Bear River and its fine valley, through which we found so many comforts which we had long been deprived of. The valley of the river is lost among the mountains to the south, while a lateral valley, without a stream flowing through it, runs northwardly towards Fort Hall. Soon after we passed a new route was explored across the western range, to avoid Fort Hall, and saving ninety miles of travel; but the first twenty-five miles is without water. This became the principal road; but as it was not known at the time of passing, we took the road to Fort Hall. Turning north around the point of a rocky spur at the extremity of the Bear Valley, we slowly continued our journey.

Nearly two miles on the plain west, we observed the craters of two extinguished volcanoes, and in company with my friend, Doctor Hall, I walked out to the southernmost one. Its form was conical, about eighty feet high, the crater being oval shaped, and probably two hundred feet in its greatest diameter, and about forty feet deep. Around its sides are black, burnt rocks and cinders, which have fallen off in places, leaving only a portion of its glazed, perpendicular walls standing, while a thin crust of soil at the bottom afforded a foothold for a small growth of sage. The crater on the north is about half a mile from this one, and is covered with grass within and without. The length is about the same, but it appears much older, and near it are three or four tumuli, which looked as if they were thrown out when the volcano was in active operation. They all stand isolated on the plain, with high mountains all around in the distance. The direct approach from the road to these craters was somewhat difficult. There were lines of rocky ledges of basalt, miles in length, having wide, continuous cracks in them, and occasionally funnel-shaped holes, sometimes quite small, and of which we could not determine the depth; and although we descended fifty feet into one of the chasms, we could not see the bottom. This main chasm ran parallel with the road about two miles, and then turned towards the mountain, the road crossing it on a natural bridge, of basaltic rock. Six miles from the Soda Springs we found another with a natural basin, formed by its gradual deposits of lime, and though its waters were sparkling, it was warmer and not so pleasant as those we had just left. Night brought us to the banks of a little mountain brook which ran across the valley, but we could see no outlet, and it was probably lost in the volcanic chasms of the valley. Distance, eighteen miles.

JULY 15.

About noon we had reached the end of the valley, and then passed through an ascending defile towards the top of the dividing ridge, between the waters of the Bear and the Columbia Rivers. For a few miles the road was uneven, with several sharp hills, and in some parts of the defile there was quite a growth of cotton-wood and shrubby trees, and when we attained the highest point, the descent, though not bad, was precipitous. During our morning drive, we were told of the misfortunes of Mr. Lindley, of whom I spoke when on the Platte. Since we parted there I had heard nothing from him, except what we learned from one of his men who overtook us.   He reported, that of five yoke of cattle, all had died but three head; that Mr. Lindley was obliged to throw away all his goods; and having constructed a cart from the fore wheels of his wagon, was trying to get through.   I subsequently saw him in the valley of the Sacramento, and he told me that he was enabled to buy another ox and a light wagon, and finally succeeded in getting through.   Night found us encamped in the Pass, near a fine stream which broke out of the mountain, and was of sufficient capacity to turn a mill.   Distance, fourteen miles.

JULY 16.

It was nearly night when we got through the defile.   In passing a grove of young poplars which stood by the road-side, we saw names of many acquaintances written on the white bark, with the different dates of their arrival ; among them was that of the Dayton company, dated July 13 — three days before us.   On emerging from our narrow road upon the barren plain, which was surrounded by high mountains, we encamped on the banks of the Neuf, about a day's drive from Fort Hall.   Distance, seventeen miles.

JULY 17.

We had become excessively weary with our long continued traveling, and the daily routine of duty became tiresome.   Not unfrequently, after a long or hard day's toil, we had to perform the task of gathering wood — which was only a few sticks, picked up perhaps at the distance of a mile, to be carried in our arms — or of bringing a pail of water half a mile, to make our coffee.   Under such circumstances, it was almost impossible to feel entirely good natured ; and bickerings would break forth ;

yet the duties were performed as a matter of course, and on the whole we got along well, and were weary, weary, weary. We contemplated one day's rest at Fort Hall, and therefore started off as early as possible, over a heavy sand-road, which continued four miles. Beyond this the plain was low, and filled with large and beautiful springs of the purest water, from many of which considerable streams flowed into the Neuf.

About noon we reached a barren bayou, which led into the Columbia, here called Snake, or American River, where there was excellent grass, and clouds of mosquitoes; and understanding that there was no grass, but plenty of mosquitoes at the fort, we concluded to halt for the day. The afternoon was variously employed. Some writing with yearning hearts to friends at home, others washing, mending clothes, airing provisions, making repairs to wagons; and others still, fishing, for fish were plenty in the stream — the first we had met with since leaving the Missouri — and our table, (i. e. the ground,) was abundautly supplied. Of all miserable work, washing is the meanest; and no man who has crossed the plains will ever find fault with his wife for scolding on a washing day. Rubbing in the soap and rinsing a shirt is not much; but when it comes to getting out the stains, dear reader, you will agree with me.

JULY 18.

We reached Fort Hall about nine o'clock in the morning. Its form resembled that of Fort Laramie, although it is much smaller. It belongs to the Hudson Bay Company, who, by treaty at the cession of Oregon to the United States by England, was allowed to retain possession nineteen years, in order to close its affairs, five of which have expired. We had hoped to obtain some supplies here, but were disappointed. The company were even purchasing bacon and flour from the emigrants who were overloaded. The fort stands on the left bank of the American Fork of the Columbia, sometimes called Snake, and formerly Lewis and Clark's River, which is here perhaps five hundred feet broad. On the west, nothing is seen but a vast barren plain, as far as the eye can extend. On the north, at an apparent distance of thirty or forty miles, high buttes and mountains rise to the clouds, with nothing in the view to cheer the traveler; and this we felt more keenly after having passed through the fine valley of Bear River.

On applying at the fort, we were courteously told we could leave our letters, and they would be forwarded by way of Oregon the first opportunity, but there was no certain communication with the States, and that our surest way was to take them ourselves to California. While thanking them for their frankness, we felt disappointed at not being able to send our remembrances to our friends. Subsequently we learned that no intelligence of us reached home, until four or five months after we left the Missouri. It was therefore anticipated that some accident had befallen us.

Around the fort were several lodges of Snake Indians, and a shirt was their only dress. The honesty of the Indians was so proverbial, that in traveling through their country we had relaxed in our discipline, and did not consider it necessary to keep night guard — a confidence which was not misplaced.

We were informed that it was eight hundred miles to the settlements in Oregon, and seven hundred to Sutter's Fort in California. About six miles below Fort Hall, we crossed Panack River, a little above its junction with the American. It was here an hundred and fifty feet broad, and so deep that it was necessary to raise our wagon boxes to prevent our provis ions from getting wet. Ascending a steep hill after crossing the Panack, we found ourselves upon a barren, sandy plain, where nothing but the interminable sage and greasewood grew. In the sultry sun, and through suffocating clouds of dust, we drove on till night. Our cattle found good grass below a steep hill on the bottoms of the American, after a drive of seventeen miles.

JULY 19.

Through burning sand, and in dense clouds of dust, we pursued our way, with the scenery of the plain but little varied. We frequently drove along the banks of the river, and it was always pleasant to view its sluggish current. About twenty miles below Fort Hall, it was nearly one-eighth of a mile wide, with rocky, perpendicular banks of black trap-rock, and rapids were frequent. The American falls were the first of these, and is caused by a dyke of black trap-rock, extending across the river in a horse-shoe form, making nearly a perpendicular fall. Near this are scattered on the ground, black volcanic *debris*, resembling somewhat anthracite coal, but which is merely melted matter, thrown to the surface. Laving the falls, the road was broken and hilly, with steep pitches, but we got over safely, without trouble, and reached our place of encampment before sundown. It was a barren spot, half a mile from the river. We found poor grass about a mile to the left, on the hill-side. After supper I went to the river, and descending an almost perpendicular rocky bank, I found, growing from a little beach, some of the finest red currants I ever saw. They were like the English currant, nearly as large as a cherry, and grew on bushes at least ten feet high. Their flavor was excellent, and I enjoyed a feast. While busily engaged in discussing their merits, I was startled by a strange, puffing noise, and looking to the river, I saw several Indians swimming and pushing a frame-work of willows before them. On their landing a little below me, I found they had fish, and came over for the purpose of trade. I tried my hand at making a bargain on reaching the wagons. They wanted a shirt for a small string and one fine salmon trout. I exhibited my stock, but they were unfortunately too small. I next offered them money, and quite as much as they were worth, but that they considered worthless. Some bright buttons were no better, but they offered to take a blanket worth five dollars. This was too hard a bargain for me, and I gave it up for a bad job, but finally I bought the whole lot for six fish hooks, both parties being equally well satisfied with their bargain. On their return, Hittle, Humpstead and Morrell swam over to their village with them, and were received in the most friendly manner. Distance, eighteen miles.

JULY 20.

Our Indians had promised to come over this morning and bring a pony, for which I had promised a blanket, but they did not make their appearance, and instead of a gallant steed, I was compelled to ride shank's horse, as usual. We crossed Fall Creek, a fine clear little stream, having a succession of falls, which have been erroneously, I think, called petrified beaver-dams.

Although there were some steep ravines, the road was better than we expected, and we found it unnecessary to use ropes in letting our wagons down hill. We met a train of five hundred mules, from Oregon, loaded with supplies for the fort. There were both men and women in the train. The half-breed squaws, with sun-burnt faces, soiled buckskin clothes, and wild, half-savage looks, made a strange appearance.

A long drive brought us to Raft River, or creek, for it is only two rods wide, flowing through a valley three or four miles wide, with good grass near the stream. Here the road forks, one leading to California, the other to Oregon. Distance, eighteen miles.

JULY 21.

Our course now lay southerly, up the creek, and during the day we crossed it three times. Last night two horses were stolen from an accompanying train, and the first impression was that the theft had been committed by the Indians, but subsequently it was believed that white men were the thieves. We began to see many traveling on foot, begging their way — having broken down their animals, and having no way to get forward but to walk. Most of the emigrants were disposed to render them all the aid in their power, but the supplies of the majority were only adequate to their own wants. The valley of Raft Creek was like all others in the country, a level, barren plain, except in the immediate bottoms. On either hand were high hills, rising abruptly from the sides, with black trap-rocks protruding from the surface, destitute of vegetation, except occasionally a few fir and cedar trees, and bunch-grass growing on their summits. It was quite dark before we found a small spring, a mile from the road, and although the road had been good during the day, general weariness had prevented a long drive. Distance, sixteen miles.

JULY 22.

Our traveling now became somewhat monotonous, with but little variation of scenery. One fact, however, was somewhat remarkable. Since leaving Green River we had heard of

G   10 scarcely an accident from fire-arms. When we first crossed into the Indian territory above St. Josephs, every man displayed his arms in the most approved desperado style, and rarely thought of stirring from the train without his trusty rifle. But no enemies were seen. By degrees the arms were laid aside, and by the time we reached Fort Laramie all were abandoned except a knife, and sometimes a pistol, which might be seen peeping from a pocket. Our train soon left the valley of the Raft, at the point where I have since been told the new road from the Soda Springs, found by Myers, comes in. Turning up a small branch between high hills, we traveled all day in a small valley, the road ascending all the way, and night over-took us before we had gained the ascent of the ridge, where we found a spring, about a mile to the right of the road. We were looking with some impatience for that "good time coming," when we might catch a Leprechaun, or gold-giving spirit, scarcely doubting that we should eventually capture him. Distance, fifteen miles.

JULY 23.

There were a large number of trains now traveling together, and for days we saw the same faces, and talked with the same men, while the scenery varied but little in its general outline. The course of long travel, however, like true love, "does not always run smooth," and so I found during the day to my cost.

On reaching the top of the ridge, which we did after pro-ceeding about a mile, we saw a large basin, surrounded by high mountains, the road apparently running around at their base, to avoid, as we thought, marshy ground in the valley, and from which a pretty creek took its rise. From the place where we stood we could see a line of dust all around the basin, with wagons moving on the opposite side. It seemed as if the road led out between a gap in the mountains to the south-east, in the direction which the creek ran, for we could trace its course by the willows. At a point nearly opposite, we judged the distance to be about twelve miles; and as it was the intention of the train to reach that place about noon and halt, I thought I could save six miles travel by walking straight across, which I concluded to do. When going out alone I usually put a luncheon in my pocket, to guard against contingencies; but with the *straight forward* prospect before me, I deemed it unnecessary at this time, and accordingly started off across the plain alone, unarmed, and without provisions. I trudged along leisurely, stopping to eat red and yellow currants, which grew in great abundance, when, as I jumped over a little gully, my ears were suddenly saluted with a terrible, hissing noise. Looking forward about six feet, I saw a monstrous, hissing snake, with its head elevated from the ground at least two feet, its eyes flashing with anger, and apparently in the act of springing upon me. The temptation of Eve must have been from a different kind of serpent from this, for as it ran out its forked tongue, and issued its loud hiss, there was more of defiance than of pursuasion in its tones and manner. On seeing the infernal reptile, I did just what anybody else would do on glancing at such play-things — I jumped aside about six feet, and then, ashamed of my own cowardice, I sprang towards him, as he was elevating his head still higher, either for fight or flight, (I could not tell which,) and brought him a blow with my trusty cane, which set the monster to groveling in the dust; a few more strokes put him in a condition not to disturb the walks of future travelers. He was over six feet long. When the deed was done, I found my heart was palpitating somewhat faster than a lovers on confession, and with an eye out for anything like snakes, I plodded on.   At the distance of about four miles I reached an elevation, from which I could see wagons moving in the basin around me on three sides, and satisfied that I could reach our noon halt long before our train, I lay down in* the scalding sun, covering my eyes with my hat, and was soon sound asleep.   I slept over an hour, and getting up I started on, but from the wet nature of the ground, was obliged to make a detour of nearly a mile below the place I intended to reach. On coming to the road, there were no trains in view, and oddly enough, the tracks of all the animals showed that they were going west instead of east.   I was in a quandary, and hesitated for a while to determine my course.   I finally concluded that the wagons would be above me, so I turned and followed the tracks.   After going about a mile, I caught a sight of six wagons, standing near the road side, and said to myself " all right," but I soon discovered that their hind ends were turned towards me, as if they were going back.   I could not understand it.   Advancing still nearer, I saw that they were not our wagons, but those of another train.   I did not know what to make of it ; and on going up I inquired,

" Have you seen the Ottawa company pass ?"

" No."

" How long have you been here ?"

" About an hour."

" Why, they must have passed in that time.   I saw them coming around the base of the hills not an hour ago, and they must be near.   Are there no trains camped near you ?"

" Not any."

"You certainly must have camped near us last night, and we have been traveling together for some days, I imagine. What time this morning did you pass the Ottawa train?"

"We do not know any such company."

"Did you camp last night on the ridge, or on the branch?"

"We camped on this branch, about ten miles below."

"Below! how can that be? The road follows *down* the branch."

"No — we came *up* the branch."

"Are you going to California?"

"Yes, we are on that road."

"Then *I* must have got turned around in my sleep. I thought I was bound for California too, but I may be on the road to Sodom, for aught I know. Why, I came directly across the valley, and the road follows around the base of the hill from yonder point."

"Not this road," replied the speaker, who began to comprehend my dilemma.

"Why — what road is this? How did you get here?"

"This is the road from Salt Lake, and we came that route."

"Ah! oh! — the mystery is explained. I find that instead of walking in my sleep, I have only been making a pleasure excursion into the country for the benefit of air and exercise. O Lord!" I exclaimed, as I thought of the long miles to be retraced before overtaking my train. I had walked across the valley and got into the Salt Lake road, and no one could tell how far it was to the junction, but I concluded to follow it, as I could stand it one day without provisions. I had a box of matches in my pocket, with which I could kindle a fire to shield me from the cold night air. It appeared, as I subsequently learned, that the Fort Hall road turned off from the basin, through a narrow gorge which we could not see, and the Salt Lake road, with its flying dust and moving trains, gave us the impression that our road was there.   Understanding my very agreeable mistake and situation, they kindly invited me to dinner, when we mutually gave all the information in our power to each other about the respective routes, and I gained much information about the Mormon City and its vicinity.   After dinner I left my kind entertainers, determined to keep that road to its junction with the other, which I concluded could not be more than a day's travel at the furthest.   The afternoon was excessively warm, and the plain over which I was passing was destitute of water.   I began to be thirsty.   By degrees my mouth became dry and parched, and I experienced much torture. On the left, nearly a mile from the road, I saw a line of willows, which experience had taught me was on the banks of a creek.   Suffering intensely, I dragged myself to it, and found, alas! the bed perfectly dry.   I could not find a single drop. My tongue began to swell; my mouth was dry, and I could scarcely articulate a word.   I had often gone all day without water before without much inconvenience, but now, for some reason, it seemed as if the very fountain of moisture was drying up.   In this miserable state I dragged myself along for three miles further, thinking I must use a last resort, when I caught sight of a cluster of willows growing near an outcrop of rock. With but small hope I went to it, and directly at the foot of the rock a soft, miry spot showed indications of water.   Stooping down, with my hands I scooped out the mud, and to my great delight water began to run in.   I could not wait for the mud to settle, but lay down to drink — faugh! the water was so strong of sulphur, that, under any other circumstances, it would have made me vomit, but I drank enough to revive me, and then scooping the hole larger, I waited until it had settled, and then took a long and hearty draught. Nauseous as it was, it appeared the most delightful draught I ever had. After drinking and resting a short time, my spirits revived, and I continued my journey.

About a mile beyond I came to the junction of the roads, where there were many sticks set up, having slips of paper in them, with the names of passengers, and occasionally letters to emigrants still behind. A mile distant, on the Fort Hall road, there was a singular outcrop of rock, which was a curiosity. There were three points, in the shape of sugar loaves, sixty or eighty feet high, and these were surrounded by many lesser ones of the same shape, and I could compare them to nothing else but heathen deities, surrounded by their kneeling worshipers.

Soon after passing the junction of the roads, I met Rood, one of our train, who had been riding forward in search of grass, and by whom I learned that notwithstanding my erratic course, I had got ahead of our train. He had found a place for encamping in a basin about four miles farther, and I continued on to the appointed spot, where I arrived two hours before our company came up. I probably had gone only about five miles out of my way, and the road I came was much the best. We camped on the western side of the basin, where a small brook sank into the ground. Drive, fourteen miles.

JULY 24.

My predilection for going ahead afforded a subject of fun for the company. Henderson insisted that I must wear a guide-board on my back, or I would get lost altogether. Another said if I did not stray away I surely would be stolen; while a third advised me never to go out again without a sack of bread and a side of bacon. Ascending a narrow ravine to the rim of this basin, we found a rough country, with steep and sidling passes, while at every step, as we advanced, indications of high volcanic action became more apparent. Cones and colored hills, rocks which appeared as if they had been rent in twain, deep gullies in every rocky and rugged shape, were presented to our view. Yet the road lay over the most eligible ground, and we proceeded without accident till noon, when we descended to a little branch of Goose Creek from a steep cliff, down which many let their wagons with ropes.

Here we found one train whose mules were nearly worn down, and being unable to draw their wagons farther, they were constructing pack saddles, hoping to get through with life. They had abandoned all their wagons and much valuable property; but this was nothing new. We almost daily saw wagons thus left, together with chains, bars, and various utensils, which nobody thought worth picking up. After our noon halt we ascended a hill and drove on to the wild, strange valley of Goose Creek.

From the summit of the hill, a fine and peculiarly interesting view was afforded. It had evidently been the scene of some violent commotion, appearing as if there had been a breaking up of the world. Far as the eye could reach, cones, tables, and nebulæ, peculiar to the country, extended in a confused mass, with many hills apparently white with lime and melted quartz — some of them of a combination of lime and sandstone — perhaps it might be called volcanic grit; while others exhibited, in great regularity, the varied colors of the rainbow I have seen the broken hills exhibit, in parallel lines, white, red, brown, pink, green and yellow, and sometimes a blending of various colors. It is an interesting field for the geologist, as well as for the lover of the works of nature. We were told that men were digging gold on Goose Creek, but this was untrue; yet it is far from improbable that gold, or valuable mineral, exists in those seared and scarified hills. On reaching the valley of the Creek, B. R. Thorne and myself, tired as we were, climbed to the top of a high table mountain which stood on the right of the road, and found the surface flat, and covered with melted *debris*, such as I have seen among the cinders of a blast furnace.

The road up the valley was excellent, and night brought us to good quarters on the bank of the Creek. Smith, with a view of having extras for supper, collected a quantity of fresh-water clams and crabs. The latter were very palatable when boiled, but even with a hungry stomach and long confinement on salt bacon, I could not relish the clams. Distance, seventeen miles.

G*

CHAPTER X.

HOT SPRING VALLEY — POST OFFICE — DESTITUTE EMIGRANTS — CHILL AND FE-
VER — A PARTY OF DIGGER INDIANS — ANECDOTES — THE GREAT BASIN —
HUMBOLDT, OR MARY'S RIVER — WILD FOWL — APPETITE AND PROVISIONS
— NEWS FROM THE PLATTE — SICKNESS AND ABANDONMENT OF MR. WARE —
INCIDENTS BY THE WAY — INDIAN DEPREDATIONS — MARY'S RIVER —
NIGHT TRAVEL — MORE TROUBLE FROM THE INDIANS — WOLVES — SLEEP-
ING IN THE OPEN AIR.

JULY 25.

Our route to-day was through a narrow vale, called Hot
Springs Valley, occasionally opening into basins, with high,
bare and rocky mountains around us. The hills were either
white with lime, or presented the bleak aspect of the black
trap-rocks in high and perpendicular cliffs. We passed several
springs which were so warm that the hand could hardly be
borne in them; yet within a few feet of one was a spring of
pure, cold water.

The grass was abundant and good, and we went on in as
good spirits as our way-worn condition would allow. A little
after noon we reached the extremity of the valley, where the
road entered a rocky pass. Here we were told there was neither
grass nor water for fifteen miles; and as it was too late to drive
through, we halted on the creek, which had dwindled into an
insignificant stream. A little time before stopping, we overtook

the Hennepin company, but they passed on, having determined to enter the cañon. They had lost three cattle since leaving Green River, but otherwise had got along well.

Near the close of the day, as I sat reading in the shade of my wagon, I was surprised at seeing Mr. I. Schaffer, an old Indiana acquaintance, ride into camp on horse back, in company with a gentleman named Beckwith, from Rock Island, Illinois. Mr. Schaffer informed me that they had started with three yoke of cattle and ample supplies, but finding themselves in the midst of a great crowd, and the grass so scanty as hardly to afford subsistence for their cattle, rather than run the risk of losing all, they disposed of them and purchased horses, and with the little they could carry, started off, to get through as best they might. They eventually succeeded, but with much exposure and great suffering. They fully corroborated the account given by the express rider, of the sickness on the Platte, and the lamentable condition of the emigrants. One whole family were swept off by the cholera, except one little girl, who was kindly taken care of by strangers, and brought through. They shared the meagre fare which we could afford them, with shelter in our tent — the best we could give. Distance, fifteen miles.

JULY 26.

" All hands ahoy ! — up and away," was shouted in our ears by day-break, and as soon as the cattle had sufficiently filled themselves, we entered the narrow gorge of Hot Springs Valley.

In a few miles it opened upon a barren, rolling, rocky country, though on the whole the road was good. In passing up the gorge, I attempted to jump across a narrow stream, but like thousands of others in the world, I missed my mark, and fell into the water, a remarkable subject of disappointed ambition, although I "looked before I leaped." Squash, squash — I had my boots full of water, and should have drank it with pleasure while on the Mormon road, but here, my want of taste, and a recurrence to more refined ideas, would not permit; so I emptied my boots on the ground, and trudged on ahead of the train. About ten miles in our progress, I saw, a little off the road, a natural circular wall of rock, shaded by a single tree. The strange sight of a cooling shade led me up to it, and I found it to be an emigrant's post office. Several newspapers lay on the natural stone seats within the walls, with a written request to "read and leave them for others." Scrupulously complying with this request, I looked them over, carefully folded and replaced them, and went rejoicing on my way. It was a long walk in the hot sand without water; but after crossing the hills I found myself on the rim of another basin, and from the appearance of many wagons standing together on the plain below, I knew water was near. A mile more brought me to them, where I found a small stream of lukewarm water, flowing in a trifling brook under the point of a rock. I drank freely, and then want an hundred rods and lay down under the shade of a lage sage bush, which screened my head from the sun. I soon began to feel stupefied and exhausted, and very sick at the stomach. I could not tell whether it was caused by the water I drank, or from a bilious attack, but it came upon me almost instantaneously, and when my wagon came up I crawled in, unable to do anything more for the day.

At night, a man came to our camp who had taken a passage at St. Louis in the Pioneer line of spring wagons, which were advertised to go through in sixty days. He was on foot, armed with a knife and pistol, and carried in a small knapsack all his worldly goods, except a pair of blankets, which were rolled up on his shoulders. He told us that at Willow Springs their mules gave out, and there was a general distribution of property, a small proportion of the passengers only obtaining mules, the rest being obliged to go a thousand miles without supplies, in the best manner they could, trusting to luck and the emigrants for provisions. The passengers had each paid two hundred dollars for their passage, but now, like the Irishman on the tow-path, were obliged to work it out. No emigrant would see him suffer under such circumstances, and we cheerfully shared our poor fare with him. At the first water I parted from Schaffer and Beckwith, who pressed forward on their long and dubious journey. On leaving the brook, we journeyed on over a plain, where there was grass but no water; and when night at length compelled us to stop, we found water by digging shallow wells in a moist place, but there was no grass at this point, and our cattle fared badly. The wind blew cold, and our condition was cheerless enough. Even the sage bushes were not plenty near the water, but our excessive weariness soon drowned all our troubles in sleep, after a hard drive of twenty miles.

JULY 27

At daylight we were astir, and five miles brought us to grass, but without water. We halted four hours to let the oxen graze, and then proceeded across a plain a few miles, where we found brackish water in pools in the dry bed of a creek. The ground in many places was white with an effervescence of salt. Night found us on a broad valley with abundance of grass, and near a spring of pure cold water, ten feet deep. No one can fully appreciate the luxury of a good spring, without crossing a desert plain, destitute of this essential comfort for the wants of man. Distance eighteen miles.

I felt extremely well this morning, and starting off in advance of the company, I walked about four miles, when I came to a pretty brook, fringed with willows. I took the tin cup which hung from a string in my button hole, and drank a hearty draught, and then lay down in the thick shade of bushes. Very soon I began to feel cold chills creeping along my back, and became satisfied that a day within the wagon was my fate. I felt almost discouraged when I reflected that that fell disease was gnawing at my heart; but there was no help for it, and when my wagon came up, I turned in under the influence of chill and fever. During the day we left this valley, passing some hot springs, and then by a gentle ascent, came as usual into another basin. The scenery was but little varied, and I was too ill to take notes. There was but little grass, and the water was poor and brackish. The days were excessively warm, and the nights cold — ice being frequently found in our buckets half an inch thick. Drive, twenty miles.

I was under the operation of cathartics, and spent a most disagreeable day. It is indeed hard to be sick in a wagon, while traveling under a burning sun, with the feelings of those around you so blunted by weariness that they will not take the trouble to administer to your comfort. At our noon halt we found good water, and a cup of tea revived me so much that I was able to walk some during the afternoon. Near our halting place we saw a party of Digger Indians, and I went over to them. As I approached, they advanced to meet me, offering their hands, and pronounced in good English, " *How de do*," followed by " *Whoa haw!* " They had picked up these few words from the emigrants, and pronounced words after us with surprising correctness. They were entirely naked, except a breech-cloth — of a dark complexion, nearly as dark as a negro, and showed considerable obesity. Their stature was about five feet six to five feet eight inches, with well formed limbs. Each was armed with a bow and a quiver of arrows, neatly made, tipped with iron. They saluted every one who came up in the same way, laughing immoderately, and seemed a merry set of mountain rovers.

An amusing story was told of Hudspeth's company, when crossing the mountains from Bear River. His guide took them by the shorter route from Bear River, avoiding Fort Hall. The Indians had mostly retired to the hills, but they had learned a few English words from the teamster's vocabulary. On Hudspeth's approach, they met him in the most cordial manner with, " How de do — whoa haw! G – d d — n you! " It was in fact the most common language of the drivers. In short, the most profane swearing was the common dialect of a great majority of the emigrants, and the poor Indians only used it as a welcome to the whites. On another occasion a party were inquiring for a good camping ground. They were assured that there was " plenty of grass for the *whoa haws*, but no water for the G – d d — ns!"

We fell in company this afternoon, with a poor fellow who was working his way to California on foot, his sole supplies being a small bag of flour on his back. His cattle had died, and he had bought a horse. This, too, had died, and with a lame leg and a cancer on his hand, he was limping his way to that bourne which was to salve all his aches and pains — the valley of the Sacramento. At our usual camping hour, we reached a beautiful valley of good grass, and a good spring of water, and turned off the road to it. Several of the teams were unyoked, when a thick coating of carbonate of soda was discovered among the bright green grass. A discussion took place respecting it, some declaring it was salt. I took a handful, and mixing it with water in a cup, applied a little tartaric acid, when it foamed and effervesced equal to any soda in the world, showing its nature at once. In ten minutes the cattle were reyoked, and we were moving from this valley of death. That night six head of cattle died from the imprudence of a company who encamped on the spot, and allowed their cattle to get at the alkali. We drove on four miles, and were obliged to stop where there was grass, but no water, and nothing was left for us but to do as we had done before — leave by day-light in the morning. Distance, eighteen miles.

JULY 30.

It had long been our desire to reach the great River of the Mysterious Basin. Our guide books assured us that for three hundred miles we should find good roads, with an abundance of grass and water. We therefore felt a curiosity to see a river flowing that distance, which had no outlet. We were now in the heart of the Great Basin, spoken of by Fremont. Since coming through the South Pass of the Rocky Mountains, it had been a continued series of basins, or valleys, surrounded by a rough, broken, and sterile country; and although there was varied scenery in the route, yet here there was nothing to distinguish it particularly from what we had already passed over. There was no line of demarcation other than the Rocky Mountain range ; and this is in fact the eastern boundary of the Great Basin.

By sunrise we had driven two miles, when, in sight of hundreds of wagons, we reached the celebrated Humboldt, or Mary's River, where we made a long halt for breakfast and forage. Here we again overtook the Hennepin company, on whom we had gained a day and a half since leaving Green River. The Humboldt is a small stream, perhaps thirty feet broad at this point, having a good current and pure water. It flows generally through a valley, several miles wide, with high and barren mountains on each side, which, occasionally coming near each other, the valley is contracted to rocky caverns which cannot be traveled. At such points the road leads over spurs of high hills, several miles across. Generally, on the margin of the stream and its immediate bottom, good grass is found, but sometimes the deep sand extends quite to the river, and forms its banks. Game began once more to appear. Sage hens, ducks, wild geese and cranes were very numerous, and easily killed. A few fish were in the streams, but we were unable to catch any with the hook. I was weak from continued disease, still I was able to walk slowly nearly all day, and kept along with the train without much difficulty.

It was a strange thing for us to have as many comforts as we found here, such as wood, water, grass and game ; and the sage hens and ducks made a delicious repast. To-day our sugar was used up, and from this time we were obliged to drink our tea and coffee without sweetening. It is astonishing what appetites we had, and how much the stomach could digest. It seems almost insatiable. I have frequently ate four slices of bacon and drank a quart of coffee at a meal, and still felt a desire for more ; and I have seen one of my mess drink half a gallon of coffee

11

at a sitting. This inordinate appetite, with the quantity of salt meat used, is probably one principal cause of the frequent cases of scurvy on the road.   Fortunately, we had a large supply of vinegar and acid, which, together with our getting out of bacon sometime before our arrival in California, prevented any such disease in our company.   When laying in my supplies I bought one hundred pounds of sugar for four men, and it lasted only ninety days.   Distance, eighteen miles.

JULY 31.

This was a day of *rest*, and, as usual, we were busy all day in renovating and repairing sundry goods, wares, and merchandise — washing and mending clothes, together with all such interesting occupations.

AUGUST 1.

The thought that another month would end our journeying, together with the *rest* which we had enjoyed, put us in good spirits this morning as we started off, and we made a good forenoon drive.

As we were leaving our noon halt, we were agreeably surprised at seeing an old Ottawa acquaintance in the person of Charles Fisher, who rode up on horseback.   Finding himself behind, in a great crowd, with a doubtful chance of getting through, he had sold his oxen and wagon at Fort Laramie, and purchasing a pack and riding horse, had come ahead.   As he left home nearly a month later than we did, his news was interesting to us, although it was but little more than that our friends were well.   He confirmed the accounts of the sickness of which we had previously heard, and told us that the cholera extended as far as Chimney Rock.   By him we learned that Mr.

Chipman, (formerly a merchant of Ottawa,) had lost his cattle in the great storm on the Platte, and had not found them when he left, and was remaining by the road side. He, however, recovered his cattle subsequently, and got through. I afterwards met him under melancholy circumstances on Feather River. Many had abandoned the idea of reaching California this fall; some passed on with the intention of wintering at Salt Lake, while others turned about and returned to the States, discouraged. Those who did come on suffered incredible hardships in crossing the California mountains. But the most lamentable case was that of the abandonment by his companions, of Joseph E. Ware, formerly from Galena, but known in St. Louis as a writer, and if I recollect right, the publisher of a map and guide-book to California. He was taken sick east of Fort Laramie, and his company, instead of affording him that protection which they were now more than ever bound to do, by the ties of common humanity, barbarously laid him by the road side, without water, provisions, covering or medicines, to die! Suffering with thirst, he contrived to crawl off the road about a mile, to a pond, where he lay two days, exposed to a burning sun by day and cold winds by night, when Providence directed Fisher and his mess to the same pond, where they found him. With a humanity which did them honor, they took him to their tent and nursed him two days; but nature, overpowered by exposure as well as disease, gave way, and he sank under his sufferings. He told Fisher who he was, and related the story of his company's heartlessness. He was a young man of decided talents. Fisher was confident that if he had had medicines and proper attendance he might have recovered. What misery has not California brought on individuals? — and this is but one of the many tales of suffering which might be told. This being my night to guard the cattle—a practice which we had resumed on getting into the Digger country — I shouldered my rifle, and wading the river, commenced my rounds. Distance, eighteen miles.

AUGUST 2.

Mr. Fisher took leave of us this morning; and, as he intended to go to San Francisco, we gave him the letters which we had prepared at Fort Hall, to be mailed on his arrival; but they never reached the States, and the first intelligence which our friends obtained from us was by letters written after our arrival in Sacramento.

Mr. Fredenburgh was very successful in hunting to-day, and returned at noon, loaded down with ducks and sage hens, and we fared sumptuously. At night we encamped near where there were two roads — one leading through a rocky point, which can be traveled in low water by fording the stream several times, the other a mountain road for ten miles, without grass or water. Distance, fifteen miles.

AUGUST 3.

Walking on in advance of my companions, without being aware at the time that the road around the mountain was passable, and seeing all the wagons of other trains turning up the mountain gorge, I also followed it up an ascent of three miles, when, on arriving at the summit, as usual, a barren and rough country lay before me, with the deep cañon of the river far below. Reposing under the shade of a sage bush lay a member of the Hennepin company, whose name I forget, but a very clever fellow by the way, and joining him we walked on. Soon we became so thirsty that we were obliged to descend the steep side of the mountain to the river, which we found was a some-what intricate and toilsome task. Here we found the other road, which was level and good, with plenty of grass, and we followed it several miles to the junction of the two roads.

Our train did not come up, and we became so hungry that we applied to a company encamped on the river, who were from Columbia, Lancaster county, Pennsylvania, for dinner, which was cheerfully given, and I found Colonel Halderman to be a well educated gentleman, to whose hospitality I was in-debted. It seems that our train discovered the cañon road, and preferred it, thereby saving many hard hills and something in distance, having good water all the way. Finding a good encampment, they halted for noon three miles below, and did not come up in three hours. There was a good deal of vexation among the emigrants who took the mountain road, on learning the character of the lower one, and they immediately called the long, hard, mountain trail the Greenhorn Cut-off — a name which it still bears. Our afternoon drive was on a good road, along which the valley resumed its usual breadth and character. Mr. Bryant speaks of cotton-wood trees and willows, which fringed the banks of the Humboldt. The place at which I dined was the only point where I observed anything that could be called a tree in the whole length of the river, all the rest being shrubs of a few varieties, and willows. Manifestations of Indian hostility began to appear. We saw an ox which had been shot during the night with arrows, which were found stick-ing in him in the morning. The same company lost several head of oxen the same night, and taking their trail into the mountains, found the remains of two, which the Indians had slaughtered and eaten. Drive, eighteen miles.

AUGUST 4.

One of the most disagreeable things in traveling through this country is the smothering clouds of dust. The soil is parched by the sun, and the earth is reduced to an impalpable powder by the long trains of wagons, while the sage bushes prevent the making of new tracks. Generally we had a strong wind blowing from the west, and there was no getting rid of the dust. We literally had to eat, drink, and breathe it. Two miles below our encampment the mountains again reduced the valley to a cañon, which was impassable for wagons, and we were obliged to cross a spur, eighteen miles in extent, before we reached the river again.

I was taken with dysentery during the night, and being too weak to walk, I had to take up uncomfortable quarters in my "moving lodge." On arriving at the river, after passing the rough mountain, I felt much better, and spreading my buffalo skin in the open air, slept well. From this time till we reached the valley of the Sacramento, I discarded the tent altogether, and from choice slept in the open air without inconvenience, and indeed long after I reached California. Distance, twenty miles.

AUGUST 5.

The weather was excessively warm during the day, but the nights were cool, and we determined to change the order of our traveling; that is, to lay by during the day, and travel at night. For the purpose of arranging this, we made only a short drive, and then lay up on a fine bottom. Distance, six miles.

We started off a little before sundown. The evening was cloudy, but the moon gave light enough for us to see our way, and in the cool air we made excellent progress. There were no trains moving but our own, and it was decidedly more pleasant than traveling in the hot sun. I walked forward some miles, with my blankets on my back, when, coming to a crossing in the river, I lay down and slept till the train came up. After crossing I resumed my solitary walk. The road at one point lay along the bank of the river, and Henderson, who drove the cattle, being nearly asleep at the moment, walked off the bank where it was six or eight feet high, and brought up " all standing," knee deep in water, skinning his nose against the willows, and cooling his nether extremities with a sudden and involuntary bath. However, he scrambled out right side up, and with his usual " whoa haw," &c., was plowing the ankle-deep dust again. I made a compromise with him, offering my old ox, of Green River memory, against his Mary's River bath, thinking that in the way of joking it was " a long road that had no turn." By daylight we had made twelve miles.

AUGUST 6.

The day was chiefly spent among the willows, or in the shade of our wagon, in the service of Morpheus, until the sun was about two hours high, when, lashing my blankets to my back, in company with Charley Traverse, I set out on my night's walk. The road was down a level valley, bounded by high mountains, as usual, and the river very serpentine in its course. We advanced at a good pace for some hours, when we came to the point of a mountain, on going around which we found the road stony and bad for a mile. After that every step was in dust ankle deep, making the walking extremely laborious.

Indian depredations were becoming frequent. The utmost vigilance became necessary in guarding cattle and mules. The Indians seemed to have as *cruel* a taste for beef as the Irishman's cow had for music, when she ate Paddy the piper, pipes and all.

We fell in company with a Missouri train, who the night before had five head of cattle stolen. The Indians had run them up a bank, so steep that it hardly seemed possible for an animal to go up. The company followed their tracks twenty-five miles, when they found them with all the cattle slaughtered, and preparations for a grand feast going on. The Indians, however, did not wait to welcome their unexpected guests, but fled at their approach to save their own bacon, for the men would most assuredly have shot them had they remained. Scarcely a night passed without their making a raid upon some camp, and for five hundred miles they were excessively troublesome. If they could not drive the animals off, they would creep up behind the sage bushes in the night and shoot arrows into them, so that the animals would have to be left, when they would take them after the trains had passed. During the night it became a common practice for those on duty to discharge their firearms frequently, to show the Digger banditti that they were on the alert, but this precaution was not always effectual, and as we advanced, the tribes became more bold. They cannot be seen in the daytime, but at night they prowl about like vicious beasts, and pounce upon their prey with comparative safety.

After walking about twelve miles we turned aside from the road and lay down in a water-worn gutter, our train passing us about one o'clock, intending to go about eight miles across the plain to the river, where we joined them at breakfast in the morning. Distance, twenty miles.

AUGUST 7.

The Hennepin company lost five head of cattle and two horses during the night. As soon as the loss was discovered, sixteen men set off to the mountains in pursuit. After going up a gorge something like six miles, they recovered four head. The Diggers had killed one ox, and succeeded in getting off with the horses. Another company lost ten head, and another four, in spite of all their vigilance. Not a day passed without hearing of similar depredations, and the emigrants resolved to pursue and chastise the robbers, if possible, in every instance.

In some cases this led to severe combats, and it was found that instead of being frightened at the sound of a gun, they would often stand and fight man to man with the most desperate courage, though they were usually defeated on account of the superior weapons which the emigrants used. If under any circumstances the Indians came into a camp, they were hospitably treated, and provisions given them, but war was declared to the knife when they made an inroad.

Captain Fredenburgh was my companion for the night, and after a walk of fourteen miles over a smooth road, we spread our blankets by the road side among the sage bushes. The night was " made hideous " by the incessant howling of wolves all around us, who often came within a few rods of us, keeping up an infernal serenade ; but as they did not otherwise molest us, we returned the compliment by letting them alone. At the dawn of day, we roused up, and left the river. Passing around the point of a small hill, we again came upon the broad valley. Beyond this, for many miles, there was nothing but sage, except the willows which marked the course of the river. The ashy dust was very deep, and when we turned aside to find better walking, the parched and dry alkaline crust broke under our feet like frozen snow, making it excessively fatiguing to walk.

A walk of six miles brought us to camp. The boys were enjoying a quiet snooze, and we cooked our own breakfasts, which we relished much. The valley was about fifteen miles

H

wide, with grass growing only along the borders of the river. We began to observe a difference in the volume of water in the river at intervals. Sometimes it decreased materially, then again it was full and deep. The water began to be warm and slightly brackish, but still it answered all purposes for use, without deleterious consequences. Distance, twenty miles.

AUGUST 8.

Reports of Indian depredations continually reached us, and perhaps one cause of our own good fortune in not losing cattle, was on account of traveling at night — thus having them constantly under our charge at the hour when they were most likely to be stolen. At the usual hour for setting out at night, Charley Traverse accompanied me in my walk, and we went at least fifteen miles without halting. Scarcely had we spread our blankets and lain down before the wolves commenced their usual music, and they approached so near that sleep was out of the question. Several times they came within two rods of us, and our pistols were cocked to give them a salute, but on rising up they retreated so far that we could not hit them, and we felt unwilling to throw away a shot. Fires were kept burning in camps not very distant, and the discharge of firearms was almost continuous, so that between the discharge of musketry, and the howling of wolves, sleep was impossible, tired as we were. As soon as the faint streaks of day began to gild the horizon, we set out to follow the train, as usual, which had laid over about six miles beyond us.

We passed through a narrow valley, made by the approach of the mountains to the river, where we saw the palace of a "merry mountain Digger." It was simply a cleft in the rocks — a kind of cave, strewn with wild grass, and might have served equally well for the habitation of a Digger king, or a grizzly bear. On leaving home it looked like a hardship to sleep upon the ground, but habit had changed us so completely that I could sleep as well and sweetly on a bare rock, as upon a bed of down. After our sumptuous meal of bacon and hard bread, we enjoyed the luxury of a quiet snooze in the thick shade of the willows along the bank. Distance twenty miles.

CHAPTER XI.

BROKEN SURFACE OF THE COUNTRY — VISIT TO LIEUT. THOMPSON'S CAMP — COL. KINKEAD — BAD NEWS FROM THE SINK — PASTIMES — LEFT THE HUMBOLDT RIVER — JOURNEY OVER THE DESERT — SUFFERINGS FOR WANT OF GRASS AND WATER — A MOTHER'S AFFECTION FOR HER CHILD — THE OASIS IN THE DESERT — HOT-SPRINGS.

AUGUST 9.

THE scenery during the last two days had been growing more interesting. The hills were higher and much more broken, showing the upheavings to have been much greater, and the dislocation of black trap-rock more prominent than at points higher up the valley. Sometimes valleys seemed to cross each other at right angles, affording extended views in opposite directions, while the mountains seemed jumbled into a confused mass of sharp points, cones, and nebulæ. The river, from being fifty or sixty feet broad, was now but about twenty, and instead of its original purity, its water had become discolored like the Platte. Its bends are often circuitous, and as grass was found only along its banks, we accordingly followed its course, increasing the distance much beyond the amount actually gained. The soil continued much the same. A quarter of a mile from the river it was a sand, or ashy plain, bearing nothing but sage or greasewood bushes, without water of any kind. As no one seemed disposed to accompany me this evening, I set out alone,

"Here, my child, here is water!"—*p.* 185.

having first put my pistol in good shooting order. For ten miles the road was over deep quick-sand. Thinking that to walk barefoot would be easier, I pulled off my boots and stockings, but the dry sand, grinding between my toes, soon made them so sore that I was glad to resume their covering. We now found that other trains had adopted our course of traveling at night. That day and night the road was thronged with moving emigrants. I had gone only twelve miles, when, being worn out by the labor of walking in the sand, I scooped out a bed with my hands, and laid down and slept so soundly, that I did not know when the train passed me. Towards daylight it became so cold that I could not keep warm, and when the morning star showed itself, I rolled up my blankets and set forward. A little after sunrise, on coming to a lateral valley, which extended many miles on the right, I discovered two objects lying in the road nearly in the wagon track, and coming up, found that it was Brown and Charles Traverse, who were quietly enjoying a sleep, where they could be conveniently run over by some passing wagon. Rousing them up, we followed the main valley about two miles, where we found our company encamped nearly a mile from the road, on the bank of the river. Distance, eighteen miles.

AUGUST 10.

Reports began to reach us of hard roads ahead; that there was no grass at the Sink, or place where the river disappears in the sands of the desert, and that from that place a desert of sand, with water but once in forty-five miles, had to be crossed. In our worn-out condition this looked discouraging, and it was with a kind of dread that we looked to the passage of that sandy plain. At the same time an indefinite tale was circulated among the emigrants, that a new road had been discovered, by which the Sacramento might be reached in a shorter distance, avoiding altogether the dreaded desert; and that there was plenty of grass and water on the route. It was said, too, that on this route the Siérra Neváda Mountains could be crossed with but little difficulty, while on the other it was a work of great labor and some risk. Near us was encamped Lieutenant Thompson, of the Navy, who had been in California, and who had once made a trip overland to the States. As it was an object to avoid the desert spoken of, we thought it worth while to gain all the intelligence possible on the matter; therefore, Colonel Kinkead, of Missouri, who was emigrating with his family, Mr. Fredenburgh and myself visited Lieutenant Thompson, for the purpose of making inquiries. The Lieutenant was on his return to California with his family, having leave of absence, and was now on his way to join his ship at San Francisco. His information was simply the report of others — that there was a good road leading into the upper part of the valley somewhere; that the desert would be avoided, and that grass and water were plenty; but that the Indians were very bad. On the whole, this prepossessed us with a favorable opinion of the route, but we did not make up our minds on the subject at the time, yet we did soon enough, however, as the sequel will show.

On leaving the camp, alone, I walked ten miles. Becoming tired, I scooped a hole in the sand, and slept till the cold morning air awoke me, when I walked with stiffened limbs into camp. Distance, fifteen miles.

AUGUST 11.

In consequence of the reported hard route before us, the boys again shortened the running-gear of the wagons to eight feet, to make them run easier, but as for our loads, they were light enough.

Although our outfit had been ample, while traveling along the Platte, Henderson became so alarmed at its weight, that he insisted on throwing away much bacon, which he did by trying out the lard for wagon grease — a measure which I foolishly consented to, not knowing the capability of our cattle, but which eventually proved a subject of regret to our mess. The scenery continued much the same; the atmosphere began to be smoky, and I will observe here that it continued more or less so — indeed, until the rains of the succaeding winter cleared it off. There were a great many men daily passing, who, having worn down their cattle and mules, had abandoned their wagons, and were trying to get through as they might; but their woe-begone countenances and meagre accoutrements for such a journey, with want and excessive labor staring them in the face, excited our pity, wretched as we felt ourselves. Our own cattle had been prudently driven, and were still in good condition to perform the journey. Although our stock of provisions was getting low, we felt that under any circumstances we could get through, and notwithstanding we felt anxious, we were not discouraged. Reports here reached us that the emigrants were cutting grass twenty miles above the Sink to feed their cattle with on the desert — a measure which we intended to adopt, should we conclude not to take the *cut-off* by the northern route. Distance, fifteen miles.

AUGUST 12.

We concluded to return to our old practice of traveling in the daytime instead of at night, and therefore remained in camp until morning.

AUGUST 13.

We made but a short drive, and encamped on a high sandy plain, with a good grassy bottom below, near Colonel Kinkead. Our guide books told us that our next day's drive would be fifteen miles, over deep sand, without grass or water — a kind of intelligence no way agreeable to us. Drive, fifteen miles.

AUGUST 14.

Contrary to our expectations, we discovered an excellent road along the river. There were, in fact, two roads — the upper, or sand road, was traveled when the river was overflowed, as it was in the early part of the season; and most of the trains took it now through ignorance, but we were fortunate in getting on the lower one, where we had the comfort of water. By noon we reached a capital encampment, twelve miles from our starting point of the morning.

Among the pleasant acquaintances which I made on this journey, was that of Colonel Kinkead and family. He was originally from Kentucky, but had removed to Platt county, Missouri, where he had a fine plantation, and was well established. The information which he received from California, of its climate, soil, and various advantages, gave him a desire to make it his permanent residence; and having an opportunity of selling out to advantage, he embraced it, and with his family and several negroes belonging to him, joined the grand emigration of 1849. He was a gentleman of education and much urbanity, and was fully imbued with that hospitality which is characteristic of his native State, and which times of scarcity and trial cannot change. He had, with ourselves, a favorable impression with regard to the new route, and more especially as his cattle were much worn down, and it was somewhat problematical if they could pass the desert. As our camps were contiguous at our noon halt, I stepped over to confer with him relative to some new information, or rather rumors, respecting the northern road. His eldest son was a tolerable performer on the violin, and while sitting in his camp he gave us a few tunes to while away the time. When I was about returning, he invited me in such a hearty, cordial manner to stay and dine, that I could not refuse. Had it been at his home, I should have felt no delicacy in accepting the invitation; But here, three or four hundred miles from any supplies, where but few have more than they actually required for themselves, I felt like an intruder; but the Colonel would accept of no apology.

In addition to our usual traveling fare, with an excellent cup of coffee we had a delicious pie, made of a nameless (to me) fruit, which grows in abundance along the river in this part of the valley. It is about the size of a currant, growing in clusters on shrubs from four to ten feet high, and its taste partakes of the flavor of both the currant and cherry. It is as agreeable as either, and made into pies, or stewed, is delicious. Miss Kinkead presided at our table, (which was a buffalo skin spread on the ground,) and certainly with as much ease and grace as if it had been in a drawing room, at a mahogany table with brass castors. My dear reader, if you ever travel across the plain, by the time you reach the Humboldt you will know how to appreciate a good dinner, and manners approaching to anything like elegance. Ah! pork and bread and long travel are sad levelers of refinement.

We made a long noon halt for the benefit of our cattle, in order to keep them in good order to cross the desert, provided we should conclude to do so. We now heard what proved to be true, that great numbers of cattle had perished there;

that the road was lined with their carcasses, and the effluvia arising from their dead bodies was insufferable, and that there was much sickness among the emigrants. While Colonel Kinkead and Mr. Traverse rode ahead to find an encampment, Mr. Fredenburgh and I went on foot about five miles, and at dusk came to the spot selected by our pioneers for camping. It was near several trains — one from Lexington, Missouri, Captain English; another from Bloomington, Illinois. Soon after our arrival, a Mr. Hammer, belonging to the latter company, brought out a banjo and gave quite an amusing concert of negro songs, and we had a merry time by the light of the fire. While Hammer was playing, one of Colonel Kinkead's negroes came in, and notwithstanding he had been walking all day, he found the music irresistible. He "jumped Jim Crow" in a perfect break-down style, amid shouts of laughter and cheering from the whole crowd. From here to the Sink it was said there was but little grass, it having been consumed by the trains in advance. Distance sixteen miles.

AUGUST 15.

Learning that the northern road turned off about three miles below, we moved down, and turning our cattle out, held a consultation with regard to our course. A man on horseback reported that he had rode thirty miles out on the route; that in ten miles there was grass, in twelve grass and water, and in twenty, grass and water in abundance; and on reaching Rabbit Springs, a distance of thirty-five miles, all difficulty would be ended. Others said that for thirty-five miles there was neither grass nor water; that the road did not go to California at all, but to Oregon, and that the Indians were troublesome and bad. Some said that only half a dozen trains had gone that way;

that they were led by McGee, a man who had lived in California, and was well acquainted with the country, and who expected to find a route over the mountains.

Colonel Kinkead was anxious to take this route, but his family becoming alarmed on hearing of the hostility of the Indians, and the doubts and perplexities of going through an unknown, mountainous country, finally induced the Colonel to abandon the idea, and keep on the old beaten track — a measure which was most happy for him, and proved that woman's fears are at least sometimes well-grounded. It was decided, finally, that we would go the northern route, although some of our company had misgivings. The younger portion being fond of adventure, were loud in favor of the road.

As we had been assured that there was grass and water on the way, we did not think it necessary to provide against these contingencies, any further than filling a small vinegar keg with water, for the purpose of getting over the first thirty miles, which, as it appeared a little doubtful in the way of essentials, we concluded to drive at night. Yoking up the cattle a little before sunset, and bidding adieu to Colonel Kinkead and family, we started off, Mr. Fredenburgh and myself walking ahead. We left the Humboldt sixty-five miles above, where it disappears in the sands, continuing down its valley for two hundred and thirty-five miles. A lateral valley led far to the north, and in the middle, towards the northern boundary, tall, irregular buttes arose, while high mountains were on each side. Our course was in a north-west direction, across the plain, towards a gorge, through which the road ran. The soil had the appearance of fine dry ashes, or clay, without its tenacity — rendering the walking hard. At the distance of ten miles we entered the gorge, but instead of grass there was only the wild sage on a discolored soil.   As we slowly wound up the gorge, scarcely able to crawl from fatigue, we felt the dubiousness of our experiment.   The thought of our Namaha wanderings came upon us, and we did not altogether relish the idea of becoming Israelitish again.   It was eleven o'clock before Mr. Fredenburgh and I reached the springs, which were a mile off the road; and suffering from thirst we took our cups and quaffed the first draught of pure, cold water which we had drunk for many days. We found a mule train camped around it, and, spreading our blankets, we soon forgot our weariness in sleep.   Distance, twelve miles.

AUGUST 16.

Daylight showed us nothing but rugged, barren mountains, and instead of the grass we had been assured of, there was not a blade to be seen.   All that there had been grew on a little moist place, irrigated by three small springs, and this trifle had all been consumed by advance trains.   The water from the springs sank into the ground within five rods of their source, and entirely disappeared.   It was now twenty miles or more to Rabbit Springs, the next water.   Our wagons had passed during the night, and were far in advance, so that we had the prospect of a late breakfast before us.   Taking a parting drink from the pure fountain, we pursued our way in a north-west direction up the gorge to the ridge, and then following down another ravine.   At the distance of five miles from the spring we were upon the north-eastern rim of another barren sand-basin, in view of a broken country far beyond.   About the centre of this basin, we overtook a wagon, standing by the road-side, when we begged for a drop of water; but, alas! they had none for themselves, and we were obliged to go on without.   Crossing the basin and ascending a high hill, we overtook our train, just entering another defile on the north-west, when we refreshed ourselves with a cup of tea, made from the acid water of our vinegar keg. It revived us, and we pushed forward, anxious to reach the promised spring, for our cattle as well as ourselves stood greatly in need of water. The day was excessively warm, yet we hurried on, and descending a couple of miles through a defile, we passed the most beautiful hills of colored earth I ever saw, with the shades of pink, white, yellow and green brightly blended. Volcanic mountains were around us, and under ordinary circumstances we could have enjoyed the strange and peculiar scenery. Turning westerly, we pressed on through a small basin beyond the defile, when, after ascending a little elevation, the glad shout was raised, " I see where the spring is !" Several wagons had stopped in the road, and a knot of men were gathered around a particular spot, which marked the place of the glorious element, and with parched tongues we went up. Judge of our disappointment, when we found the promised springs to be only three or four wells sunk in the ground, into which the water percolated in a volume about the size of a straw, and each hole occupied by a man dipping it up with a pint cup, as it slowly filled a little cavity in the ground. Each man was taking his turn to drink, and we had ample time to get cool before our turn came to taste the muddy water; and as to getting a supply for our cattle, it was out of the question. Beyond us, far as we could see, was a barren waste, without a blade of grass or a drop of water for thirty miles at least. Instead of avoiding the desert, instead of the promised water, grass, and a better road. we were in fact upon a more dreary and wider waste, without either grass or water, and with a harder road before us. We had been inveigled there by false reports and misrepresentation, without preparing for such a contingency, as we might have done, in some measure, by cutting grass on the river. Our train came up, followed by others. What was to be done? It was thirty-five miles to the river and about the same distance to the spring ahead. Should we go back? Our cattle had already gone without food or water nearly thirty hours. Could they stand it to go back? Could they possibly go forward?

While we were deliberating, four wagons came in from the west on their return. They had driven ten miles on the plain, and seeing no probability of reaching water, they commenced a retrograde movement for the river. A few of our older men hesitated, and were of the opinion that prudence dictated that we should return to the river, where we were sure of the means of going forward, rather than launch out into the uncertainties before us. But the majority, without knowing anything of the geography of the country, decided that they might as well go forward as back — trusting to luck more than to judgment — a measure which reduced us to weeks of continued toil and increased hardships. We came to the determination that we would wait till near sunset, as the cattle could travel better without water in the night than by daylight.

During the afternoon a poor fellow from Illinois, named Gard, whom we had traveled with on Goose Creek, and who was emigrating with his family, came in, after having gone on to the desert about six miles. His cattle were exhausted, and it was impossible in their present condition to go either forward or backward, and it appeared to us all that his case was sad indeed, with a family of small children. If his cattle had given out entirely, the emigrants would have done all they could; yet, in a burning house each one is apt to think more of his own safety than of his neighbor's. While standing at the well, I recognized Colonel Watkins, who, with all his judgment, had fallen into the same trap with us. He had driven over the desert about four miles, when the cattle of his train gave out. Two of them he got back to the spring, and got a little water for them, which, with a small quantity of flour, revived them so that they got through. One dropped down in the road, when the Colonel took two pails and returned to Rabbit Springs twice in a day, for two successive days, and carried water, which he dipped up with a pint cup, and gave the exhausted animal, thus saving his life. The other cattle were unyoked and driven through to Black Rock Spring; when, after recruiting a day, they were brought back, and hauled the wagon in.

While laying by during the day at Rabbit Springs, I had a visit from my old enemy, chill and fever, but luckily it was slight, and although it weakened me I was able to walk after it. We started about six o'clock, with anxious hearts and sad forebodings, on our perilous journey. We were on a level plain of ashy earth, where nothing grew but a few stunted sage and greasewood bushes, with barren mountains shading the horizon in the distance on the north and south. Our cattle traveled well, for they had thus far been prudently driven, and were in good heart, and we began to think it possible for us to get through without leaving our wagons. About midnight, becoming worn out, I turned aside from the road, and spreading my blankets, was lost to the world and to myself in sleep, till the morning sun was shining on my eyelids. Even the wolves did not awake me. Distance from first spring, forty miles.

AUGUST 17.

As I walked on slowly and with effort, I encountered a great many animals, perishing for want of food and water, on the desert plain. Some would be just gasping for breath, others unable to stand, would issue low moans as I came up, in a most distressing manner, showing intense agony ; and still others, unable to walk, seemed to brace themselves up on their legs to prevent falling, while here and there a poor ox, or horse, just able to drag himself along, would stagger towards me with a low sound, as if begging for a drop of water. My sympathies were excited at their sufferings, yet, instead of affording them aid, I was a subject for relief myself.

High above the plain, in the direction of our road, a black, bare mountain reared its head, at the distance of fifteen miles ; and ten miles this side the plains was flat, composed of baked earth, without a sign of vegetation, and in many places covered with incrustations of salt. Pits had been sunk in moist places, but the water was salt as brine, and utterly useless. Before leaving Rabbit Spring I had secured about a quart of water, in an india-rubber flask, which I had husbanded with great care. When a few miles from Black Rock Spring, I came to a wagon, standing in the road, in which was seated a young man, with a child. The little boy was crying for water, and the poor mother, with the tears running down her cheeks, was trying to pacify the little sufferer.

" Where is your husband ? " I inquired, on going up.

" He has gone on with the cattle," she replied, " and to try to get us some water, but I think we shall die before he comes back. It seems as if I could not endure it much longer."

" Keep up a stout heart," I returned, " a few more miles will bring us in, and we shall be safe. I have a little water left: I am strong and can walk in — you are welcome to it."

"God bless you — God bless you," said she, grasping the flask eagerly, "Here, my child — here is water!" and before she had tasted a drop herself, she gave her child nearly all, which was but little more than a teacupfull. Even in distress and misery, a mother's love is for her children, rather than for herself.

The train had passed me in the night, and our cattle traveled steadily without faltering, reaching the spring about nine o'clock in the morning, after traveling nearly forty hours without food or water. If ever a cup of coffee and slice of bacon was relished by man, it was by me that morning, on arriving at the encampment a little after ten.

We found this to be an oasis in the desert. A large hot spring, nearly three rods in diameter, and very deep, irrigated about twenty acres of ground — the water cooling as it ran off. But we found the grass nearly consumed, and our cattle could barely pick enough to sustain life. The water in the spring was too hot for the hand; but around it there was formed a natural basin, with the water sufficiently cool to bathe in, and I, with many others, availed myself of the opportunity to take a thorough renovation, which we found exceedingly refreshing.

Everything around bore the marks of intense volcanic action. A little above the spring was the mountain which we had seen from the plain, a bare pile of rock, that looked like a mass of black cinders, while at its base were fragments of lava and cinders, which resembled those of a blacksmith's forge. Desolation reigned around in the fullest extent. The desert and the mountains were all the eye could view beyond the little patch of grass, and the naked salt plain which we had crossed, proved to be the dry bed of Mud Lake. After the snows melt on the mountains, and the spring rains come on, the plain is a reservoir for the waters, making an extensive lake, which the hot sun of a long summer evaporates, leaving its bed dry and bare. Far to the south was another gorge, bounded on the east by a light gray granite mountain, which led to Pyramid Lake, and was the route taken by Fremont to California, on his return from Oregon. Beyond the Black Rock Mountain were other peaks, which united with a chain north of us, and along the base of which we were to travel in a westerly course. Learning that two miles beyond there was another and larger oasis, towards evening we resolved to go to it. Just before starting, I climbed to the top of Black Rock hill. As I ascended towards the summit, the air grew cold, and on the top I was met by a rain and hail storm, which chilled me through, though only a few drops fell at the base. I was glad to hurry down into a warmer climate, and follow in the wake of our train. At the second oasis we found better grass, but it was so filled with boiling springs, that there was danger in leaving cattle there. In one spring we saw the hide and horns of some poor ox that had probably fallen in and boiled to death, and in some places we had to tread with care, lest we should step into one ourselves, through the tall grass. We were told of another fine oasis, five miles beyond this, where there was every requisite for a good camp, and we drove on with the intention of giving our cattle and ourselves rest at the first good stopping place. Distance, twenty-two miles.

CHAPTER XII.

HOT SPRINGS — APPLEGATE'S ROUTE — ONWARD OVER THE DESERT — MORE INDIAN THEFT — IN PURSUIT OF THE INDIANS — DISTRESSING REPORTS FROM THE DESERT — QUANTITIES OF DEAD CATTLE AND HORSES — RE-MARKABLE CURIOSITY — CANON THROUGH THE MOUNTAINS — STANDING SENTRY — TRAVELERS FROM OREGON — LAKE OF SALT WATER — FRESH BEEF.

AUGUST 18.

ON looking around us we saw a beautiful plat of green grass, covering about an hundred acres, which was irrigated by the water of several hot springs. Two of these were very large, and from them ran a rivulet of sufficient capacity to turn a mill; but fifty rods below the brook was too hot to bear the hand in. The water in the springs was clear and deep, and hot enough to boil bacon. We boiled our coffee by setting the coffee-pot in the water. Near them was one of lukewarm wa-ter, another of magnesia, and one that was quite cold. All these were within the space of a quarter of an acre. We found about fifty teams lying over to recruit their cattle, after having lost a good many in the transit to Black Rock Spring. McGee had left his team here and gone forward to explore the road, and as he owned two or three wagons, loaded with goods, we could not doubt his intention of leading us through if possible.

We ascertained, on coming up, that we were on Applegate's route of 1846, when he went with two parties, one of which went to California — succeeding in getting through, though after experiencing much hardship; and the other, after losing all their wagons, animals and goods in the Cascade Mountains, were rescued from death by parties sent out from Oregon to relieve them. A guide book was afterwards published by authority, and a copy happened to be in one of the trains; but we could not learn that there was any traveled route to California. We learned that McGee's intention was to strike Feather River in a more direct line, and with less travel than by the usual route by Truckee River and Sutter's Fort; but as this seemed to be a matter of doubt and perplexity, much uneasiness was manifested by the different companies.

During the day most of the trains drove on, while a few came in from Black Rock, and among them Colonel Watkins. He was in possession of all the latest maps of California and Oregon, as well as Fremont's narrative, and by them we saw that we could follow Fremont's old trail to the south, through the Granite gorge by Pyramid Lake, and strike the old trail on Truckee River, losing but little if anything in the distance. This plan was suggested to our company, but met with no favor from the majority, who ridiculed the prudential motives of those who advised it. Everything with regard to a road being opened from Oregon to California was unknown, and the country had only been traversed by the small company in 1846, and their route was not known after leaving the trail that we were on. But the word was " Drive ahead; if McGee can go it, we can ; " and the man who hesitated was set down as a coward, when his objections were merely dictated by prudence.

By Colonel Watkins we learned that Gard had found a little

grass in a ravine two or three miles from Rabbit Spring, and that more water was found near there, and after laying over a day, he abandoned one wagon, and putting seven yoke of cattle on the other, succeeded in reaching Black Rock just before the Colonel left.

We had yet another dreary part of the desert to cross, over deep sand for twenty miles, without water ; and having it now in our power, we provided against the trials which we had already encountered, by cutting a good supply of grass with our knives, and filling our kegs with water. The latter was hot, but it cooled in the chilly night air, and was very sweet and good. Our cattle being recruited, we left about sunset, and were soon plowing our way ankle-deep in the yielding sand. Quite a number of men walked ahead ; and finding the traveling so difficult, we occasionally turned from the beaten track to find more firm footing, but without effect. It being all alike, we finally returned, and doggedly stuck to the path. When we arrived where we thought our morning walk would be easy, we lay down in the sand to rest, but the cold night air and the howling of the hungry wolves, who would have made us *bosom* friends if they could, prevented sleep.

AUGUST 19.

Before the dog-star glimmered in the east we were again on the way, and although the train had passed us more than two hours, we overtook it, and reached a place for halting two hours before it, with keen appetites for breakfast. This paradise was in the sage bushes by the road side. A little water and grass having been found a mile off the road, we stopped for breakfast, and to let our cattle graze, and then hurried on. Our course from Black Rock had been west of north, and parallel

with the chain of mountains we wished to cross. Many supposed that we were within fifty miles of the head waters of
Feather River, and some talked of shouldering a pack and striking across the mountains to it. So little did they understand
the distance, or appreciate the difficulties of mountain traveling.
The measure would have been perfectly suicidal, for it was four
weeks before we reached the first settlements, although we all
supposed we were not more than ten days' travel from them:
and had the attempt been made, situated as they were, certain
death must have been the result. After breakfast we continued
on, and about noon we arrived at a kind of wet valley, containing several hundred acres of excellent grass and plenty of good
water, which was a matter of rejoicing to all.

We were now across the desert proper, although we subsequently found long reaches of sand, and the highlands were as
barren as the plain. Instead of avoiding the desert, as we had
fondly anticipated when we left the Humboldt; instead of getting rid of a forty-five-mile sand-plain, we had actually crossed
the desert where it was a hundred miles broad, and in com-
parison, we should have looked upon the other route as a play-
spell. Nearly all the trains which had preceded us were encamped on the beautiful oasis, recruiting their worn-out animals,
and cursing the hour in which they were tempted to leave the
old trail. The first *agreeable* news we heard on getting in, was,
that the Indians were very bold and troublesome, having succeeded the night before in killing a horse and mule in the camp,
and driving off several head of cattle. The horse lay near the
road, and the gentlemen Digger Epicures had cut off his head,
and taken a large steak from a hind quarter — generously
leaving the remainder of the poor, raw-boned carcass for the
maws of the white devils who had brought it so far to grace

an Indian board. I well know that the air of the salt plain over which we had just passed, is rather peculiar in producing good appetites, and I should hardly have had much choice between a turtle soup and a horse-head stew ; but never mind : the bacon was not all gone yet, though it was fast disappearing. Distance from Hot Springs, twenty miles.

AUGUST 20.

We kept a strict guard during the night, and all the companies were on the alert; yet, notwithstanding all our caution, the Indians came down from the hills and drove off one cow and horse, and badly wounded two more horses, all belonging to a Mr. Watson, from Independence, who was emigrating with his family. One of the horses was shot in the side, and died during the day ; in the other, the stone-pointed arrow had completely perforated the back bone, and protruded six inches beyond — with such amazing force do they shoot these arrows. A volunteer party, as usual, was formed, to pursue the robbers. They followed their track several miles along a latteral valley, when they turned up a gorge, which the party followed two or three miles, and found themselves enclosed by high rocks and precipitous hills. Suddenly they were brought to a stand by a loud noise above them, and looking up, they saw the marauding party on a high rock a thousand feet above, making signs of derision and defiance at them. It was deemed useless to follow them farther, for by the time they could reach the height, the Indians might be a mile from them, by taking paths known only to themselves. The party, therefore, returned without obtaining satisfaction. We concluded to lay up for the day, and moved only about a mile lower down, where the grass was better, and where the majority of the wagons stood.

Through the day there was a constant arrival of wagons, and by night there were several hundred men together; yet we learned by a mule train that at least one hundred and fifty wagons had turned back to the first spring west of the Humboldt, on learning the dangers of crossing the desert, taking wisely the old road again. This change of route, however, did not continue long, and the rear trains, comprising a large portion of the emigration, took our route, and suffered even worse than we did. It was resolved that several trains should always travel within supporting distance of each other, so that in case of an attack from the Indians, a sufficient body of men should be together to protect themselves. We united with the Missouri trains, led by Watson and Bacham. Reports again reached us corroborating the great loss of cattle on the desert beyond the Sink. The road was filled with dead animals, and the offensive effluvia had produced much sickness; but shortly afterward, our own portion of the desert presented the same catastrophe, and the road was lined with the dead bodies of wornout and starved animals, and their debilitated masters, in many cases, were left to struggle on foot, combatting hunger, thirst and fatigue, in a desperate exertion to get through. Distance, one mile.

AUGUST 21.

There were about twenty-five wagons which left their encampments this morning, resolved to move on within supporting distance of each other. The road turned due west, over a sand hill and sage plain, and after traveling four miles, we came to the entrance of one of the most remarkable curiosities among the mountains. It was a cañon, or narrow, rocky pass through thy mountains, just wide enough for a smooth, level road, with intervals of space occasionally, to afford grass and water. On each side were walls of perpendicular rock, four or five hundred feet high, or mountains so steep that the ascent was either impossible, or extremely difficult. From this main avenue lateral cañons frequently diverged, and upon ascending a mountain, with much labor, the traveler reached a desert mountain plain above, where his progress was likely to be suddenly impeded by finding himself on the brink of a narrow chasm, one hundred or more feet deep, having its own branches and ramifications, sometimes extending quite through the hill to a basin, or open space among the high hills. Without this singular avenue, a passage across the mountains in this vicinity would have been impossible, and it seemed as if Providence, forseeing the wants of his creatures, had in mercy opened this strange path, by which they could extricate themselves from destruction and death.

Soon after crossing the oasis where we had been encamped, I went a little off the road; through a small lateral valley on the left, I observed an opening in the rocks, which looked as if it might be a cave, or chasm, and, on descending, I found it a narrow pass, leading in the general direction which the wagons were taking, and therefore followed it. It varied from ten to twenty feet in width, with perpendicular walls of trap-rock, towering up to a height of sixty or eighty feet, sometimes nearly forming an arch overhead. My progress, in a few instances, was impeded by perpendicular falls, six or eight feet in depth, but I clambered over these, resolving to see the end, if time allowed. In this manner, I followed the rent a mile and a half, without seeing the end, when, fearing the train would get too far ahead, I took advantage of a small open space, and climbed out by clinging to jutting fragments of rock. I fired my pistol in this singular chasm, and the sound was louder than

I   13

that of a musket in the open air. On coming out of the chasm, I found myself near the road, and where there was an Indian snare for catching hares. This was sage bushes, set about four feet apart, propped up with stones, and extending in a line at least a mile and a half over the hill, as I was told by a hunter who followed it. The hares, when alarmed, fled to the cover of these bushes, when the Indians shot them with their arrows. Pursuing my way a little more than half a mile, I came to a steep hill, down which the wagons were let with ropes into the cañon; and what was my surprise, on descending, to find myself at the mouth of that very chasm which I had been following. It was the outlet of the great cañon to the valley of the oasis which we had just left, and had I continued a little farther, I should have gone quite through the hill into High Rock Cañon, through which our road now lay. Between the high, rough walls of rock, we sped onward perhaps four miles, when we came to an opening of probably two miles in circumference, enclosed by rocky ledges, when it closed again with higher rocks than before. Threading our way onward, about twelve miles from our last encampment beyond the cañon we came to an opening of forty or fifty acres, covered with clover and wild oats taller than my head, when, with most of the other trains, we laid up for the day. A short distance before we reached our halting place, we observed a cave on the right, at the foot of the wall. It was twenty-five feet long by ten or twelve wide, with an arching roof fifteen feet high, and the remains of fires, grass beds, and burnt bones, showed it to be the habitation of the miserable race of beings who dwell in these mountains. In the rocks around our encampment were other similar clefts, and from their number, we named it Digger Town. From the meadow, there were lateral chasms leading out, one of which some of the men followed a mile without finding the end. The evening before our arrival, the Indians made an attempt to steal the cattle from a small train encamped at this place, and several shots were exchanged between the Indians and guard. The Indians were finally driven off, having some of their number wounded, and no further damage was done. Posting a strong guard, the companies retired to rest. Distance, twelve miles.

AUGUST 22.

As we drove along the cañon, we found good grass and water at convenient distances, and the traveling was agreeable. Near our noon halt, we came to a lower mass of rocks on the left, where a hill, six or ight hundred feet high, had been broken by a chasm, which had the appearance of having been melted; and its whole surface was glazed and run together like earthen ware in a furnace. With much difficulty I ascended to the top of this, which was probably more than three hundred feet high, and found the same appearance to continue half a mile. It looked as if it had hardly had time to cool. Even the most skeptical could not have doubted that it had at some period been subject to the most intense fires.

As our train passed on, Messrs. Fredenburgh, McNeil and myself followed the lateral cañon a short distance, when, coming to a place where we could ascend the mountain, we scrambled up to take a view of the country, killing, in our ascent, a large rattlesnake, which had the impudence to show its ugly face to its natural enemies. We stood upon a mountain plain, with no sign of vegetation but stinted sage. At the distance of five or six miles were towering mountains, which limited our view, while the plain was cut up by chasms and gulches, which made it difficult for us to travel in a direct course. We could trace the course of the principal cañon to a large opening some miles beyond, with a desolate view of red mountains, still farther on. The lateral cañon we traced quite through the mountain to an arm of a valley, which we reached the next day by a circuitous road; and could we have driven through this cañon, it would have shortened the distance more than one half. We followed the course of the main cañon perhaps two miles from this, and in passing a knoll of burnt lime, I picked up a beautiful petrifaction of sage. The lines of the wood were so perfect that I at first passed it, supposing it was a piece of dry bush; but my eye having caught it in a certain position, when the rays of the sun were glancing from it, I was induced to pause, when I discovered the truth. The plain was strewen with quantities of junk bottle glass, as pure as that made into bottles, and sometimes there were pieces nearly as transparent as common window glass. From a point on which we stood, we saw a grassy valley before us, into which the cañon led, and we perceived several tents and wagons standing in it, and concluding that our train would reach them, we left the mountain and descended to the camps. After waiting nearly two hours, as the train did not come up, we made a retrograde movement, and found them laid up behind a point of rocks, half a mile below where the cañon opened into the valley.

It was my turn at duty on guard after midnight, and at the hour I took my stand. The cattle were restless and uneasy, for we did not tie them to the wheels, and they were much inclined to wander away. I passed the time variously, in watching the stars, or in running after some old ox who appeared to be possessed of as many devils as the hogs which were driven into the sea. The moment I began to look at the stars, and think about their twinkling over the dear ones I had left behind, with all the sweet remembrances which followed, scanning anon my wild life of the last four months, and the causes which had induced me to lead it, some one of the horned species would start off at a gallop, followed by a score of long-tailed fools in his wake, when my sublime or moralizing cogitations would be scattered in an instant; and while pursuing the runaways at my utmost speed, all sentimental reflections would wind up with a " Whoa, haw !" &c. In one of these interesting flights, whether of legs or of fancy I leave the reader to judge, I suddenly found myself in a deep pit, standing midsides in water. This was standing guard and moralizing with a vengeance. Calling to another sentry, he came and pulled me out of what was truly " a predicament," and did double duty, while I started for the wagons to get a change of clothes. I had not gone ten rods in the dark before I plunged, " body and breeches," into another pit, proving to the life that " he who travels in the dark may fall into a pit." When daylight appeared, it showed, much to my satisfaction, that I had taken the only possible direction to fall into these water holes, and had I diverged ten feet, I should have escaped them altogether. Distance, twelve miles.

AUGUST 23.

As the grass was much better about five miles farther on, we drove to the extremity of the little valley, where we halted to graze our cattle and get our breakfasts. A fine spring brook coursed through the basin, and flowed down a lateral valley to the north, and we could mark its course by the willows some miles, till the whole seemed to be surrounded by the hills. After a three-hours halt, we again entered the cañon, which was now rocky and bad, with the creek flowing through it, which we crossed many times.

This last cañon was about two miles long, and just as we were coming out, we were greeted with the sight of a drove of fat cattle, and a party of men and wagons going to the east. It was a strange sight to meet travelers going in an opposite direction, and we mutually halted to make inquiries. We found it to be a relief party from Oregon, going to meet the troops on the Humboldt with supplies; but it was with much satisfaction that we learned that there was a good and feasible wagon road, leading from Goose Lake, beyond the Siérra Neváda, to California, which was opened last season; that the passage of the great mountain was not difficult, and that now there was grass and water all the way. This ended all our doubt and perplexity on the subject, and lightened many a heavy heart. The best news of all was, that we should reach the gold diggings on Feather River in traveling a little over a hundred miles. Alas! how we were deceived, for "the end had not yet come;" but the tale gave us infinite satisfaction for the moment.

On emerging from the cañon, an open sage plain greeted our view, with occasional strips of grass in the depressions of the country. A drive of eight miles brought us to a small ravine, where we found tolerable grass, and good water in the bed of a creek, nearly dry. Colonel Watkins had arrived a short time previous, and we often traveled together after this. Distance, fifteen miles.

AUGUST 24.

The day was smoky, and our view was limited and indistinct, but we could see in the hazy atmosphere the bold line of the Siérra Neváda, which divided us from our anxious desires. As Colonel Watkins and I walked on together in the morning, we were attracted by a large body of steam to several hot springs near the road on the right, which were throwing off a vapor in the cool air ; but there was nothing remarkable about them, aside from what we had already seen. As the day advanced the weather became sultry, and we had fifteen miles to go before reaching water. We had gone on a desert plain about twelve miles, when before us we saw a pond of clear water, perhaps five miles in circumference, and we all hurried to the muddy beach to quench our thirst, and eagerly dipped up our cups full. " Salt," roared one — " Brine," echoed another — " Pickle for pork," said a third ; and with thirsty throats, we resumed our toilsome march. Turning an angle at the salt lake, from north-west to north, we continued on ; entering a gorge, we began to ascend over a ridge about two miles long, when, coming to good grazing and water, we encamped. The mountains began to assume a more elevated outline on our left ; cedars and fir were growing on their sides, and the appearance of trees once more, although at a distance, excited pleasurable sensations, after having been so long without seeing them. Our bacon, flour, meal, sugar and vinegar, were all gone, and we had to take felon's fare — hard bread, and water — and this we felt to be much better than nothing ; indeed, we were much better off than many others on the road. Mr. Watson had an old cow that the crows had been quarreling over for a long time ; and thinking a little fresh beef, (save the mark !) might be acceptable, he slaughtered her. There could not be more rejoicing around the carcass of a camel by the Arabs on the desert, than we evinced around the poor, worn out, " knocked down" brute, and we looked upon it as a sort of

God-send, and like to have surfeited ourselves. Being out of meat, it seemed as if our stomachs only craved it the more, and our appetites grew sharper at every halt. Distance, eighteen miles.

"He slowly sank to the ground, striking wildly and with savage determination at Elliot.'—p. 215.

CHAPTER XIII.

THE SIERRA NEVADA IN SIGHT — DRY BED OF A LAKE — EXCURSION TO THE MOUNTAINS — NARROW ESCAPE FROM AN INDIAN'S ARROW — MOUNTAIN SCENERY — CROSSING THE MOUNTAIN — SALT LAKE — PITT RIVER — A HILL OF MAGNESIA — MOUNT SHASTA — A NOBLE ACT OF RELIEF — MAGAZINE ROCK — HEROIC FIGHT WITH THE INDIANS — ADVENTURE AMONG THE INDIANS.

AUGUST 25.

OUR road continued through the defile for five or six miles, when we came upon a broad track, barren, as usual, over which we proceeded ten miles to the first water — a warm spring which made an oasis. On the highest peaks of the Siérra Neváda snow still lingered, and the air felt like autumn more than summer. As we approached the base of the great mountain, over which we were to pass, we observed the valley, or basins, began to be more contracted and irregular, being broken by ravines and gulches, and points extending from the hills, and we became aware that we should soon be in the California mountains, and on the last end of our tedious journey. On arriving at the spring, and finding good grass and plenty of sage for firewood, we laid over for the day. Distance, fifteen miles.

AUGUST 26.

The Siérra Neváda — the snowy mountain so long wished for, and yet so long dreaded! We were at its base, soon to

I*

commence its ascent. In a day or two we were to leave the
barren sands of the desert for a region of mountains and hills,
where perhaps the means of sustaining life might not be found;
where our wagons might be dashed to atoms by falling from precipices. A thousand vague and undefined difficulties were
present to our imaginations; yet all felt strong for the work,
feeling that it was our last. Yet the imagined difficulties were
without foundation. Instead of losing our wagons, and packing
our cattle; or, as some suggested, as a last resort for the weary,
mounting astride of an old ox, and thus making our debut into
the valley of the land of gold — we were unable to add a single page of remarkable adventure across the mountains more
dangerous than we had already encountered.

A drive of four miles brought us to the baked, dry bed of a
lake, which I estimated to be twenty miles in circumference,
surrounded on three sides by the mountains. Towards the
upper end of this lake the Siérra Neváda seemed to decrease
much in hight, and we could see even beyond the plain over
which our road lay, that it seemed to blend with other hills on
our right, and a low depression appeared, as if an easy passage
might be made in that direction — even easier than at the point
where we crossed — where the bed of the lake was about five
miles wide, and the ground smooth and level as a floor. About
a mile from the base of the mountain, and on the bottom land
of the lake, were many acres of fine grass, with a fine mountain
brook running through it, which sank as it reached the bed of
the lake; and a little way from our place of halting there were
perhaps an hundred hot springs, which induced us to call this
Hot Spring Lake.

It was now only eight miles to the Pass, and the grass being
excellent, the company halted for noon, with the intention of

driving on in the afternoon to the crossing. I availed myself of the opportunity to make an excursion to the mountains, not only with a view of gratifying my curiosity, but hoping a chance shot might add something in the way of flesh to our larders. At the foot of the mountain I was joined by two young men from a Missouri train, and we commenced the ascent. On the sides of the mountain we saw a species of nectarine, growing on dwarf bushes not more than twelve or eighteen inches high; but they were sour and acid, not yet being fully ripe. In the ravines were an abundance of wild, black cherries, but those were not very good. Pines grew to a great height, and we were refreshed by their cooling shade.

I had preceded my companions along the border of a deep ravine, and was about fifty rods in advance, when the ravine terminated in a perpendicular wall of rock, hundreds of feet high, around which there appeared to be a craggy opening, or passage. While I was gazing on the towering rock before me, I momentarily changed my position, when the front part of my coat was grazed by something passing like a flash before me. Glancing at the base of the rock, I saw two naked Indians spring around a jutting, and I comprehended the matter at once. I had been a mark, and they had sent an arrow, which grazed my coat, but without striking me. I instantly raised my rifle and discharged it at the flying Indians, and sprang behind a tree. The noise of my piece soon brought my companions to my side, and going cautiously to the rock, a few stains of blood showed that my aim had not been decidedly bad; but we saw nothing more of the Indians.

Crossing a deep ravine, we climbed to the top of a rocky out-crop, from whence we ascended in a diagonal direction towards the road, which we reached in an hour by sliding, roll-

ing and tumbling along the ravine.   We were about four miles
from our train in the direction of the pass; and under the impression that the train would come up, I continued with my
companions to their camp at the foot of the pass.   The day
finally closed, and our train did not come, and I was indebted
to the hospitality of strangers for a blanket, supper and breakfast.   Distance, fourteen miles.

AUGUST 27.

Taking my rifle in my hand, I turned my course up the defile of the far-famed mountain.   The ascent was easy generally,
but occasionally there were benches which were to be overcome;
still the passage was far from difficult — indeed not as bad as
many hills which we had already climbed.   Grass was growing nearly to the summit; pure, ice-cold water was flowing in
little rivulets along the path, and about half-way up, near a
little stream that flowed into a grassy basin a short distance on
the right, was a most beautiful cluster of dark pines, which shut
out the glancing rays of a hot sun.   Beyond this the ascent of
another bench led to another basin, or small valley, and a little
further on arose the back bone of the father of hills.   For
about a quarter of a mile the ascent was somewhat steep, and
here was the only thing like difficulty.   Even over this many
wagons passed without doubling teams.   On each side of the
road at the summit, the ground rises higher, and the path passes
over a depression in the ridge.

Once arrived at the summit, the view of mountain scenery is
grand and beautiful.   Below, on the west, at the distance of a
mile, is a broad, green and grassy valley, abounding in springs.
The valley is enclosed by high, pine-covered mountains, which
seem to kiss the clouds; and at the distance of ten miles, at

the extremity of the valley, is seen the broad, beautiful, blue water of Goose Lake, adding a charming variety to the scene. Turning to the east, and looking beyond the pines already passed, the dry basin of the lake, with its gray bed, seems to lay at our feet, surrounded by barren hills, which extend in a broken, and irregular manner as far as the eye can see, and on each side the rocks and cliffs stand out in bold relief — the portals of the huge gate by which we enter the golden region of California.

Having gratified my curiosity in viewing the country, I returned to the bottom of the hill, where the train arrived soon after. They had found the forage so good at Hot Spring Lake that they concluded to remain all day — a determination which they came to after I left to go to the mountains. It was two miles to the summit, and they drove about half way up and halted for noon, in the deep shades of the pine grove — a perfect luxury, after having been so long deprived of the sight of trees.

After dinner came the last pull. At the steepest part our company doubled teams; but many did not, and the summit was gained without difficulty. The time actually spent in traveling from the base to the summit was not over one hour and a quarter, and the dread we had so long indulged of crossing this great mountain, died away at once at seeing the few difficulties of the passage. The descent on the west is rather precipitous, but not dangerous, and the hill is probably near a mile long. My impression is that a little further north, a still better passage might be found. A little before sunset we were encamped on the green valley, about a mile and a half from the base of the mountain, near a fine brook, and beyond arrow-shot from the pines skirting the base of the hill to the left. Distance, twelve miles.

AUGUST 28.

The road lay through the valley for three miles, when it turned into the pines over a low point, to avoid an out-crop of trap-rock, and soon rose to a higher plain, which continued until we reached the hill bordering the lake. It was the intention of several companies to lay over a day at the lake, and our boys made great calculations on bathing and fishing; but on reaching the hill their anticipations were blown to the winds, for the whole shore was white with carbonate of soda, and the beach a perfect quagmire, so that it was impossible to reach the water, except by throwing down sticks to walk on. The water was salt and soda combined, and was very nauseous to the taste. At the bottom of the hill were springs of pure, fresh water, and there was grass enough for our catttle at a noon halt.

The road now led south along a broad valley near the shore, with discolored and broken hills on our left; and a mile below where we descended to the lake, I observed the first out-crop of slate, which, in California, indicates gold. The character of the country began to change. The soil of the valley was a rich mould; pines and fir covered the hills, and the sage gave way to other shrubs, and appeared only occasionally. About four miles below where we descended to the lake, a ledge of rocks bounded the valley near us on the left, and on going to it I found it to be a strata of serpentine, the green and gray stripes beautifully blended, and the lines as delicately drawn as if done by the pencil of the artist. Along the base of the ledge the drift wood and water-washed weeds showed that during the flood season the ground was overflowed. The lake extended many miles south, which I estimated as it then was, to be twenty miles long by eight or ten broad. Night brought us to the end of the lake, yet the valley still continued, and but little above the water level, and we laid up on a mountain brook where the road forked — one branch going to Oregon, the other to California. Distance, fifteen miles.

AUGUST 29

We remained in our excellent camp till noon, and then drove down the smooth valley, crossing two fine creeks which made down from the mountains, and halted for the night in a cluster of willows, on the margin of another creek. While strolling through the willows, by paths which led to the brook, our men found a basket hanging to a tree; which contained perhaps two bushels of small fish, dried in the sun — a portion of the winter stores of the savages. In the absence of meat, we roasted some of these on the coals, and found them very palatable. A mile from camp, under the mountain, were half a dozen dwellings of the Indians. These were conical in form, about ten feet in diameter, built of grass thrown over a light framework of willows. I wandered out to them, but they were untenanted, having probably been vacated on the appearance of the first trains. Distance, eight miles.

AUGUST 30.

During the evening, on looking to the west side of the plain, we discovered a number of fires, six or eight miles distant, and in the morning several of the men were positive that they saw wagons and cattle moving along in that direction. It was supposed that the road leading from Oregon to California came in near there, and that what we saw were trains from Oregon. Being anxious to get supplies, if possible, I determined to walk forward to the junction, to meet those trains, and accordingly set out, alone. We found that, although our provisions had given out, our appetites rather increased than diminished, and it was desirable to stop the grublings of the stomach.

I walked very fast for six miles, when I came to Pitt River, the principal branch of the Sacramento, which arose four or five miles in the mountains east.   Here it was only a little brook, which I jumped across, but its numerous affluents made it a considerable stream in a very few miles.   I still walked on, and soon came to a high, rocky cañon, through which the river flowed, and the road led over a hill on the left to the valley below.   As I descended on the other side, I saw a train of six wagons, which I hoped were from Oregon; but on approaching I found they were from Davis county, Missouri — a company with whom we had previously traveled.   Instead of the road from Oregon coming in here, I became convinced that the camp fires seen by our men was the grass set on fire by the Indians; the wagons, merely clusters of bushes—and the clouds of dust which had been remarked, was that taken up by whirlwinds from naked spots of soil — a circumstance very common on the dry and dusty plains.   My hope of supplies was blasted, and not an ounce of food could be procured; we were therefore compelled to stick to our hard bread.   Some of the men of the Missouri train reported that there were plenty of fish in the stream, and a proposition was made to make a seine and drag the river.   This party I joined with pleasure; and taking an old wagon cover, we proceeded to a beaver-dam, and while a party went above to drive the fish down, we waded in the deep water with the primitive net.   In three hauls we caught fifty-five fine trout, and going with them to their camp, we had a delicious feast, made the more acceptable by a sharpened appetite. While there, three footmen came up, begging to buy a little flour. They had belonged to a pack train, and their horses and mules had all been stolen by the Indians at the little salt lake between High Rock cañon and the Siérra Neváda Mountain, and they were getting through in the only way which was left. They had pursued the Indians twenty-five miles into the country, north, where they came to a large lake of fresh water in the mountains, but here they lost all traces of the marauders, and were compelled to relinquish the pursuit. Being supplied with a small quantity of flour, they hurried on. Near the place of our halt were several singular out-crops of volcanic sandstone. There were between forty and fifty of these, standing isolated from·each other, in the form of cones, being from ten to fifteen feet high, and some of them were filled with yellow mica, which glitters in the sun like gold. Our general course from Goose Lake was a little west of south, up to the close of this day, and we again found excellent quarters in the broad valley on the banks of the river. About half a mile from our encampment I observed a hill, which was of a bright white color, and which was washed at its base by the river. I strolled down to it, and what was my surprise to find before me a hill over a hundred feet high, of as pure magnesia as I ever saw in a drug store. With some difficulty I climbed nearly to the top, and detached large blocks, which, rolling down into the water, floated off, as light and buoyant as cork until the they became saturated. It seemed as if there was enough for the whole world. A little below were other banks, partially discolored with ochre, and more impure, but we found the banks of the river and the knowls in the vicinity, for two or three days' travel, to be highly impregnated with the carbonate of magnesia. Distance, fifteen miles.

14

The road led to a table plain above the valley, over Magnesia Hill, and then turned nearly west into the valley again, in about a mile. From the brow of the hill we had a charming prospect. The great valley extended many miles before us, and at the limit of vision, perhaps eighty miles distant, a high and apparently isolated snowy peak lifted its head to the clouds, like a beacon to travelers on their arduous journey, and the clear water of the Pitt was sparkling in the morning sun, as it wound its way, fringed with willows, through the grassy plain. The high, snow-capped butte was Mount Shasta; and though it appeared to us to be on a plain at the extremity of the valley, it was in fact surrounded by a broken and mountainous country, far from the course of the river. We crossed the river twice during the day by easy and safe fords, and found the volume of water increasing every hour.

We were overtaken at our noon halt by three *packers*, who told us that the emigration had again turned upon this road, in consequence of the failure of grass on the old road; that there was much suffering on the desert, and that the Indians were excessively bold and troublesome. If there was much selfishness shown on the road, there were occasional cases of genuine benevolence. They told us of one family, in which there were several small children, whose cattle had all become exhausted, and had given out entirely. They were thus left destitute and helpless on the desert plain, without the possibility of moving. A company of young men came along, who were touched with compassion at their deplorable condition, and immediately gave up their own team to the distressed family, and traveled on foot themselves. I regret that I could not learn the names of these true philanthropists.

After crossing the river the second time, the plain was sandy and rolling, but we found a beautiful encampment on the bank of the river. A mile from our camp we passed a singular rock, of perhaps a quarter of an acre in extent, lying near a small pond, or marshy ground, that resembled a powder magazine. Its roof was regular, and the western end appeared like the gable end of a building. The roof seemed to project over the sides, while the earth was apparently banked up around it. From its singular form we named it Magazine Rock. Distance, nineteen miles.

SEPTEMBER 1.

The character of the country continued much the same, till about three o'clock in the afternoon, when our course changed to a southerly direction, leading into a cañon having some hard passes. When within three miles of our place of encampment, it again opened into a small valley. There were indications of Indians all around us, and we kept a vigilant guard, firing our guns and keeping lights burning around our cattle all night long. Distance, nineteen miles.

SEPTEMBER 2.

The Davis County train were encamped about a mile below us, and after broad daylight, their sentinel had started for the camp, when an Indian suddenly rose from the bushes and discharged an arrow at one of the oxen. The sentinel gave the alarm, and a force instantly set out after the Indian. They pressed him so hard that he was obliged to throw away his bow and quiver of arrows, two hatchets, and a pair of bullet moulds. Thus lightened, he succeeded in making his escape. The ox was slaughtered at their noon halt, and we were again regaled with desert beef. We still continued in the cañon for eight miles, though at one point passing over a hard hill to avoid a towering cliff five hundred feet high ; and had we not seen High Rock Cañon, this would have been a curiosity of itself.

We crossed and recrossed the river at least a dozen times. Three miles from our noon halt, after passing over the point of a hill, the valley again expanded, and here we came to the junction of the Oregon and California road. From the appearance of the Oregon fork, no teams had passed since spring, and all hope of further supplies was at once cut off; but we now felt sure that we were within two or three days' travel of the valley of the Sacramento. So strong was this opinion among the emigrants, that after we had encamped in a fine place on the river, a man came along on horseback, and on being invited to stop, he replied, that "we were within ten miles of the diggings," and (with an oath) said "he would not get off his horse till he got to them." I do not know whether he stuck to his horse all the while, but he did not reach the diggings in ten days. Distance, fifteen miles.

SEPTEMBER 3.

Three miles from our encampment we entered a spacious valley, at least twenty miles broad, with a rich soil, which only required irrigation to make it very productive. A little before reaching this, McNeil, Mr. Pope and myself, seeing that the road crossed the river, and supposing that it would soon recross to this side, resolved to continue under the mountain along the bank, rather than wade the river so many times as we had been compelled to do the previous day. On the right was a high ridge of trap-rock, and between it and the river a narrow bottom, rocky and covered with a chaparral of willow, wild cherry and plumb bushes. After a laborious walk of a mile through the chaparral, tearing our clothes and scratching our faces, McNeal and Pope gave it up, and waded the river, while I clambered up the crags to the top of the ridge. I found myself on a desert plain, without vegetation, and a little below the valley spread out to the right a long distance. Walking about a mile, near the edge of the cliff, I found several circular walls of stone, which had probably been the winter dwellings of the Indians.

In descending from the ridge to the valley, I lost my revolver, which probably dropped from my pocket while clambering over the rocks, but I did not discover the loss until it was too late to return and look for it. As I was walking through the tall grass near the river, Doctor Hall beckoned to me from the opposite side, and I waded across. He told me that they had just met a small mule train on their return from California to Oregon, and from them gained the information that we were still two hundred and fifty miles from the mines, and at least two hundred from the nearest settlement. This was a damper, when we expected that we were within one day's travel, at most, from Lawson's. We still had hard bread enough, but there was a tremendous cry within for flesh, flesh, flesh! Distance, fifteen miles.

SEPTEMBER 4.

Learning from the *packers* that after ten miles we should come to a hard mountainous country, we concluded to make only that drive, lay over the rest of the day, and commence the mountain road early in the morning. We accordingly halted at a point a little above where the river entered a rocky cañon, and where we were to part with it.

While we lay there, some horsemen came up, who gave us an account of a fierce combat, which had occurred a few days before between a small party of whites and the Indians. The latter had become very bold and troublesome, not only on the Humboldt, but on the plains, and in the mountains this side. On the Humboldt they had made a foray, and driven off all the cattle belonging to a man who had a family with him. A call for volunteers was made, and a party at once formed to pursue the robbers. After tracing them some miles in the mountains they found five head, which had been slaughtered, and the meat all picked from their bones. Here the party separated, and four men, two of the name of King, a Mr. Moore, and Mr. Elliot, taking a direction by themselves, while the others proceeded another way. Captain King, with whom I became well acquainted subsequently in the mines, corroborated the statement. His party had not gone far, when, on turning around a rock, they came in contact with four Indians, who drew their bows at once. Each man selected his antagonist, and a desperate fight for life commenced.

Elliot wounded his man mortally, though he commenced a flight. Moore had also wounded his, but he still continued to discharge his arrows before Moore could reload, who, to avoid the arrows, bent his head, but was severely wounded; while King, after wounding his, advanced, and after a desperate conflict dispatched him with his knife, after firing his pistol. The cap on Captain King's rifle exploded without discharging his gun, and his adversary discharged his arrows with great rapidity, without giving the Captain time to put on another cap. He however managed to dodge in time to avoid the arrows, and rushing up, caught hold of the Indian's bow with one hand, while the Indian seized the Captain's rifle. Thus they struggled until, becoming somewhat exhausted, they paused a moment, when King kicked his gun from the grasp of the Indian, and sprang after it. He avoided a second arrow, but as he was adjusting the cap, another arrow grazed his hand, inflicting a slight wound. His turn now came; the rifle was discharged, and the deadly weapon did its duty — the Indian fell dead. Elliot, being released by the death of his antagonist, rushed up to assist Moore, (who, though badly wounded, was still fighting desperately,) and shot the Indian with his pistol. Finding the odds now too great against him, the savage turned to retreat, but Elliot followed him with his knife, and inflicted a ghastly wound in his neck. Wounded as he was, the Indian now turned upon Elliot, who, with a pass of his knife, inflicted a wound in the Indian's abdomen, through which his bowels protruded, when he slowly sank to the ground, striking wildly, and with savage determination, at Elliot, with his own knife, and finally fell backwards in the agonies of death. The Indian was a hero, worthy of death in a better cause; but this desperate fight proved that the whites were heroes too, and that they were men of nerve and resolution. Moore, though badly wounded, eventually recovered, and though the cattle were never recovered, the emigrants by contributions furnished the plundered family with cattle, which enabled them to get through.

At about the same time, and in the same vicinity, the Indians took nineteen head of cattle and three horses from another train; the horses belonging to the gentleman who gave me the information. A party of fifteen men went off in pursuit, when on crossing to a rocky gorge, twenty-five Indians rose from behind the rocks and commenced an assault with their arrows, wounding some of the men, but not mortally. The company, finding their reception so warm, commenced a retreat, and were glad to get back to the valley with the loss of their cattle. The gentleman who owned the horses had taken another path alone, and in the course of the day, without knowing anything of the circumstances which had transpired, came upon his horses in a little valley, and as he was endeavoring to catch them, the Indians suddenly rose and bent their bows. He immediately advanced towards them, entirely unarmed, and by motions told them that those were his horses, and if they would assist him in catching them, he would give them his shirt. His resolute bearing seemed to have its effect, and signs of hostility ceased, when they made him understand that they wanted fish hooks. By good luck he had a gross in his pocket, which he distributed among them, after which they tnrned and caught his horses, and escorted him nearly to the valley, when, taking off his shirt, he presented it to the one who appeared to be the leader. On leaving them, he had gone but a few rods, when turning his head he saw several of them fitting arrows to their bows, but on seeing that he observed them they replaced them, and allowed him to ride off unharmed. More than an hundred head of cattle had been stolen on the Humboldt, and many wounded so that they had to be left. Distance, ten miles.

CHAPTER XIV.

LEAVING THE VALLEY OF PITT RIVER — FALSE ALARM — GOOD FORAGE — FEATHER CREEK — TIMELY HOSPITALITY FROM A BROTHER ODD-FELLOW — AN UNDER-GROUND RIVER — GAME — COOKING A BEEF STEAK — PROSPECT ING FOR GOLD — VENISON — EFFECTS OF STARVATION — DEER CREEK — STARTING ALONE FOR THE VALLEY OF THE SACRAMENTO — INCIDENTS BY THE WAY — THE VALLEY IN SIGHT — SENSATIONS — COL. DAVIS' HOUSE — LAWSON'S SETTLEMENT — PRICES OF PROVISIONS — EMIGRANTS.

SEPTEMBER 5.

WE bid farewell to the fine valley of the Pitt, and took our course in a west-of-south direction over a long hill, the precursor of a hard, rocky road. It was twelve miles to the first water, and fourteen to the first grass. The day was too smoky to obtain an extended view, but what we saw showed us a rough, mountainous country all around. For the first time, we found on the hillsides some oak shrubs, and as we descended at one point into a gulch, they were large enough to be called trees. We had been assured by the Oregon packers that, on reaching the mountains we should be among a tribe of honest Indians, who were neither hostile, nor would they steal our cattle; yet the first thing that met our gaze on arriving at our camp ground, were the remains of five head of cattle, which they had killed the night before. Of course our vigilance was

J

not relaxed, and that same night an attempt was made to drive off cattle, but happily for us, it proved unsuccessful.

We found a good encampment for the night, in a valley in which a fine mountain stream arose.   Distance, fourteen miles.

SEPTEMBER 6

We made a short drive of only six miles to-day, over a rough, hilly road, and as the next water was fifteen miles, we encamped. Distance, six miles.

SEPTEMBER 7.

Our information with regard to the distance to the next water, proved incorrect; for, six miles from our encampment, we found an excellent spring, about twenty rods to the right of the road.   The days were very hot, while the nights were so cold that ice formed in our buckets half an inch thick.   The road during the day was quite good, and before night we arrived at a wide opening, or valley, in the mountains, where there were lateral valleys opening into it, with high mountains on the sides, which gave us an extended view.   One of the accompanying trains slaughtered an ox, and the science of cooking was never displayed to better advantage than in the camps around us, as well as in our own.

About sunset, the general conversation turned upon Indians; and the course which each man would pursue in case of an attack, was being discussed.   Watson had a moment before come over to inquire about some arrangement respecting the night guard, when a cry was raised — " Indians, Indians !   They are coming towards us ! "   Looking down the valley, we distinctly saw three coming up, and as they approached, we saw they were squaws.   " Get the guns, boys — shoot the Diggers," was echoed, and several jumped for their rifles. "No, no. Don't shoot! Don't shoot squaws," was replied. "Let them come up; perhaps they are friendly." Every man was on his feet, and generally prepared for any exigency, while every eye was strained in the direction of the coming savages, endeavoring to ascertain their disposition, whether friendly or not.

As they approached within a little distance, we were at once attracted by a loud, guffatory "haw, haw, haw!" from Watson, and looking again, we saw that the hostile squaws were none else than his own wife and a daughter-in-law, in company with another woman belonging to his train. "Thunder!" "Gracious!" and a variety of similar interjections escaped the mouths of our valiant men, as they recognized their neighbors, who had only strolled down the valley, and were now returning; but whose sun-burnt faces, soiled and dilapidated garments, had made them look more like mountain wanderers than civilized beings. No harm being done, a hearty laugh ended the horrible catastrophe. Drive, eighteen miles.

SEPTEMBER 8.

About noon we found ourselves about eight miles from our last stopping place, on a fine creek which arose in the mountains a short distance off, but sank in the sands of the valley after a course of five or six miles.

The road was excellent, but the day was excessively warm. After our noon halt Colonel Watkins and I walked forward, and at the distance of five miles, came to a broad valley, near a lake of water, so filled with insects and animalculæ, that a cupfull could not be dipped up without having multitudes in it. It seemed as if every insect that lives in water was there. The only way it could be used was by digging wells near the margin, and letting the water filter through the ground, and then it proved to be sweet and good.

We passed, during the day, some of the most magnificent pines I ever beheld, some of them being over two hundred feet high, and at least six feet in diameter.   Mr. Gard and his family came up with us here, entirely destitute of provisions; but the emigrants freely shared with him, although he had no money; thus enabling him to get safely through.   He had lost eight head of cattle, but the others had recruited, so that he got along with one wagon.   We found a beautiful place to encamp, under a grove of tall pines, and our cattle fared sumptuously.   Distance, fifteen miles.

SEPTEMBER 9.

It was reported that it was twenty miles to the next water; we therefore started early in the morning.   We found the road good, and at the distance of fourteen miles, there was a little grass.   It was understood that the train would drive the twenty miles, which would bring us to the first tributary of Feather River; and with Colonel Watkins I had walked to the fourteen mile point.

As the train did not come up, however, I concluded to go on alone to the branch.   The whole distance was finely wooded with magnificent pines.   Occasionally volcanic rock protruded above the ground, and the soil was discolored with ochre.   It was nearly sunset when I descended a steep pitch to a small valley, through which flowed the Feather Creek.   While I sat near a camp, patiently awaiting the arrival of my company, with an anxious longing for a crust of hard bread, the shades of night began to darken, and no train appeared.   The prospect of no supper, and a bed without blankets, were rising before

me, producing no very pleasant feelings, when a gentleman approached, and stopping before me a moment, observed,

" You are alone."

" Yes, I am in advance of my train,·which was to come to
this place; but I fear something has detained them."

" No matter," he replied ; " I want you to go with me, and
spend the night at our camp. Come," said he, as I hesitated,
knowing that none were well supplied with provisions ; " you
must go and share what we have. No excuse — no ceremony."

I followed him, and such as they had I freely shared, and the
evening was whiled away in such pleasant conversation as well-
bred and well-educated gentlemen know how to introduce.
Gentle reader, if there is any mystery in all this, it may be
explained by saying, they were Odd-Fellows ; yet in all my
journey, when circumstances have taken me from my own
train, I have never, in a single instance, been denied the rites
of hospitality ; and although at this time, when our route had
been lengthened nearly three weeks — when every individual
had scarcely supplies enough for himself, and when a single meal
was an item of consideration, the courtesy of a civilized land
was extended, and the weary and hungered were not denied the
enjoyment of hospitality, such as Messrs. Cox and C. C. Lane,
of Flemingsburgh, Kentucky, extended to me.

The train did not come up. It appeared that, as they came
to the fourteen-mile halt, a beautiful lake had just been discovered, a mile and a half east of the road, and that they had
driven to it, where, finding luxuriant grass, they had concluded
to lay up all day. Distance, twenty miles.

SEPTEMBER 10.

That branch of Feather River where I spent the night, is a Rocky-Mountain stream of ice-cold water, about two rods wide. In the small valley in which we lay, another creek nearly as large gushed out at the base of the mountain. We had expected, on reaching Feather Creek, to find auriferous indications, but the formation was a kind of green-stone along the stream, and trap-rock in the mountains, with neither quartz nor slate.

The train came up early, and we went on. Ten miles, over a rough road, brought us to a paradise in the mountains, which is the principal head of the main fork of Feather River. A low, broad valley lay before us, probably twenty miles or more in length, and ten miles or more in width, apparently enclosed by high, pine-covered mountains. Into this flowed the mountain creek already named, through a deep gorge in the hills. A mile above, where the road led into the valley, was a curiosity indeed. At the very base of the hill the water gushed forth, forming at once a stream of crystal clearness, and cold as ice, six rods wide, and eight feet deep. In fact, it was an underground river, which had burst into the light of day, of sufficient capacity to float a small steamboat. From a little height we could trace its serpentine course through the tall grass of the valley for two or three miles, until it united at nearly right angles, with Feather River, which moves with a slow, even current, through the broad bottom, a clear, beautiful and navigable river. Many miles below it entered the mountains through a high, rocky and almost impassable cañon, being joined, however, by another affluent of nearly the same size, flowing from the northeast, through a broad lateral valley, and then by a long series of rapids and falls, after a circuitous course of between two and three hundred miles, it emerged from the foot of hills, through a rough cañon, into the broad valley of the Sacramento. From the indications along the edges, this valley is overflowed by the rains of winter and the melting snow of spring — thus making a broad but shallow mountain lake, of from sixty to eighty miles in circumference. Ducks, swans and wild geese covered its waters, and elk, black-tailed deer, and antelope were numerous on the bottoms; while the tracks of the grizzly bear, the wolf and cougar, were frequent on the hills. We halted for the night on this beautiful bottom, after a drive of sixteen miles.

SEPTEMBER 11.

It was rather late before we started, this morning; and proceeding down the valley, crossing some bad hills, over spurs which put down from the mountain on the right, before noon we came to the lateral valley before mentioned, which is only an arm of the main one, and through which flows the principal affluent, which rises in the hills in sight, at the upper extremity.

This part of the valley was about five miles wide, and besides the river there were several deep sloughs, through which we had to wade, and from the hills on the western bank other creeks and branches took their rise. About one o'clock, we reached the western side of the valley, where there was an encampment of a hundred wagons, laying over to recruit their cattle, for it was known that it was seventy miles to Lawson's, in the valley of the Sacramento, and also, that fifty miles of the distance was over a rough, mountain desert, destitute of grass and water. Lawson himself had passed the day before with an exploring party, and had left directions what course we were to take to reach the valley, as well as a table of distances to water, which was posted on a tree by the roadside above our camp.   Distance, ten miles.

SEPTEMBER 12.

We were now in the valley of plenty.   Our poor teeth, which had been laboring on the filelike consistency of pilot bread, had now a respite, in the agreeable task of masticating from the " flesh pots" of California.

As we determined to lay over during the day, our wagon master, Traverse, concluded to butcher an ox, and the hungry Arabs of our train were regaled with a feast of dead kine. Feeling an aristocratic longing for a rich beef steak, I determined to have one.   There was not a particle of fat in the steak to make gravy, nor was there a slice of bacon to be had to fry it with, and the flesh was as dry and as hard as a bone. But a nice broiled steak, with a plenty of gravy, I would have — and I had it.   The inventive genius of an emigrant is almost constantly called forth on the plains, and so in my case.   I laid a nice cut on the coals, which, instead of broiling, only burnt, and carbonized like a piece of wood, and when one side was turned to cinder, I whopped it over to make charcoal of the other.   To make butter gravy, I melted a stearin candle, which I poured over the delicious tit-bit, and, smacking my lips, sat down to my feast, the envy of several lookers-on.   I sopped the first mouthful in the nice looking gravy, and put it between my teeth, when the gravy cooled almost instantly, and the roof of my mouth and my teeth were coated all over with a covering like hard beeswax, making mastication next to impossible.

" How does it go ?" asked one.

" O, first rate," said I, struggling to get the hard, dry morsel down my throat ; and cutting off another piece, which was free from the delicious gravy, "Come, try it," said I; "I have more than I can eat, (which was true.) You are welcome to it." The envious, hungry soul sat down, and putting a large piece between his teeth, after rolling it about in his mouth awhile, deliberately spit it out, saying, with an oath, that

"Chips and beeswax are hard fare, even for a starving man."

Ah, how hard words and want of sentiment will steal over one's better nature on the plains. As for the rest of the steak, we left it to choke the wolves.

We were successful in killing ducks, and our evening meal was more palatable. At night a hunter came in and reported that he had seen an out-crop of slate on a mountain bordering the valley below, and from his description we thought there were indications of gold, and a small party was organized for prospecting the following morning.

SEPTEMBER 13.

How long we might be out in prospecting we could not tell, but putting up a two days' supply of bread and coffee, a party of six of us started off, under the guidance of the hunter, to the mountain, while the train took the road toward Lawson's, after cutting grass to be used on the desert. Three miles traveling brought us to a lofty mountain, and about midway up its sides was a small out-crop of light gray slate, standing about ten degrees from a vertical position, the dip in the rock being to the south-east. We made some slight excavations, and washed some of the earth, but obtained nothing, and concluded to return to the road in a diagonal direction, so as to save distance in overtaking the train. Three of the party, Hittle, Tuttle and Jackson, took a different direction, and crossed a ridge to the valley below, when they became bewilered, and were out all

J*   15

night. This little prospecting tour was the origin of a report to emigrants behind that there was good gold diggings near, and at one time a party of forty men started out and spent several days in searching for the lucky mines. Some penetrated to the cañon of the river, and a few followed it down many miles, climbing rocks and stupendous mountains, crossing gulches, and forcing their way through chaparral — suffering hunger, thirst and fatigue — until they were compelled to relinquish their golden hopes, and make for the road again. On reaching the road we walked briskly on for eight miles, over a somewhat rocky road, and coming to a fine mountain stream, called Deer Creek, we stopped in a beautiful cluster of trees. Here we made coffee in our prospecting pan, and satisfied our appetites on our hard bread. Two miles beyond we found our train encamped, and the boys out hunting. They were successful, and several black-tailed deer were brought in, and several grizzly bears were seen. Distance, twelve miles.

SEPTEMBER 14.

The success in hunting the previous day induced our company to remain in camp to-day, for the purpose of killing more deer, but they obtained only one. A short distance from the camp, whortle and goose berries were abundant, but they were not very good; however, they were very acceptable. Hittle, Tuttle and Jackson came in about noon, pretty well used up with fatigue and hunger, having ate nothing since they parted with us. We heard of one poor fellow who got lost while hunting, and was out six days, roaming over the mountains, and who had gone three days without eating. On approaching the road he seemed to be bewildered, and by his strange conduct, attracted the attention of a passing train. His impulse seemed to be to fly, as they approached, and then return; but he finally allowed some of the men to approach him, when, with a wild, hysterical laugh he told them where he had been. They took him to their wagons and fed him, and after resting quietly through the night, he became perfectly composed again, and followed after his train, which was about thirty miles in advance, having given him up as lost.

SEPTEMBER 15.

Six miles below, along the valley of Deer Creek, we came to the last grass, and where the mountain desert of fifty miles commenced. We now began to feel that our long, toilsome journey was coming to a close. We felt, too, that we could reach the settlements under any contingency which was likely to arise. Although we were worn down with fatigue, and want of nutricious food, our spirits were elevated because our monotonous travel was coming to an end. Our future course began to be talked of, yet we expected that our company, on reaching the valley, would dissolve, as the object of association would then be accomplished; still, no one could mark out a course for himself, to be persued with any certainty. As a matter of course, all would go into the mines, and the best mines, if such could be ascertained. To ascertain what could be done on our arrival, I determined, at the request of several members of the compny, to go ahead to the valley, to gain any information which might be useful to us. After dinner I took a check shirt, and tying the sleeves together, made a kind of knapsack, in which I put three days' supply of bread, jerked venison and coffee, and started on my solitary walk across the mountain desert. Twice, in as many miles, I waded Deer Creek, and then through a dark forest of tall pines I persued my lonely

walk, over a sideling and very rocky road.   Five miles beyond
I came to an open glade, where there was an encampment
of troops, who had come out to afford aid to the emigrants, if
necessary, and from them I learned that three miles beyond
there was a spring.   It was nearly sunset when I again entered
the deep wood, but my anxiety to get in sight of the abodes of
civilized man impelled me forward, choosing to risk a night
alone in the woods, among the wild beasts which swarmed in
that region, rather than not gain the distance.   The road now
led over long hills, over rocks, and among tall pines, and it soon
began to grow dark.   In the faint twilight of evening I discovered a fresh track, which I concluded was that of a negro's foot,
and I felt satisfied that some train was at no great distance before me.   I followed the track a mile, when it suddenly turned
into the bushes, and while I was examining it with some curiosity, a deep, low growl a short distance in that direction convinced me that I was in close proximity to a grizzly bear.
Even if I had been armed, it would have been dangerous to meet
such an enemy alone.   Having only my hunting knife, I did
not desire a closer acquaintance with the monster.   I therefore
walked on without the ceremony of leave-taking.

While I was congratulating myself on my escape, and had
walked over half a mile, I saw the glimmer of a light through
the trees.   It was now pitch dark, and I was hastening on, in
order to light a fire at the spring, to lay down by ; but on
coming up I found a bright fire blazing before an encampment
of several wagons, and I was familiarily hailed by a well
known voice.   It proved to be the Davis County train, and
I was cordially welcomed, and invited to spend the night in
their camp — an invitation too agreeable, under my present circumstances, to be slighted.   Distance, fourteen miles.

SEPTEMBER 16.

By sunrise we had breakfasted, and gathering up my blankets and knapsack, I bid farewell to my kind entertainers, and walked on. I had not gone a mile from the spring, when the tracks of two large bears were seen in the road, and a few rods farther, about ten rods off the road, I saw the monsters standing near the trunk of a fallen tree. But as they showed no disposition to molest me, I felt grateful for their forbearance, and left them in peace, hoping they would show the same kindly feelings to future solitary travelers. Before leaving the spring I had filled my flask with water, for it was said that there was none to be found in the day's travel. A short distance from the spring the road ascends to a high ridge, with gulfs on each side more than a thousand feet deep, and in some places only wide enough for the road, and seldom over fifty rods. The country around is a confused, broken mass of mountains, to the utmost limit of vision, and is highly auriferous, with stupendous out-crops of slate and white quartz. The road continues along this ridge nearly twenty miles, though there are occasional indentions, which make hard, rocky and sideling hills for wagons to pass. Eight miles from the spring, a notice on a tree informed me that water had been discovered over the bank on the right, and a note to myself on the same tree from Colonel Watkins, also informed me that he was in advance. At length I passed the apex of the ridge, and began to descend gradually on the other side, when I found the pines began to give place to ever-green oaks; and I observed many trees that had been cut down, so that the poor, hungry cattle could browse upon the tender branches — a substitute that would scarcely sustain life. About noon my stomach admonished me that it was dinner-time, and kindling a fire in the shade of some oaks by the road-side, I boiled coffee in my tin cup, from water in my flask, and made a sumptuous meal of my hard bread and jerked venison, with a zest which even Robinson Crusoe might have envied.   It was now six miles before water could be obtained, and after resting I plodded on to that favored spot, where I found thirty or forty wagons on the ridge, with weary and exhausted cattle, to which they were trying to give water, by driving them a mile down a steep rocky hill, into the gulf on the south of the ridge.   There was not a blade of grass, and the labor of descending and ascending was nearly equal to a day's travel, yet all the water which could be obtained was from this source.   Tired as I now was, I was compelled to go down and fill my flask before I could think of going on, and when I had done so I could hardly walk from fatigue.

On coming up the hill I found Colonel Watkins, who was just ready to move on, and he kindly invited me to go on and share a part of his bed.   We here left this ridge, and crossed by a deep ravine to another on the right, and proceeded a couple of miles, when he encamped among the rocks by the roadside.   There was not a drop of water in the camp, and the Colonel made an excellent cup of tea from that which I carried in my flask.   Yet such was the desire for water, that two of his men each took a pail and walked over the hills two miles to procure some.   Distance, twenty-five miles.

SEPTEMBER 17.

We used the last water in my flask to make our morning beverage, and I left the Colonel on my last day's travel to the valley.   It was six miles to the only water that could be had near the road.   I was stiff and sore from the exertion of the previous day, but hope impelled me on with ardent fervor, and suffering from thirst, I was desirous of gaining the point where it could be assuaged. This was half a mile distant, at the foot of a steep hill — a part of the way over perpendicular ledges of rock, from which I let myself down with difficulty. On reaching the brink of a fine mountain creek, now called Cow Creek, I kindled a fire, and prepared a refreshing draught of coffee. Anxious as I was, I could not prevail upon myself to leave the delicious stream for two hours. After filling my flask, I again climbed the hill to the road. Ascending to the top of an inclined plain, the long-sought, the long-wished-for and welcome valley of the Sacramento, lay before me, five or six miles distant.

How my heart bounded at the view! how every nerve thrilled at the sight! It looked like a grateful haven to the tempest-tossed mariner, and with long strides, regardless of the weariness of my limbs, I plodded on, anxious to set foot upon level ground beyond the barren, mountain desert. I could discern green trees, which marked the course of the great river, and a broad, level valley, but the day was too smoky for a very extended view. There was the resting place, at least for a few days, where the dangerous and weary night-watch was no longer needed; where the habitations of civilized men existed, a security from the stealthy tread of the treacherous savage; where our debilitated frames could be renewed, and where our wandering would cease. Perspiring and fainting from exertion, I reached the foot of the last hill, and stood upon the plain. Yet here I was disappointed, for instead of the high grass and rich soil that I expected to find, for four or five miles after reaching the valley the earth was dry and baked by the sun; the scanty vegetation was dried and crisp, and the ground was strewn with round stones, which seemed to have been thrown there by volcanic force, or washed by the floods from the hills. But onward I pressed, till I reached the first trees which I had seen from the mountains, and found that they grew along the margin of Deer Creek, which I followed a mile, when the sight of a chimney attracted my attention. It was the house of Colonel Davis, eight miles from the foot hills. My sensations were singular on approaching the house. Although it was a simple abode, standing within a rough paling, it was the first peaceful dwelling of civilized man which I had seen for months. While I hurried to it, I felt an almost irresistible repugnance to approach, and when at length I sat down in the porch, I felt lost and bewildered with a degree of astonishment at seeing men and women moving about at their usual avocations. I could only give short replies to interrogatories which were made. and after sitting nearly an hour in a kind of half stupidity, I found resolution enough to inquire where the trains were encamped.

"About a mile below," was the reply, and I got up and walked off, leaving, probably, no very favorable impression as to my conversational powers.

On reaching the encampments below, and seeing the hundreds of white tents and wagons, with multitudes of cattle cropping the grass, I felt once more at home : all uneasy sensations vanished, and I wondered how I had been so perfectly stupid at the house. I met many traveling acquaintances, and was soon invited to share the hospitality of friends for the night.

Lawson's was on the opposite side of the creek, and a little before evening I went over, and found two or three small adobe buildings, one of which was called by courtesy a store, having a little flour, whisky, and a few groceries for sale. Around the trading post were lounging gangs of naked Indians of both sexes, drunken Mexicans, and weary emigrants, enjoying respite from excessive fatigue in the flowing bowl; and take it all in all, it did not give me a very flattering impression of the morals of the citizens of the first settlement. My first act was to provide for the creature comfort; and purchasing a little beef, bread, sugar and cheese, I returned to the camp, to enjoy a feast to which I had long been a stranger.

The following are the prices current paid for provisions at that time at Lawson's: Flour, per 100 pounds, $50,00; fresh beef, $35,00; pork, $75,00; sugar, $50,00; cheese, per pound, $1,50.

The emigrants, as a matter of course, were all anxious to find where the best mines were, and were busy seeking intelligence; but there seemed to be such a variety of opinions, nothing certain could be learned, and the consequence was that they scattered in all directions, as fancy dictated. Some were going direct to the mines, some to Sacramento City for supplies—a place which was not in existence when we left home, but which had sprung up in the meantime, and now contained several thousand inhabitants, with an immense trade. Some were arriving, some departing; and the camp and trading post looked more like the dépôt of an army, than the first halting place for the toil-worn emigrant. Distance, twenty miles.

CHAPTER XV.

SUFFERINGS OF THE EMIGRANTS ON THE JOURNEY IN THE FALL OF 1849 AND 1850 — DESTITUTION — CHOLERA — EMPLOYMENTS IN THE MINES — NARRATIVE CONTINUED — ARRIVAL IN THE VALLEY — BROKEN CONTRACTS — SEPARATION — IN PURSUIT OF SUPPLIES — INDIANS AT THE RANCHES.

It will be as well to speak here of the emigration in the latter part of the fall of 1849. Those who started from the Missouri late in the season, or who, by the vicissitudes of the plains, could not arrive till November, experienced almost incredible hardships. The previous trains had consumed all the grass, and thousands of cattle perished by the way. The roads were lined with deserted wagons, and a vast amount of other property; the Indians grew still more bold and troublesome by success; and many families were reduced to the utmost distress, with no means of getting forward but to walk. Provisions, which had been abundant at the commencement of the journey, had been thrown away, or abandoned with the wagons, and the last part of the emigration resembled the route of an army, with its distressed multitudes of helpless sufferers, rather than the voluntary movement of a free people. Worn out with fatigue, and weak for want of nourishment, they arrived late in the season in the mountainous region of the Siérra Neváda, where still greater struggles stared them in the face. The rains and snow commenced much earlier than usual, and fell to an unprecedented depth; and it seemed utterly impossible for them to get through. In addition to other calamities, many suffered from scurvy and fevers — the consequence of using so much salt or impure provisions ; and while many died, others were made cripples for life.

Reports of these sufferings reached the settlements, when the government, and individuals, who contributed largely, sent out a detachment to afford all the relief they could, and to bring the suffering emigrants in. The last of the emigrants had reached Feather River, on the Lawson route, when the government train reached them with mules. Some had been without food for two or three days, and with others a heavy body of snow lay on the ground. Three men made a desperate effort to get through. For some days they had been on an allowance of but one meal a day, when, packing up all the bread they had left, which was only a supply for two days, they started for Lawson's, a distance of seventy miles. The snow was between two and three feet deep, yet they waded through it for a few miles, when they came to a wagon containing two women and two or three children, who had eaten nothing for two or three days. With a generosity which was rare, under such circumstances, they gave all they had left to these helpless ones, and went on without. They succeeded in reaching Lawson's. Many knocked their exhausted cattle in the head, and lived upon them until the government train reached them. Women were seen wading through the deep snow, carrying their helpless children ; and strong men dropped down from utter exhaustion. The only food they had was their animals, and men became so famished that they cut meat from the mules and horses which had perished from hunger and thirst by the road side. When the government train arrived, the women and children were placed upon the mules, exposed to a furious snow storm, in which many of the animals perished ; but the emigrants finally succeeded in getting through, when the government furnished boats to carry them to Sacramento, as the roads along the valley had become impassable.

In the succeeding year, the emigration was quite as large as in 1849. The reports of the error of the emigrants of the preceding year, in loading their wagons too heavily with provisions, had reached the States, and very many took the opposite extreme. This was a most unfortunate mistake, which led to horrible results, in addition to other calamities. On reaching Fort Laramie, the provisions of many were consumed; but with a headlong determination to persevere, they went forward, depending on chance for supplies — a step which the reader can now well understand was entirely desperate, in the country through which they were compelled to pass. Many others were well supplied until they reached the Humboldt, when their stores became exhausted. Another difficulty was, that many started with horses, and in their anxiety to get forward, drove too fast, so that when they arrived at the barren wastes beyond the Platte, their animals were worn down with fatigue, and gave out by the time they reached Green River, and they were thus obliged to leave both wagons and supplies, with a long, doubtful, and dangerous journey still before them. Added to these causes of suffering, another existed, which did not the previous year. In 1849 there was more grass than had ever been known before. Traders who had been in the country fifteen or twenty years, assured us that they had never known such a plentiful season, and that grass was then growing in abundance where they never saw any before, and they universally said that had not such been the case it would have been utterly impossible for such an emigration to get through. There was an unprecedented fall of snow and rain the following winter, but the weather was dry and hot in the spring; and when the second emigration came on, the grass was dried up in many places where we had found it good, and the melting snows rendered the streams so high, that they were crossed with much difficulty. The lower valley of the Humboldt, where we found a smooth, level road the previous seasons, was now (in 1850) overflowed, presenting one vast lake, and the emigrants were compelled frequently to keep the hills or uplands, either in deep sands, or among rocks and ravines, with their worn-out animals, while the overflowed valley afforded no grass. Long and laborious detours were necessary, to avoid lateral valleys, now under water; and on the Humboldt there was one point where they had to go thirty miles over difficult mountains, where we made the distance in six. In traveling down that river, grass was obtained frequently only by wading or swimming to islands, and cutting it with a knife. In one instance, which came to my knowledge, a man paid an Indian fifteen dollars to swim to a little island and get enough to feed his mule. In addition to all these unfortunate circumstances, the cholera broke out among the emigrants, and reached from Fort Kearney to Fort Laramie. It raged with dreadful violence, marking the road with the graves of the unfortunate victims.

Although many came through well and safely, is it to be wondered at, that horses, mules and cattle broke down, that provisions were exhausted, hundreds of miles from the settlements, and far from human aid, and that men, women, and children, were left destitute, without a mouthful to eat, and without the means of getting forward, exposed to a burning sun by day, and the chilling cold of night? Perhaps an exhausted, worn-out horse, or mule, might be left to carry a remnant of supplies;

yet even without this slender aid, mothers might be seen wading through the deep dust or heavy sand of the desert, or climbing mountain steeps, leading their poor children by the hand; or the once strong man, pale, emaciated by hunger and fatigue, carrying upon his back his feeble infant, crying for water and nourishment, and appeasing a ravenous appetite from the carcass of a dead horse or mule; and when they sank exhausted on the ground at night, overcome with weariness and want of food, it was with the certainty that the morning sun would only be the prelude to another day of suffering and torture.

Is it strange, then, that under such destitution and trial, when for weeks a draught of good water could not be had, some should become desperate, and commit suicide, rather than continue a living death? In one day, on the Humboldt, three men and two women drowned themselves, having become frantic from suffering. The men were observed, and once rescued; but they persisted in declaring that death was preferable, and finally succeeded in committing the desperate deed. The women had families, and unable longer to witness the suffering of their children, with no prospect of relief, chose the dreadful alternative. It can scarcely be realized by those who have not been placed in such situations, to what desperation the human mind may be excited; yet, from what I have witnessed myself, I can readily understand their perfect despair under the circumstances.

By the earliest arrivals, in June and July, of those emigrants who reached the valley, the sufferings and destitution of those behind were made known, and the government and individuals once more extended the hand of relief. San Francisco, Sacramento City, and Marysville made large contributions, and trains loaded with provisions were dispatched to meet them. In addition to this, traders pushed their way over the snows to Carson's Creek, and Truckee River, and even to the Sink of the Humboldt, with supplies ; and although much good was done, and many lives saved, yet aid could not be rendered to all. Indeed, it seemed as if this aid was scarcely felt. Five pounds of flour was doled out to a man, from the free supplies, which was afterwards reduced to two and half, and with this they had to travel over the mountains two hundred miles before they reached the settlements. The traders asked and obtained two dollars and a half per pound, for flour and pork. Hundreds had no money, and if they had, a large amount would have been required to sustain a family. Some parted with their horses and cattle for a few pounds of flour ; while others lived upon the dead carcasses of animals by the road side. When at length the emigrants arrived at the end of their journey, destitute and exhausted, they were attacked with fevers and bloody flux, and many perished miserably, after having endured all but death in crossing the plains. Were the personal adventures of a moiety of the emigration of 1850 to be written, they would furnish a volume of absorbing interest, forming a sad commentary on the California gold-seeking mania, which produced more wide-spread misery than any similar occurrence in the annals of mankind.

But a small portion of the emigration this year, came this northern or Lawson route. The character of this route was now generally understood, and but few attempted it, fortunately. Those who did, almost without exception, suffered severely. The Indians on Pitt River were very hostile. In one night they stole twenty-seven mules from one train, which so completely broke it up, that the emigrants were compelled to leave their wagons, and on the few mules that were left they packed what things they could, leaving their wagons and goods to be plundered by the savages. One gentleman told me that he walked three days without a mouthful of food, leaving three companions, who fell exhausted in the road, one day's journey from Lawson's ranch. Supplies were sent back, and they were rescued. Another company of seven men were surrounded by a band of two hundred Indians, stripped of their clothing, and driven into the river, when they were assaulted by a murderous discharge of arrows. The whites had but a single gun, with which they dared not commence any defence, hoping that after being robbed the Indians would spare their lives. Six of them were killed, and the seventh badly wounded, when providentially two men, who were hunting along the river, unconscious of the horrid butchery going on near them, discharged their pieces at some ducks. This alarmed the Indians, who thought a force was at hand, and they fled precipitately. The wounded man crawled out of the river, and being discovered, was taken to their train, and eventually recovered from his wounds. These are only among the many incidents of that eventful year. From the Sink of the Humboldt, across the desert to Truckee River, like that of the previous year, the road was covered with the putrefied carcasses of dead animals, and the effluvia arising from them poisoned the atmosphere, and produced disease among the emigrants, and on their arrival in Hangtown, one of the lower mining districts, the cholera broke out, and raged with violence, thus adding pestilence to their other misfortunes. A large portion of the emigration of 1849 explored and occupied the northern mines, while those of 1850 either stopped in the central, or proceeded to the southern diggings, and the two emigrations wrought a change in California, wonderful as the magic influence of Aladin's lamp.

The difficulties of prospecting for gold, with the consequent exposure attending it, and the difficulty of obtaining food and shelter, in a great measure vanished. As soon as placers were discovered on the mountains, roads were opened; ranches and trading posts were established, and public houses opened at convenient distances on the road; so that in twelve months it was no longer necessary to carry blankets, even into the lower mines. Still, at this moment, no new discoveries are made in isolated regions without exposure and privation. These things will appear in the course of my narrative in their proper places, and although my own adventures are more particularly described, they are only a single instance of what thousands passed through.

The emigrants of 1850 were not exposed to the same difficulties after their arrival, as those of the previous year. Provisions the first year could scarcely be had in many places, and were enormously high; but competition and the means of access scattered them through the mines, so that the second year there was no danger of starving.

It was a common error which emigrants generally fell into on leaving home, that little or no money would be needed on the route, and that in the land of gold it would be more an incumbrance than otherwise; and many who might have provided themselves sufficiently, neglected this important consideration. They found, however, that money was necessary to pay ferry-age across streams, to buy provisions on the road, when accident or circumstances reduced their own supplies, and often to replace their worn-out and dying animals, which could occasionally be done. And when at length they had successfully passed desert and mountain, and reached the grand haven of wealth, weeks, and sometimes even months elapsed, before they

K   16

were successful in digging enough to pay their daily expenses, while many were taken sick immediately on their arrival, and for a long time were unable to help themselves. The consequence was, that starvation and misery stared them in the face, after all the trials they had encountered on the plains; for, notwithstanding public and private charity was extended for their relief to a great degree, their numbers were too great for all to be relieved, and many suffered and died for the want of the care and proper nourishment which their way-worn and debilitated frames required. Many were happy at first in getting employment to pay their board; even those who never had been accustomed to labor at home, and who had been surrounded by the luxuries of life, were glad to get any servile employment adapted to their constitution and abilities. It was found, too, that talent for business, literary and scientific acquirements, availed little or nothing in a country where strength of muscle was required to raise heavy rocks and dig deep pits. It was strength, absolute brute force, which was required to win the gold of the placers, and many a poor fellow, unable to endure the severe labor under a scorching sun, was finally compelled to give it up in despair, and seek employment more congenial to his former habits of life.

California proved to be a leveler of pride, and everything like aristocracy of employment; indeed, the tables seemed to be turned, for those who labored hard in a business that compared with digging wells and canals at home, and fared worse than the Irish laborer, were those who made the most money in mining. It was a common thing to see a statesman, a lawyer, a physician, a merchant, or clergyman, engaged in driving oxen and mules, cooking for his mess, at work for wages by the day, making hay, hauling wood, or filling menial offices.

Yet false pride had evaporated, and if they were making money at such avocations, they had little care for appearances. I have often seen the scholar and the scientific man, the ex-judge, the ex-member of Congress, or the would-be exquisite at home, bending over the wash-tub, practicing the homely art of the washerwoman; or, sitting on the ground with a needle, awkwardly enough repairing the huge rents in his pantaloons; or, sewing on buttons *a la tailor*, and good-humoredly responding to a jest, indicative of his present employment — thus:

" Well, Judge, what is on the docket to-day ? "

" Humph ! a trial on an action for *rents* — the parties prick anew."

" Any rebutting testimony in the case ? "

" Yes, a great deal of re-*button* evidence is to be brought in, and a *strong thread* will uphold the suit."

— Or, to the ex-Congressman at the wash-tub — " What bill is before the house now ? "

" A purifying amendment, sir : one that will make a *clean* sweep of the vermin which infest the precincts of our constituents."

" Will not the bill be laid on the table ? "

" At all events, a thorough *renovation* will take place; for the state of things requires a *soap*-orific modification of existing evils."

But I resume the regular course of my narrative from Lawson's.

Having long been deprived of the comforts of life, I found it impossible to restrain my appetite from over indulgence in fresh meat, on my arrival in the valley; and a strong hankering for something sweet made me imprudent in eating sugar and the consequence to me was what it is to almost every one else, on first getting in — I was seized with diarrhœa, which reduced my remaining strength at once. I had no tent, as our wagon had not arrived, but I found Colonel Watkins, who came in the day following, and he insisted, with his characteristic benevolence, that I should take up my quarters with him, and under his kind care the disease was checked in a few hours, and I was again whole.

Our wagons arrived on the 10th, after a laborious and excessively fatiguing passage across the mountain desert, in which the men and animals suffered for water. And now the object of our association was gained. We had reached California, and were about to part, each to pursue the course which seemed best. Smith and Brown, whom I had brought across the plains, and with whom I had a written agreement to continue in my employ, taking advantage of circumstances, where there was no law to enforce the fulfillment of their contract, immediately left me, and I never received one farthing by way of remuneration. Indeed, insult had been heaped upon me in my defenceless condition on the plains, yet I bore all patiently, hoping that a latent sense of justice on their arrival would prompt them to do what was right, but instead, like many others who assisted men in crossing to California, I was met not only by heartless ingratitude, but bad faith. Henderson, though often brutal and overbearing, was possessed, naturally, of many good qualities, and faithfully performed his part of the contract, which was to drive the team to the valley ; and it gives me pleasure to record his good faith, though Heaven knows he caused me much pain on the road, without the least provocation, as the company can well attest.

The only place where a supply of provisions could be had,

was at Sacramento City, an estimated distance of one hundred and thirty miles, and before going to the mines it was necessary that some of the company, myself included, should go down and procure them. Nearly all the others decided to go to the Yuba, and this would keep us in company a day or two longer. Between Lawson's and Sacramento City, there was at this time only six ranches, or stopping places, viz: Potter's, Neal's, on Butler Creek; Charlie Burch's, near Feather River; Nye's, near the mouth of the Yuba, where Marysville now stands; Nichols', on Feather River, where Nicolans has sprung into existence; and Vernon, at the confluence of Feather River with the Sacramento.

On the morning of the 21st of September, I bade adieu to Colonel Watkins — not as a casual acquaintance, but as one with whom a kindred taste, mutual hardships, long and weary travel, and sympathy amid toil and suffering, had awakened feelings of genuine friendship. We parted with regret and esteem for each other, yet resolved to meet again, if consistent with the uncertain and varying current of California life. For twenty miles, our first day's travel, we passed over a dry and barren plain, destitute of water; and we found but little sign of vegetation along the whole distance to the city, except in the immediate vicinity of streams or sloughs, the course of which were marked from the mountains by a line of trees on their banks, and where the soil could be successfully cultivated only by irrigation. As Henderson had joined Fredenburgh, with his cattle, Mr. McNeil hitched his with mine to my wagon, and Mr. Pope was to drive them to the city; therefore, for the present, it was not necessary that I should undertake the new business of driving team, and I walked on to Potter's in advance, where I arrived a little before nightfall, tired and hungry. It had been

nearly six months since I had sat down to a table, and the sight
of a clean cloth awakened old recollections, and although my
purse, like my person, was gaunt and spare, I could not resist
the temptation, and with as much complacency as if I were in
possession of thousands, I ordered supper.

A long time elapsed before it was ready, for the landlady
seemed disposed, like " Miss Lucy Long," to " take her time."
It was set on after a while, and although it consisted only of
cold boiled tongue, bread and butter-milk, to me it was a feast,
which cost me one of the five dollars which remained in my
possession in the land of gold, and I am not quite sure but I
really ate a dollar's worth, such as it was. The following day
we halted at Neil's, where I indulged in purchasing two small
biscuits, for which I paid twenty cents ; but finding that at this
rate I should be without a farthing on reaching the city, I resolved to stick to my wagon larder of dry pilot-bread, which
had become nauseating enough, but would sustain life, hoping
that some adventitious circumstance would arise by which my
fare might be mended. I am more particular in narrating these
little circumstances, as it illustrates the condition in which we,
as well as thousands of others were placed, on our arrival in
the happy valley of the Sacramento. Here I parted with the
rest of our company, who resolved to stop one day, and then
go to the Yuba mines. In company with my friend, Doctor
Hall, and Mr. Rood, who were going to the city for supplies, I
proceeded, Mr. Pope driving my team, with one yoke of Mc-
Neil's cattle. McNeil decided upon going to the Yuba mines,
on a prospecting tour, and was to meet us on our return at
Nye's ranch, where we all contemplated meeting, to be governed in our future operations by his report; but it was destined that months should elapse before we should again be

united. I am compelled to be thus precise in this uninteresting portion of our journey, in order to keep up the train of circumstances as they occurred. McNeil, Mr. Pope and myself had agreed to work together, after I had succeeded in getting supplies.

With a portion of our company we parted with regret, but from those from whom we had experienced abuse, and who indulged in the most disgusting ribaldry and profanity, and outrageous behavior, when under trials that should have called forth the best feelings of men, we were glad to be separated; and it seemed a happy transition, to drive on without having our ears saluted every moment with disgusting oaths and opprobrious epithets.

In passing down the valley, instead of an abundance of grass and water, which we had expected, we generally found the first only at long intervals, in the streams which made from the mountains, and the latter, as I have before mentioned, only in sloughs, or near the banks of the streams. The earth was dry and parched, with wide cracks two or three feet deep, bearing nothing but weeds, except in the places just mentioned, which afforded no nourishment for animals; but where there was grass, although dry and crisp, it was rich and nutricious.

In traveling from Lawson's south, towards Sacramento City, our course was generally parallel with the Sacramento River, varying the distance according to its sinuosities, from five to fifteen miles, and we forded Feather, Yuba, Bear, and the American Rivers, besides several creeks.

On reaching Bear River, we understood that we had a dry plain to cross, thirty miles in extent, without grass, and with water but once, and we provided for the contingency by cutting grass on the rich bottom, and filling our kegs with water. Near every ranch we found a village of naked, filthy, lazy Indians, of whom I shall speak at length hereafter. On the fifth day after leaving Lawson's, we encamped on the bank of the American River, where there was a broad, grassy bottom, and where there were thousands of emigrants encamped, and it seemed as if we were again transported to the plains, amid the universal emigrant army.

CHAPTER XVI.

ARRIVAL AT SUTTER'S FORT — PLANS FOR THE FUTURE — MEET CAPTAIN
GREENE AND DR. ANGEL — FRIENDLY AID — SACRAMENTO CITY — DEPAR-
TURE FOR THE MINES — BEAR RIVER — CAYOTES — YUBA RIVER — ARRI-
VAL AT THE MINES — SICKNESS — SUCCESS IN TRADE — RETURN FOR
MORE GOODS.

WE had driven half of the previous night to reach our resting place; and we now learned that we were within three
miles of Sacramento City and Sutter's Fort. After a frugal
dinner of hard bread and water, Doctor Hall, Mr. Rood and
myself doffed our soiled garments, and after assuming habiliments more in accordance with civilized life, we set out for
town, leaving our cattle and wagon in the care of Mr. Pope.
Taking off our clothes on reaching the ford, we waded across
the American, a clear and beautiful stream, about four hundred
feet wide, and reached the city of tents about four o'clock in
the afternoon. And here I found myself more than two thousand miles from home, in a city which had risen as if by en-
chantment since I had crossed the Missouri, a stranger, way-
worn and jaded by a long journey, half famished for want of
even the necessaries of life, practicing domestic economy to
the fullest extent, with every prospect before me of continuing

K*

in the practice of that useful science; for, on examining the state of my treasury, I found myself the wealthy owner of the full sum of four dollars! — enough to board me one day at a low-priced hotel. And I had come in the pleasant anticipation of raising a full supply of provisions, which would cost not less than two hundred dollars. This afforded me an opportunity of enlarging my views of political economy, by studying "ways and means." How the thing was to be done, I could not conceive. Dear reader, could you, under these circumstances? While I was cogitating on the strange course of human events, as exhibited in my own particular case, and wishfully eying a piece of fat pork, which was temptingly exhibited for sale on a barrel head in a provision store, I met my old Captain, Jesse Greene, who, by keeping the old route and avoiding Greenhorn Cut-off, had got in four weeks before, and made something in the mines. A short time after, I met Doctor M. B. Angel, who had been equally successful, and they, understanding by intuition the state of an emigrant's treasury, generously offered to supply me with the *quid pro quo*, verifying the old proverb that "friends in need are friends indeed;" and I think that under the circumstances, I was more rejoiced to see them than they possibly could have been to see me.

Thus, through their kindness, an arrangement was made, by which I could obtain a load of provisions, and which I designed to take to the mines, either to sell, or live upon, till McNeil and myself could make something by mining. It was with reluctance, however, that I accepted their proffered kindness, from the very uncertainty of California operations; but necessity compelled me to do so, or die, and I did not relish the idea of dying there, so far from home. While strolling through the streets during the evening, I chanced to go into a hotel, where

I met an old acquaintance, F. C. Pomeroy, who had been unsuccessful in the mines, and was looking for business. As it was necessary for me to have assistance, I immediately made an arrangement with him to go with me to the mines. Fortune seemed to be smiling on me, from a small corner of her vacillating mouth. During the two days that I remained in town, Pomeroy and myself took up our quarters under a large oak tree near J street, where we luxuriated on the fat things of a bacon cask, with a bountiful supply of bread and butter; in short, we fared sumptuously, by cooking for ourselves. One night, feeling a little aristocratic, we spread our blankets on the ground in an unoccupied tent, but the owner came in the morning before we were up, and charged us fifty cents for sleeping under the canvass roof. We thought it smacked of inhospitality, but we got used to it in time, and discovered that in California it was custom and not extortion.

Sacramento City, at the period of which I write, contained a floating population of about five thousand people. It was first laid out in the spring of 1849, on the east bank of the Sacramento River, here less than one-eighth of a mile wide, and is about a mile and a half west of Sutter's Fort. Lots were originally sold for $200 each, but within a year sales were made as high as $30,000. There were not a dozen wood or frame buildings in the whole city, but they were chiefly made of canvass, stretched over light supporters; or were simply tents, arranged along the streets. The stores, like the dwellings, were of cloth, and property and merchandise of all kinds lay exposed, night and day, by the wayside, and such a thing as a robbery was scarcely known. This in fact was the case throughout the country, and is worthy of notice on account of the great and extraordinary change which occurred. There were a vast number of taverns and eating houses, and the only public building was a theatre. All these were made of canvass.

At all of the hotels and groceries, gambling was carried on to a remarkable extent, and men seemed to be perfectly reckless of money. Indeed, it seemed to have lost its value, and piles of coin and dust covered every table, and were constantly changing hands at the turn of a card.

At high water the river overflows its banks, and a notice of a dreadful disaster of this kind will appear hereafter. For a mile along the river lay ships, barges, and various water craft, laden with merchandise and provisions. Trade was brisk, and prices exorbitantly high.

On the north side of the city is a large and deep slough, in which cattle frequently mire and perish, and at this time the effluvia arising from their putrid carcasses was almost insufferable. A little beyond the slough the American River empties into the Sacramento. This river is not navigable for vessels. The Sacramento River, though affected by the tide, is pure and sweet, and generally is better to drink than the water of the wells, some of which are slightly brackish.

On the first day of October, all things being in readiness, Pomeroy and myself, taking Mr. Pope, with McNeil's cattle, set out for *somewhere*, but with no definite location in view. Arrived at Bear River, we encamped under the trees on the bottom, and after turning out our cattle, and cooking our suppers, we placed our provision chest at our heads, and spreading our blankets, were soon asleep, despite the howling of the cayotes all around us. On awaking in the morning, we discovered that the thievish animals had been at our bedside in the night, and had actually taken the cloth which covered our provisions, and dragged it across the road, without awaking us.

These animals are of the dog species, and appear to be a connecting link between the fox and wolf. They frequently go in packs, but rarely attack a man, unless pressed by hunger, which is not often, for the number of horses and carcasses of wild cattle in the valley furnish them food, and they are not looked upon as dangerous. I have seen them stop and play with dogs, which had been set upon them, returning their caresses, and showing no disposition to fight. They would even playfully follow the dogs, which had been set upon them, to within a short distance of the wagons.

On searching for the cattle in the morning, it was discovered that one of my best oxen was missing. This was a serious loss, and although we searched two days and a half, we finally had to give it up without finding him. Nearly a mile below our encampment, there was a swampy morass, which extended a mile or more, to Feather River, into which the Bear flowed. On the last day, while searching for my stray ox, I got lost in the tangled grape and pea vines, which covered the trees and bushes in an almost impenetrable maze. At every turn I found the tracks and beds of the grizzly bear, the caugar, and black wolf, and momentarily expected to meet some of these interesting natives of California; but Providence directed otherwise. After wandering about half a day, completely bewildered, breaking my way through the thick maze with difficulty, I finally came to a stand, and commenced firing my gun, to attract the attention of my companions. I fired away all but one charge of my ammunition, without effect, and then sat down to wait until the declining sun should indicate the direction to my camp. At length this occurred, when I could take the true bearings, and I finally succeeded, with infinite toil, in getting out of the swamp. I soon met Mr. Pope, who, alarmed at my long absence, had started after me.   Further search appearing useless, the following morning we went on, and in the course of the day I was enabled to purchase an ox of an emigrant, which, though not near as good as the one lost, answered the purpose.   At night we halted near a muddy slough, where there was a little water, and set about preparing our evening meal.   While we were thus engaged, a fine, rollicing, young fellow drove up, and requested to mess with us till morning, to which we assented cheerfully.   In the course of the conversation, with some exultation, he told us that he had made fifteen hundred dollars in a short time, and taking out his purse, exhibited the money in gold coin.   As it was heavy in his pocket, he arose, and going to my bed, which was spread under a tree near by, he turned a corner of the blanket down, and then put the purse under it, leaving it there till morning, without going near it again, apparently with as much unconcern as if it had been so many chips, although we were entire strangers.   In the morning, after breakfast, and when he had harnessed his mules, he went to the bed, and taking his gold, jumped into his wagon and drove off, as carelessly as if he had run no more risk than in depositing his money in the vault of a bank.   Such was the security felt at the time from robberies.

On reaching the Yuba, we could learn nothing of McNeil. We had thought, when parting, of taking our load to Redding's diggings, above Lawson's ; but that would be to depend on his report from the Yuba.   In our course up to Bear River, we received from miners very favorable accounts from the Feather River mines, not only of the diggings, but for the sale of provisions, and we decided to go there, hoping that McNeil would overtake us, or follow us there.   As Mr. Pope did not feel at liberty to take his cattle further, he concluded to leave them with a Mr. Barham, (who crossed the plains with us, and who was temporarily stopping on the Yuba,) and then go himself in search of McNeil, up the Yuba. On finding him, he would follow us to Bidwell's bar. But we never met again; and it gives me pleasure to attest to his real worth and honesty, and kindness of heart.

Proceeding the next day to Charlie's Ranch, (familiarly known as " Old Charlie,") the route here led off the road which we had previously traveled, and the next morning we started for the mountains, after leaving a note for McNeil, which we subsequently learned he never received. It was fifteen miles across the plain to the first water, within the first gorge of the mountains. A portion of the distance we found broken by dry sloughs, which were impassable in the rainy season, but were now narrow and deep sluices, somewhat troublesome to cross. We halted for the night at a hole where there was a little water, which was surrounded by weary travelers, and which strongly reminded me of the plains. As we proceeded in the morning, the hills became higher and more abrupt, yet not difficult, and in the afternoon we reached the hill immediately above Bidwell's Bar, and descended a mile by a steep and sometimes sideling path to the lower end of the bar, known as Dawlytown, named after a young merchant, who first opened a store on that point, about two months before.

It was on the 10th of October when we reached this place of our destination, and, pitching our tent, opened a store, after sending our cattle back to a small valley where there was a little grass, trusting to luck for finding them again when we should need them.

The river was a rapid, mountain stream, flowing through deep cañons and gorges more than a thousand feet high on each side sparsely covered with oaks and pines. In this vicinity more than a thousand men were at work, with pans and cradles, who were making, variously, from five to fifty dollars per day. The bed and banks of the stream were composed of slate rock, and the gold was found in the dirt and crevices. On the bar the gravel was removed to the depth of from three to six feet, and the dirt in the immediate proximity to the bed rock was washed, and generally yielded well. The labor was quite equal to that of digging canals and wells, and the quantity of gold looked small for the large amount of dirt required to be handled. It had been our original intention, that one of us should work at mining, while the other attended the store, but I was soon visited by my old companions, chill and fever, and had scarcely recovered, when Pomeroy was taken with fever. Thus instead of digging, it became necessary for one to take care of the other. There was much sickness among the miners, especially those who had recently arrived in the country, and many lay ill with scurvy, fevers and flux, without the shelter of a tent, and our first advent in the mines presented no agreeable aspect.

We had scarcely arrived an hour before an application was made for my buffalo skin and blanket, from two poor fellows who lay ill of fever under a tree, in a rain without covering, exposed to the cold night air, destitute of the comforts of life, which their debilitated condition so much required. I cheerfully complied with their request, but it availed little, for in a few days they both expired. In Dawly's store, nearly adjoining ours, lay a poor fellow in the last stages of consumption and flux, which he had contracted in the mines — delirious with disease, raving and tossing in his agony — who, after a few days of suffering, expired. He had accumulated five thousand dollars, the result of a year's hard labor and privation, which he had buried, and never disclosed its place of concealment, so that it neither benefitted him or any one else. He had no family.

At the end of two weeks we found our profits to be about $600, with about two hundred dollars remaining on hand, and I made preparations for going to the city to replenish our stock.

We spent three days in hunting our cattle, which I fortunately found just as we had given up all hope of seeing them again; and after many little vexatious delays, I finally started on the 25th for Sacramento, with a very different feeling from that with which I had entered it a short time before, for now I had a capital of my own to commence on. With no adventure worth relating, I reached the city in four days and a half, and commenced laying in my stock.

17

CHAPTER XVII.

HARDSHIPS OF THE MINERS — UNEXPECTED MEETING WITH COLONEL WAT-
KINS — KINDNESS OF DOCTOR MORSE — DOCTOR PATRICK — CROSSING THE
YUBA RIVER — SICKNESS — SEVERE RAINS — THEFT, AND ITS CAUSE — RE-
TURNING FROM THE MINES — MELANCHOLY DEATH OF ·MR. CHIPMAN.

I SHALL avoid narrating personal adventures as much as possible ; but it will be necessary, frequently, to refer to my own
acts to form a connecting link in California life. In speaking
of my own trials, it should be borne in mind that they were
common to thousands who went through similar scenes ; and
although they may be necessarily varied, yet almost every miner, in the years '49 and '50, experienced hardships nearly akin
to those of others ; and shared alike much ill fortune. At this
time there were but few dwellings in the country, and those of
the most fail and unsubstantial character ; indeed, the great mass
of men passed one of the most inclement winters that had ever
been known, in tents, or cloth houses, obliged to sleep on the
wet ground, and, if necessity compelled them to move from one
point to another, it was absolutely necessary for them to carry
their beds, (consisting simply of thin blankets,) their cups,
plates, and frequently their provisions, on their backs, for these
could not be furnished by those whose kindness gave them a
shelter from the rain, beneath the hospitable cover of a tent.

It was all that any one could do to provide a shelter for him self, and a single meal was an item of consideration, where it could with difficulty be obtained. Having completed the purchase of my second stock of goods, in Sacramento City, on the last day of October, I was waiting for a friend, (Mr. Billinghurst,) whom I had met the day before, and who was laying in supplies for his camp, which was only a few miles from my own, when I recollected some trifling article which I wished, and stepped into a store to purchase it. While I stood at the counter, waiting the action of the clerk in serving me, a poor, emaciated and feeble form, in which the ravages of disease were prominently marked, darkened the door; and as he advanced with tottering steps, it was with difficulty that I recognized my warm-hearted friend, Colonel Watkins, the companion of my weary travel on the plains, the kind nurse in my illnesss, and counselor in an hour of trial and uncertainty, when the recklessness and utter disregard of the courtesies of life, in some of my mess on the plain, prompted me to separate from them, with the determination to travel alone, weak as I was, rather than endure longer their outrageous deportment.

"Colonel Watkins! Can it be possible. And sick, too?"

"Mr. D——, I am rejoiced to meet you. I have been very sick, and this is the first day that I have been able to get out. I have not a single acquaintance in this throng of human beings, and it is to the kindness of strangers that I am indebted, probably, for life. I want to go with you, to live with you, to be near you during the winter."

For a moment I could not reply. To see the strong man so suddenly stricken down — so weak and helpless — one, too, who had been accustomed to the elegancies of life, now like a wreck upon the heaving ocean, with but a slender chance of reaching a haven of safety — I felt overpowered by my emotions, which at first he interpreted as hesitation.

" Will you take me with you ? " he repeated ; " for with you I shall get well."

" Good heavens ! Colonel," said I, as soon as I could speak ; " I will not desert you. You shall go with me if you are able to ride, and such as I have you shall freely share ; but I fear you are still too weak to ride in the uncomfortable manner which will be necessary in my wagon."

He felt strong, however, at the moment, and I gave up leaving town that day, in order to give him time to rest, and to make his arrangements for going with me. After taking care of my cattle, I met him at his lodgings, which were at the office of that well-known philanthropist and gentleman, Doctor I. F. Morse. I soon learned, however, that it would be impossible for the Colonel to go with me, for Doctor Morse assured me that he not only had not strength to ride, but he feared the excitement of meeting me would be too much for his debilitated condition, and that the journey should not be thought of for a moment. As I intended to return to the city immediately on my arrival at the mines, it was arranged that the Colonel should remain where he was till I should return, when he would probably have strength to ride, and then he was to go with me—an arrangement which was prevented by a singular combination of circumstances, in which my own life was more than once endangered. And although we did not meet again for many months, we frequently wrote to each other, but our letters were invariably miscarried. For a long time we entirely lost sight of each other.

It gives me infinite pleasure to speak of the kindness of Doctor Morse, though nothing from my pen can add to his reputation for well known benevolence and philanthropy. He was passing near the Colonel's tent one day, when he heard the groans of a sick person within, and drawing aside the curtain, he saw a man extended on the ground, delirious with fever, who, in broken and unconnected sentences, appeared addressing his constituents, as if at a public meeting. Seeing at a glance how the matter stood; without knowing anything of his history, and governed solely by his natural kindness of heart, he had him conveyed to his own lodgings, and attended him through a course of fever, to a state of convalescence and health. Had it not been for his timely interposition, the Colonel might have died unattended and unknown in his tent, without one kind hand to give him a cup of water to cool his parched lips, as many a poor fellow did that memorable year in California.

On Wednesday morning, bidding adieu to Colonel Watkins, and feeling sure that he was in better hands than if he had been in my own care, I left Sacramento, in company with Mr. Billinghurst and a Mr. Erholtz, both of whom were going near the same point in the mines with myself. After crossing the American River, three miles from Sacramento City, our way led across a plain, which at this season of the year was dry and barren, and night was approaching before we had reached a place where we could encamp. We were tired, and with our weary cattle were suffering from hunger and thirst, and anxiously looking forward for the concomitants of a good camp ground. The sun had nearly set, when an old man overtook us, who was driving a span of smart mules before a light wagon; and accosting him, we inquired where we could find water and grass for the night. "About four miles distant," he courteously replied. "I camped there on my way down; and it is the first place you will reach where you can stop. It will be quite dark before you can reach it, but I will drive on and kindle a large fire, which you will see from the road, and which will serve as a beacon." He went on, and we followed slowly, when, on reaching the point he designated, we found he had been as good as his word; for a bright fire was blazing near the bank of the Sacramento, about half a mile from the road. We found him engaged in cooking his supper, and we soon joined him in this agreeable occupation. Though rough in his exterior, and somewhat *Californian* in his language, we soon saw that he was a well-educated man, and a gentleman, but eccentric. After spending the evening agreeably in telling stories and discussing various topics, we spread our blankets on the ground and turned in, without inquiring where each other was from. While we were breakfasting the next morning, the old gentleman dropped a remark about Indiana.

"Are you from Indiana?" I interrogated.

" Yes."

" What part?"

" Oh, from down on the Wabash, where they have the ague so bad that it shakes the feathers off all the chickens."

A vague recollection flashed through my memory, and I inquired, "Are you from Terre Haute?"

" Yes."

"Is your name Patrick?"

"Yes," said he, looking up.

" You are, then, Doctor Scepter Patrick?"

"Yes, that is my name," he replied, with energy. "Who are you?"

" You were once a student of my father — Doctor Frederick Delano, of Aurora, New-York."

"Is it possible! And you — you must be A——?"

Our knives and breakfast simultaneously dropped, as we grasped each other's hands, for in this wild place, and under such peculiar circumstances, this was our second meeting in thirty-eight years ; and now we could have but a moment to ourselves before we were to part.

" And now, Patrick," said I " situated as you were at home, with every comfort about you, with reputation as a physician, and with political honors clustering around you, what induced you to take this wild-goose chase across the plains to California ? "

" Why, I'll tell you. My health had become very poor, and I thought a journey across the plains would help me. I have improved vastly, but I came near dying on the way."

" How so ? "

" Why, I was taken with the cholera, and came within an ace of slipping my wind. I was taken suddenly, and most severely, and there was not a man near me who understood dealing out a dose of medicine, except one cursed fool of a pepper doctor. I was vomiting, purging, and suffering all the tortures of the infernal regions, when I told the steam doctor to give me a large dose of calomel, camphor and opium, nor stop to count the grains, either. But he urged me to take a dose of number-six. ' Go to the —— with your number-six — give me the calomel, quick, or I am a dead man.' But the fool kept talking about number-six — number-six, till, finally, to satisfy him, and while I was writhing in agony, I told him to pour it out — hoping that after taking *his* medicine, he would be willing to give me mine. He immediately poured out a double dose of his *liquid fire*, and I took it down. I thought I should surely die, for the remedy seemed worse than the disease. I thought my whole insides were on fire, and I roared out ' Water, water ! for heaven's

sake, or I shall be burnt up.'   But there was not a drop of water in the camp, nor any within a mile.   ' Well, then, give me
brandy — anything : fire, turpentine, live coals ;   I am dying !'
All were very much alarmed, and the doctor jumped to the
brandy jug, and poured out half a glassfull, which I nearly
swallowed before I discovered the wretch had made a mistake
in the jugs, and had given me another quadruple dose of number-six — thus adding fuel to the flame ; and now I thought
I was surely gone.   But it stuck.   It stopped my vomiting in a short time, and then he was willing to give me my
medicine ; and that stuck too ; and operated finely.   The disease was checked, and I got well ; and after all, I don't know
but the fellow's number-six was beneficial to me."

By this time our cattle were yoked to the wagons, and we
parted, to meet once more about a year afterwards in San
Francisco.

It was the third day (the 3d of November,) after leaving
Sacramento City, when within four miles of the Yuba, we were
overtaken by a heavy rain — the first which had fallen since
spring, and which we afterwards found to be the commencement
of the rainy season.   We lay weather-bound till the 4th, when
we reached the upper ford about ten o'clock in the morning, but
a heavy storm setting in, we encamped for the day.   The following day being clear, we drove to the ford, and I, being better acquainted with the crossing than the others, took the lead,
while my companions remained behind to observe my success.
I soon found that the rain had raised the stream higher than I
had ever seen it before, and the current was so swift that my
cattle could with difficulty keep up against it.   It soon became
apparent that they would not be able to strike the landing on
the opposite bank, when I jumped in, hoping to keep them suf-

ficiently up to reach it. The current was so swift that I could scarcely stand. With difficulty I reached my wagon again, and as we progressed the water became deeper and more swift, till we were within three or four rods of the opposite bank, when it was impossible for my cattle to make head against it, and yielding to its force, they turned down stream, towards a deep hole which would engulf us all. At this moment my leaders doubled around my wheel cattle, and finally stopped. I sprang into the whirling stream, for the purpose of getting my cattle again into line for the shore, when the swift water took me down in an instant, like a feather, and I saved myself by seizing hold of one of the leaders' horns, as I was being carried by, and with great exertion regained the wagon. It now became imperative to save my cattle, and getting between them, on the tongue of the wagon, I succeeded in about half an hour in getting the lightened chain loose, and they started back for the shore. But the current again carried me down, when I seized hold of the tail of one of the oxen, as I floated by, and he dragged me ingloriously to the shore. I was so chilled that I could scarcely stand; but a good fire was built up, and I soon recovered the use of my limbs. The next care was to get my wagon out. It contained all my goods, and the loss of it would be utter ruin; and if the river raised a few inches higher, it would inevitably be swept off. I went to a rancho, which was near, and stating my difficulties, a fiery young man declared, with an oath, that he could get it out, and if he were successful, I was to give him ten dollars. Mounting a strong horse, he proceeded to the ford, with three yoke of large oxen; but when he came to see the swollen river, his courage evaporated, and he dared not ride in. With much persuasion, I obtained permission to ride his horse, and succeeded in reaching the opposite bank, where I

L

found a company of men from Missouri, who kindly offered to render me assistance. With a small line in my hand, to which was attached a strong rope, I now rode to the wagon, and getting on to a wheel, I sent my horse ashore, and then contrived to fasten the rope to the end of the tongue, when twenty stout men pulled the wagon to the steep bank, a few rods below the landing. With a hatchet I cut away the thick willows, and the roots and branches of overhanging trees; then, with a pick and shovel, I dug down the bank, which occupied me busily all the afternoon. It was quite dark before I could prepare my supper, when another storm set in just as I began to eat, and I was driven to my wagon for shelter, which still stood in the water. My bed clothes were upon the opposite bank, and of course inaccessible to me, and I had no other way but to lay in my wagon all night, with no covering but my soaked garments — the pattering rain over head, and the roaring flood beneath. But my dreams were not troublesome; for, as might be expected, my sleep was light. Morning dawned slowly, when the other teams succeeded in getting across, and hitching five yoke of cattle to the tongue, my wagon was pulled up the steep bank, on dry ground.

Soon after starting, it began to rain again, and for the following five days there was not a moment's cessation. The plain which was dry and hard when I passed it a few days before, was now deep mud; and although we only drove twelve miles, our cattle were so much exhausted, it was necessary to double teams the last half mile, and draw the wagons in singly to our camp ground. Then it was with infinite difficulty that we could get a fire started, to cook our suppers and warm our stiffened limbs. We were encamped near Burch's Ranch, and when morning came, it rained so heavily that it was impossible to travel; and to add to our peculiar pleasures, I was seized suddenly and violently with bloody flux, in its worst form, owing to extreme exposure the two previous days, and from fatigue, and sleeping in wet clothes. It was thought impossible for me to survive, and for two days I suffered immense pain, when, after taking two doses of calomel and oil, an operation was produced, which checked the disease, but left me weak and helpless as an infant. We lay at this point six days, with no shelter but our wagons; and the considerate kindness of my companions have left an indelible impression of gratitude in my heart; for it is mainly to their care and watchfulness that I am indebted for life.

The rain ceased for a day, after it had continued its pelting for a week, and as I was able to ride, we went on. But we had much difficulty in crossing sloughs, which, though dry in summer, now were roaring torrents, and occasionally we were detained many hours, till the flood had partially subsided, so that we could cross.

It was not until the 15th that we reached the first foot hill of the mountain range, where Ophir, in Butte county, now stands. Beyond this, farther egress was impossible. Notwithstanding we were upon high land, the soil was so soft, that, whether in the road, or out of it, cattle sank to their bellies, and wagons to their beds. Even oxen and horses, when striving to pick up a little grass, which grew scantily in spots on the mountain, frequently were mired down, so that it was impossible to get them out, and they perished miserably in the mud. Finding ourselves thus completely mud-bound, within ten miles of our camp, we hastily erected a bush shanty, and while my companions proceeded on foot to their camp, I remained to watch the wagons. As supplies were wanted at our several camps, members of respective companies came down, and backed them up through the rain and mud; and it was not until after three weeks had passed, that the rains subsided, and the roads became sufficiently firm for us to get our wagons into camp. During this long storm, hundreds of wagons were caught out on the plain, with loads destined for the mines, but being mired down, were left till spring before they could be rescued; consequently there was a short supply of provisions, and thousands of men were forced to abandon the mines, and seek refuge and employment in the cities, where, in some instances, from necessity, in others, from depraved morals, many were induced to resort to stealing for a subsistence; and the character which California had hitherto borne for universal honesty, was suddenly changed, and it became necessary to guard property with as sedulous care as in any of the older cities at home. The winter of '49, and '50 may be set down as the era of the commencement of crime, which ultimately led the more honest portion of community to rise, and in effect to produce a political revolution, for the protection of life and property, when it was found that the law could not do it.

Daily men passed my camp on Mud Hill, who, fearing starvation in the mountains, were endeavoring to gain the towns, where a dubious prospect was before them. Some were sick, and scarcely able to drag themselves along, and having as yet done but little in the mines, had no money, and were dependent on charity for a meal. Many, though well, had no money, and the sympathies of those who had anything to eat was almost hourly excited, for who that had it in his power to relieve could see men starve before his face? Along the road there were no tents for public accommodation. When night came, the sick, the weary and hungered were obliged to lay on the wet ground, in the chilling rain; and when morning appeared, they still had fifteen or twenty miles to go, wading through the mire, or swimming deep sloughs, with an exertion for life which was enough to discourage a strong man. We had been under the necessity of driving our cattle back twelve miles upon the plain, where they could get grass, and once, when the rain had ceased for a day, and there appeared an indication of fair weather, we hunted them up at the expense of a day's diligent search, in order to try to reach our camp. But we had not been an hour in camp with them, before it began to rain again, which continued for ten days without cessation, and we were obliged to drive them back to the valley, and remain in our quarters.

One day, while I was chatting with Mr. Billinghurst, who had come down from his camp, a stranger came up to borrow our chains, to drag an ox from the mire, a little above us. On his return, Billinghurst addressed me by name, making some inquiry, when the stranger seemed struck with the name.

" Is your name D——? " he inquired.

" Yes."

" Are you from Ottawa, Illinois ? "

" Yes."

" There is a sick man at Long's Bar, who is very anxious to see you."

" Indeed. Who is he ? "

" Mr. Chipman."

" Mr. Chipman from Ottawa ? Is it possible ! I was not aware that he had come to California."

" He started after you did. He was taken with scurvy on the plains, and is now helpless, at Long's Bar. He has made many inquiries after you, without success ; and desires to see you very much.

"It is now too late to go there to-night; but tell Mr. Chipman I will see him early in the morning;" and I immediately addressed a note to him to the same effect, and gave it to the young man, who was in his employ.

Early the following morning, taking such things as I had, which I knew to be good for his disease, I started off for Long's Bar, which was three miles distant, to see my old friend. On reaching his tent I scarcely recognized him, worn down by disease as he was. One leg was drawn up so that he could not use it, and he was barely able to hobble about on crutches, and his whole appearance was changed, by emaciation and sufferings. Few can appreciate the joy of our meeting; and although we had always been on familiar terms, the peculiar circumstances under which we now met made it doubly interesting to both. Nursed in the lap of luxury, unused to anything like the toil and labor to which he had been subject in crossing the dreary wilderness of the plains — surrounded by everything at home to make life pleasant, with an intelligent and accomplished wife, who would have sacrificed her own life to promote his comfort — here, during the most inclement season of the year, he had only the dubious shelter of a tent to protect him from the storm; and suffering from insidious disease, his bed was on the damp, wet ground, in a place where money could not procure the comforts necessary for a sick man. Surrounded by strangers, who could scarcely afford to extend a sympathising hand for relief, his future seemed anything but encouraging, and dark forebodings could only be the result of witnessing his present condition. I need scarcely add that I visited him almost daily, and urged him to go to the city, where he could procure medical attendance, and the comforts he absolutely required. He finally consented. A boat was going to Sacramento, in which he secured a passage, and the morning he was to start I went up to bid him adieu. He had been taken to a more comfortable tent, where a bed was made, off the ground, by the kindness of Mr. Butts, from Michigan. On going into the tent, I inquired of Mr. Butts,

"Is Mr. Chipman still here?"

"He is."

"How is he this morning?"

"Mr. Chipman is dead."

"Dead!" I was shocked but not disappointed; for a short time before he had been taken with the bloody flux, and run down immediately. He had expired that morning, about an hour previous to my arrival. Amid the throng of busy men who were at work around, it was with some difficulty that four were obtained to carry him to his grave. He is now at rest, in peace and quiet, on one of the foot hills of the Siérra Neváda.

The day after the performance of the last sad rites to my poor friend, I broke up my camp at Mud Hill.

CHAPTER XVIII.

TROUBLE WITH THE INDIANS ON THE SOUTH FORK — FATE OF MR. HENDERSON
ON THE NORTH FORK OF THE PLATTE — HIS WIFE AND CHILDREN — PROS-
PECTING FOR GOLD — THE RESULT — DISAPPOINTED HOPES AND FAILURES
— GETTING RID OF THE INDIANS — MR. TURNER — MELANCHOLY INCIDENTS.

AT length the rain ceased long enough to allow the roads to settle sufficiently to move, when I broke up my temporary camp, and returned to my old quarters at Dawlytown. Before reaching it, however, I was taken with a neuralgic fever, and on my arrival I immediately went to bed, where I was confined three weeks, enduring much pain. Being unable to attend to the care of my provisions, the most of them were spoiled by damp, and the wet weather.

I had been absent six weeks, owing to rain and sickness, and I found a great change in the appearance of the place on my return. Some few cabins had been built, but the greater part of the town had been deserted, the miners having gone up to the South Fork of the Feather, where better diggings were re-ported. A difficulty soon occurred between them and the In-dians, which ended in bloodshed, and was the commencement of a warfare, which of course eventually terminated in favor of the whites. An Indian stole an axe from the tent of a miner, who, on missing it, went to a village a mile or two distant, and with threatening language demanded its restoration, when an

Indian who had not been guilty of the theft went into the wigwam and brought it out. The miner, instead of receiving it quietly, began to beat the Indian. This so enraged him, that when the miner turned to go, he seized his bow and shot his assailant dead. A few days afterwards two men were hunting mules in the neighborhood, and becoming separated, one of them was shot dead with an arrow, while the other being assaulted, effected his escape.

In addition to these outrages, the Indians had taken mules and cattle, and it became unsafe to risk life or property in immediate proximity with them. Under these circumstances it was deemed best to give them a severe lesson, and a party proceeded, well armed, to their village, and in a skirmish killed five or six Indians, and destroyed their houses, while the remainder of the savages made their escape higher in the mountains.

A day or two after my return to head quarters, Mr. Billinghurst arrived, sick with scurvy, which had not broken out on him till now. Although our tent was not as capacious as a temple, we made room for him, and while I was confined to my bed on one side, suffering the pain of the condemned, he lay within six feet of me on the opposite side, enjoying the same pleasure in a still worse degree; and although the music of our groans ascended in unison, the notes were rather discordant with harmony, and it is with pleasure that I record the fact, that illness, and its consequent pevishness, did not for a moment interrupt our mutual good will and friendship for each other. His comrades moved from their old station near Long's Bar, to Stringtown, a new mining settlement on the South Fork, five miles above us, where they built a comfortable log cabin. But it was spring before Mr. Billinghurst was able to join them, and it seemed almost a miracle that he escaped with life.

I found on my arrival at Dawlytown, an old friend of the plains, a companion of my desert wanderings, William McNeil, from Illinois. After having lost sight of us on the Yuba, and failing to receive my letters, he had gone to Reading's diggings, at the upper part of the valley, under the impression that we were there; but after a month's ill success in digging, he accidentally learned I was on Feather River, and came down, and with much difficulty found my camp, where, during my absence, he installed himself with Pomeroy.

In my journal scross the plains I have spoken of a Mr. Henderson, who was emigrating with his family to California, and who, after establishing a ferry on the North Fork of the Platte, sent his family on, intending to overtake them in a few days. I found his wife a resident of Dawlytown, and a near neighbor, and her amiable disposition and correct deportment gained her the respect of a large circle of friends. From her own lips I received the following sad tale.

The time set for the appearance of her husband had already passed, when one day the two men who were engaged with him at the ferry rode up to the train, and without going to see Mrs. Henderson, informed some of the company that he was detained behind in settling some matters, and would overtake them the next day, and hastily rode on. But the next day passed, and the next — still he did not come. Her anxiety and alarm began to increase, and as time winged its flight day after day, and still her husband did not appear, the uncertainty of his fate, and the helplessness of her condition, produced a state of feeling and wretchedness bordering on frenzy. By degrees the opinion was formed that he was murdered, and she left

among strangers, upon a barren wilderness, with her two helpless children, with a long, doubtful and dangerous journey before her, and all the uncertainty of an unsettled and barbarous
country on her arrival in California, if she should be so fortunate as to reach it herself. In her trying situation she found
sympathy and friends in those around her, and every possible
attention was shown her by the way-worn emigrants. She
reached the settlements in safety, and with acquaintances went
to Dawlytown, where, opening a little hotel, she not only sup-
ported herself, but made considerable money. She afterwards
went to Stringtown, and subsequently was housekeeper for
Doctor Willoughby, near Yateston, on Feather River, where
she died, leaving her children to Doctor W.'s care.

Daily accounts of rich diggings on the South Fork were received ; and as my mercantile transactions were brought to a
close, by long illness and the impossibility of keeping up supplies, owing to the flood, feeling the necessity of doing something,
on my recovery, I projected a prospecting tour in the mountains, and a party was organized for that purpose, composed of
the Hon. James B. Townsend, late of St. Louis, McNeil, Pomeroy and myself. Fifteen or twenty miles above Dawlytown
the South Fork passed through a difficult cañon, and at this
time it had not been penetrated. Our design was to go above
it, if practicable, provided we could raise a sufficient force ; for,
as the Indians had become very hostile, it was no longer safe to
venture far from the settlements, except in parties of considerable strength. Having made preparations, by baking bread to
last a number of days, and putting our arms is good condition,
we sallied forth the third of January, each man carrying his
provisions, blankets, prospecting tools, firearms and ammuni
tion. With the weight of our loads, and the high, steep hills

we were obliged to climb, we made only five miles the first day, and night found us tired enough, in the hospitable cabin of our friend Brown, at Stringtown. In the morning he joined our party, with the understanding that he and his company were to share in any discoveries which we might make.

Our intention was to locate on some unoccupied bar, if it could be found, and go into general mining operations; for it was looked upon by everybody that if a bar on the South Fork could be obtained, a dam built, and the water turned from the bed of the stream, that a rich reward for the labor would be certain; and it was thought, too, that in the region where the hills were highest and most precipitous, the richer the streams would prove; and the result of our present undertaking will show how much truth there was in the hypothesis.

Our path lay along the hill-side bordering the river, and the trail was over deep ravines, rocky and precipitous, and we were occasionally obliged to cling to projecting rocks to maintain a foothold, while at times we forced our way through bushes, scratching our hands and tearing our clothes; and then we were in danger of sliding down the steep bank among the rocks of the river. And what added much to the peculiar pleasure of our mountain ramble, about noon it began to rain. Two days of infinite toil brought us to the cabin of Arnold, Scott & Co., the last and highest of the settlements, where we were hospitably entertained for the night. Making our prospecting determination known, four of their company, viz: two Arnolds, Scott, and a jovial, fearless, good-natured fellow, nicknamed Bunkam, joined us, making a force of nine well armed men, which we deemed sufficient to repel any attack the Indians might make. We decided to reach the high land above the river, as we were within two miles of the cañon, then follow the ridge till we supposed we were above it, and strike down to the river again, for during high water a passage through the cañon was impracticable. We were now in a rough, broken, mountainous country, with steep hills a mile or more high, bordering the river. After eating our breakfast of pork and bread, we commenced the ascent. The weight of our loads made it extremely laborious, and we could climb only a few rods without stopping to rest. It required two hours of excessive toil to reach the top of the ridge, when we found ourselves upon the height of land which divided the waters of the Yuba from those of the Feather. This we found comparatively level, and practicable for a good wagon-road, which has since been built, and extends far up into the mountains, and over which a daily mail is now carried to thriving mining settlements. Indeed, a few months wrought great and important changes in this part of the country. Villages and settlements speedily arose, roads were opened, hotels erected, and comforts abounded where we nearly starved. We were only half way up the mountain, when rain commenced falling, which scarcely ceased an hour during the remainder of our journey; and although I had recently arose from a bed of sickness, and for days was constantly wet to the skin, continually sleeping in the rain, upon the wet ground, I not only gained strength, but did not even take cold — a strong evidence of the salubriousness of this climate. We found the small streams roaring torrents, often difficult to cross; but where they could be waded they offered but a small impediment to our progress; and with Bunkam's good nature and originality, and the peculiarity of our situation, we felt much hilarity, notwithstanding the weight of our packs and the inclemency of the weather. Towards night-fall, judging we were above the cañon, we began to descend towards the river, after passing a high mountain, covered with snow, and the descent was almost as laborious as the ascent, for frequently we would lose our footing, and slide down many feet, until, by coming in contact with a bush, we gained our equilibrium. Between sliding and tumbling, we at length reached the rocky banks of a stream almost hid in the deep gorge of the hills, and which we found to be a branch of the South Fork, into which it tumbled over rocks and falls, about half a mile below where we reached it.

Being a little in advance of the others, I discovered a shelf in a cleft, where an overhanging rock projected sufficiently to protect the most of us from the rain, and we resolved to pass the night here, and the boys facetiously named it "Delano's Hotel," in honor of the discoverer. Building a large fire at the mouth of our den, we dried our wet garments, and roasting our pork on the ends of sticks, we lay down on the bare rock. Although the night was cold, we were tired enough to consider it a bed of down. I never slept better.

Daylight presented two important facts for our consideration. The water was too high for making a particular examination for gold along the bank, and our provisions were nearly exhausted; therefore, unwilling as we were to give up the search, we were compelled to turn our faces homeward, for our previous experience had proved that stomachs were stubborn things, and that there was a limit to their endurance. We dreaded the ascent of the hill more than we had its descent, but as there was no help for it, after digging for gold in a few spots without success, we began the task.

Night overtook us on the ridge, and amidst the outpourings from the clouds, we spread our blankets on the wet ground, and with a guard stationed on the lookout for Indians, we snatched a little sleep during the livelong night. On resuming our march, we saw many fresh tracks of Indians in the mud, who appeared to have been prowling around during the night, but probably finding us on the guard, had not ventured an attack. Had they done so, they would have had every advantage, for owing to the wet weather, there was scarcely a piece in the company that could be discharged. At noon we parted from our friends, the Arnolds, and keeping the ridge, we followed it in a storm of snow and rain till a heavy fog set in, when, fearing we might get lost among the mountain gorges, we descended to the river, and four hours of hard walking brought us to the cabin of our friend Brown, where a hearty supper and a quiet night's rest restored our equanimity, and revived our wearied frames. On the third day, when going up, we had located a claim on a bar fifteen miles above Dawlytown, and on our return we commenced preparations for taking possesssion of it. By the law among the miners, it was necessary to commence work on a claim within ten days after it was located, and a party was detailed from Billinghurst's and our own party, to erect a cabin on our claim. It was also arranged that the two companies should join in all their mining operations, and unite the Stringtown claim with the other, to which we gave the name of Ottawa. The working party proceeded to the spot and commenced falling trees and cutting them to the requisite length, and although the weather was wet and cold, they worked incessantly day after day, till at length the cabin was raised and enclosed with a roof. The last day they worked without food, as they were determined to get the roof on before they left it, and the provisions which they had backed up being exhausted. It was then arranged that McNeil and myself should go up, and after finishing it off, go to work digging the race, until other members of the company could get ready to join us. We accordingly went up, found a track where a path for a mule could be made along the steep hill-side, over which we could get provisions on to the bar, and then commenced work. By degrees a fire-place and chimney were built, doors made, bedsteads erected, and within a week we were in possession of the most comfortable quarters which we had enjoyed since crossing the Missouri River, and we had learned by this time how to appreciate even this rude shelter. McNeil was a capital fellow — honest, industrious and energetic — although I knew all this before, our isolation together in that dreary mountain gorge only cemented still stronger the bonds of friendship which existed between us. For three weeks we lived alone, and performed prodigies in moving rocks and throwing out dirt, in which I must give him credit for superior skill and ingenuity — what appeared an impossibility in my unsophisticated judgment, he found means of accomplishing with ease.

I may as well bring the subject of our labor to a close; for dwelling upon it is not very gratifying to my recollections. We labored on till the spring raised the water so high that a suspension of work was indispensable, both here and on the Stringtown bar, and as our funds and supplies were both getting low, it became necessary for a part of our company to disperse, in order to raise the means of living. When the river was low enough, in June and July following, we re-assembled, and began the work of building the dams. I then had charge of the work at Stringtown, while Billinghurst took that of the Ottawa bar. After finally finishing my work, at an expense of sixteen thousand dollars, and getting into the bed of the stream, we did not get the first farthing for our labor and our pains. The unprecedented high waters of 1850 rendered it impossible to drain the water on the Ottawa bar, and we were obliged to abandon it, or starve; but we had the satisfaction of learning that in 1851, when the water was very low, a company of Chinese took possession of it, and took out from fifty to a hundred dollars a day for many days. So that the harvest, which was almost within our reach, was reaped by others, and they foreigners and aliens.

I have purposely omitted many details of our operations during that eventful year; but enough, perhaps, has been mentioned, to give an idea of what the miners of the first emigration encountered in the fall of '49, and the summer of '50. For forty miles along the South Fork of Feather River, the stream was dammed whenever it was practicable, some of the dams costing, in labor and necessary expenditures, fifty to eighty thousand dollars, and not one paid a moiety of its cost. Below Stringtown dam about a mile, an energetic and enterprising company erected a splendid dam, and dug a race at an expense of thirty-two thousand dollars, expending four thousand dollars which they had dug the previous fall, and all that they got when completed was fifteen cents! They were completely wrecked, and their company broke up hopelessly in debt, a portion of which was for the provisions on which they had subsisted during the winter.

And this wide-spread ruin did not fall upon the poor miner alone. Merchants who had given them credit for provisions, in the expectation of being repaid when they should get fairly at work, were sufferers, not from any design, but from the utter inability, of their poor debtors to pay, and some of them, having purchased a portion of their stocks on credit in the city, were also unable to meet their payments. Thus the failure of the miners was felt far and wide. Wherever we turned, we met with disappointed and disheartened men, and the trails and mountains were alive with those whose hopes had been blasted, whose fortunes had been wrecked, and who now, with empty pockets and weary limbs, were searching for new diggings, or for employment — hoping to get enough to live on, if nothing more. Some succeeded, but hundreds, after months and years of toil, still found themselves pining for their homes, in misery and want, and with a dimmed eye and broken hopes, sighing in vain for one more fond embrace of the loved ones who were anxiously looking, but in vain, for the return of the father and friend.

While McNeil and myself were living alone, we were one day visited by several naked, mountain Indians. We treated them kindly, giving them tobacco, fish-hooks and bread, and they left us, manifesting the utmost good nature. Subsequently, they came with others, and we began to think they might be tempted, by our isolated condition, to commit some depredations on our property, even if no acts of hostility were exhibited towards our persons, and we deemed it best to get rid of them as quietly as possible, upon any future occasion when they presented themselves.

One cold, stormy day, while sitting by our cabin fire, unable to work, the door was gently opened, and two naked savages, dripping with wet, stood before us. We invited them to the fire, and after giving them something to eat and a little tobacco, I gave them to understand that I was a conjurer, who came from the rising sun; and that I could control the elements. Occasionally, a terrific gust of wind drove the smoke in clouds down our chimney, and for the purpose of practicing on their credulity, I would jump up and wave the smoke up, which, as the gust passed, seemed to obey my behest. On the approach of another gust, I would invite it down, and by continuing my manipulations long enough, the wind appeared to obey me. When it lulled, I would stop, and the smoke came or went accordingly, till it was plain to see that their wonder was excited.

Still, they did not move. Then I began to examine their heads phrenologically, making some mysterious observations to Mac, who as gravely responded, when, under apparent excitement, they inquired in Spanish, if I was bueno. We answered that it was good, yet they still stuck by the fire. At length, after a few passes of animal magnetism, during which Mac had all he could do to maintain his gravity at my ridiculous manœuvres, I took a smooth board, and with a piece of crayon, began to sketch their likenesses, occasionally continuing my smoke-driving up and down the chimney, as the blast invited. As the figures began to assume shape and form something like themselves, they evidently became uneasy and frequently looked at the door, inquiring if it was good. We still assured them it was not bad. Suddenly, a mighty gust came, driving the smoke down with unprecedented violence, when I sprang up to the fire-place, while Mac jumped to the door, and opened it to look out, and our tawny friends, seeing an outlet, bolted outright, preferring to " bide the pelting of the pitiless storm," rather than stay longer in the den of a monster who called the storm from the clouds, and took their spirits from themselves and made them fast to a board. We never received another visit from an Indian while we remained.

When Billinghurst, Brown and Periam were crossing the plains, they found at Fort Laramie an elderly man named Turner, who had bargained with a man to bring him through ; but at this point the man sold his wagon and team, and left poor Turner to shift for himself. Without a friend to aid him, with no money or provisions, and unable to go backwards or forwards, he was like a shipwrecked mariner upon a desolate coast. Happily, Messrs. Billinghurst, Brown and Periam, from Chicago, came along, and pitying his condition, they took him on board their wagon, with all his worldly wealth — his violin, to which he clung with an affection that only an amateur knows — although their own supplies were not abundant.

On the road across the plains, Turner was taken with scurvy, and instead of being of any service to them on their arrival, he was only a continual tax upon their generosity and good feeling, where even the necessaries of life were with difficulty procured ; and though his disease had made him childish and irritable, they did not relax their assiduity for his comfort, notwithstanding it was " without the hope of reward."

He moved with them from Long's bar to Stringtown in November, and if at times he was able to draw the bow to "Auld Lang Syne," or " Sweet, Sweet Home," with plaintive melody, with tears trickling down his care-worn face, at the reminiscences they called forth, it was destined that " wife, nor children more, should he behold, nor friends nor sacred home." He gradually grew worse, and died the last of January, and was buried on the hill-side above the cabin, leaving, as the only memento of his former existence, his violin, which long hung against the rude wall, and a half-written letter to his wife, which she probably never received. Many cases equally as melancholy came to my notice. During the winter, at least thirty persons were drowned in the river. One man perished before my own eyes, and two bodies floated down the river in one day. The most cases were caused by persons slipping from logs in crossing the rivers, when, by the icy stream, they soon became benumbed and incapable of exertion, and were whirled away to death in the rapid current.

CHAPTER XIX.

STOLEN CATTLE — RAPID GROWTH OF CITIES AND VILLAGES — SPECULATION— UNCERTAINTY OF TITLES — SACRAMENTO CITY — ITS GAMBLING HOUSES — REFINEMENT — GREAT FLOOD — CRAYON SKETCHES — A SPECULATION IN TOWN LOTS — THE INDIANS.

WHEN the high water in the spring of 1850 arrested the progress of our works, and our two companies temporarily separated, I learned that cattle stealing had become common in the valley. During the rainy season, the miners who owned teams were obliged to drive their cattle to the valley, where there was grass; for none grew on the mountains. They were left there from necessity, without care, till spring. I frequently met many who had lost all their cattle — unprincipled men having seized and driven off whole teams, and either sold them, or used them to haul loads to the mines after the roads became passable. One day a teamster drove a wagon into our settlement at Dawlytown, when Mr. Billinghurst recognized one of his own oxen in the team. As he had an abundance of proof at hand, the fellow was glad to compromise the matter by paying him a hundred dollars and taking the ox. Scarcely had the thief gone twenty yards before another yoke was claimed by a miner; and before he left the diggings his cattle were all claimed and taken by their owners. The fellow had made an unfortunate mistake, and had driven his load into the very settlement where his cattle belonged. This wholesale stealing excited much surprise among us, for the almost unheard-of honesty of Californians, as it had been the previous fall, was a subject of general remark. But a change seemed coming " o'er the spirit of *their* dream," for soon we began to receive accounts of robberies beyond anything we had ever heard. In this state of things I deemed it advisable to look after my own cattle ; and taking my blankets and provisions on my back, I set out for the valley, Twenty-five miles brought me to the meadow land, and I was fortunate enough to find three out of four ; but the fourth was lost. Being unable to continue mining and have a care over my cattle at the same time, I drove them to Marysville and sold them. And here I met with a surprise. When I forded the Yuba, in September previous, there stood then but two low adobe houses, known as Nye's Ranch, but early in the following winter a town had been laid out, which, in this short space of time, had grown to over a thousand inhabitants, with a large number of hotels, stores, groceries, bakeries, and (what soon became a marked feature in California) gambling-houses. Steamboats were daily arriving and departing, which seemed strange, for it had been a matter of doubt the previous fall as to Feather River being navigable for craft larger than whale boats. On this river, a mile from Marysville, Yuba City had sprung into existence, with a population of five hundred inhabitants ; and two miles below, the town of Eliza had been laid out, and buildings were rapidly going up. The two latter places, however, were eventually swallowed up by the rapid growth of Marysville, which has become a beautiful city, while the others, at the moment of writing this, have dwindled into nothing, and are nearly deserted. Speculation in towns and lots was rife ;

and on every hand was heard "Lots for sale" — "New towns laid out" — which looked as well on paper as if they were already peopled. There seemed to be a speculative mania spreading over the land, and scores of new towns were heard of which were never known, only through the puffs of newspapers, the stakes which marked the size of lots, and the nicely drawn plat of the surveyor. Not a single town was laid out on land where the title was indisputable; and as might be expected, litigations were frequent. Squatting followed, which resulted, in many cases, in riot and bloodshed. And to this moment, when the State contains probably over three hundred thousand souls, three years from the first emigration, claims are contested, and there is a vagueness and uncertainty in the possession of lands in the great valley, and in San Francisco, which renders the purchase of landed property uncertain, and the risk so great that prudent men hesitate to invest large sums.

Before the conquest, many of the old Californians had either taken possession of lands without authority, or held grants under revolutionary governors, which were not acknowledged by the supreme government of Mexico; and in some cases, where these grants were given by an acknowledged Mexican Governor, the proprietor had neglected to have them confirmed by the parent government; and in others, if this was done, they had neglected to comply with the requisitions of the grant — so that, where there were so many loop-holes, some shots of contention would enter. Still some of the claims were undoubtedly good, and will be acknowledged by the government of the United States, while squatters, in many cases, will very likely be able to hold the land they have taken up, after it has been decided that such lands belong to our government by the Commission instituted to examine the merits of claims, and we may look forward to the time when litigation and uncertainty on the subject, shall cease, and consequent happiness and thrifty progress of the people of California ensue.

Before returning to the mines, I visited Sacramento, and the improvements not only in the city, but in the country around, which a few months had produced, astonished me. Along the road hotels and dwellings had been erected at convenient distances; and where we had traveled the previous fall without seeing a human habitation, was now the abode of civilized man. At Nichols' Ranch, near the mouth of Bear River, where then but a single adobe house stood, a town had been laid out, and buildings were going rapidly up, (but this, however, eventually declined,) and under the bank, in the river, a large brig was moored, which had doubled Cape Horn. Vernon and Fremont, at the mouth of Feather River, appeared flourishing, but subsequently shared the uncertain fate of new towns in a new country. All these may revive, as the country advances in population, and its agricultural resources are properly developed.

Sacramento City had become a city indeed. Substantial wooden buildings had taken the place of the cloth tents and frail tenements of the previous November, and, although it had been recently submerged by an unprecedented flood, which occasioned a great destruction of property, and which ruined hundreds of its citizens, it exhibited a scene of busy life and enterprise, paculiarly characteristic of the Anglo-Saxon race by whom it was peopled. An immense business was doing with miners in furnishing supplies; the river was lined with ships, the streets were thronged with drays, teams, and busy pedestrians; the stores were large, and well filled with merchandise; and even Aladdin could not have been more surprised at the power of his wonderful lamp, than I was at the mighty change which less than twelve months had wrought, since the first cloth tent had now grown into a large and flourishing city.

I regret to say, that gambling formed a prominent part in the business of the city ; and there appeared an infatuation, if not unprecedented, certainly not excelled in the annals of mankind.   Long halls had been erected, which were splendidly lighted, and beautifully decorated with rich pictures, having magnificent bars, where liquors and various refreshments were exhibited, to tempt a depraved appetite ; and along the centre and sides of the room tables were arranged, where piles of money were seductively laid out to tempt the cupidity of the unexperienced.   And to crown all, on raised forms, or finely-wrought galleries, bands of music " discoursed harmonious sounds," to attract a crowd.   These places of resort were daily and nightly thronged with men of all ages and conditions in life, eager to tempt the fickle goddess of Fortune, too often to their own ruin.   Large sums were freely staked, and often changed hands, and the hard earnings of the infatuated miner, which he had been months in accumulating by incessant toil and wearying hardships, frequently passed from his well-filled purse, to swell the gambler's bank that was spread seductively, before him.

A day or two previous to my arrival, I was told that a young man, having started for home, came to the city from the mines, with nineteen thousand dollars.   On his arrival he deposited sixteen thousand with a friend, and with the rest went into one of these splendid hells, and commenced betting at monte.   He soon lost this, and under the excitement which it occasioned, he drew the sixteen thousand from his friend, notwithstanding all remonstrance, and determined to retrieve his luck.   He returned to the table, and continued playing till he had lost every farthing,

M   19

when, instead of making his friends happy, by returning to their embrace with a competence, he was compelled to return to toil and privation in the mines. Another, with fifteen hundred dollars, began playing, with the avowed intention of breaking the bank ; but the result was, as might have been anticipated, the gambler won every dollar in a short time. With the utmost coolness the poor fool observed to the banker, " You have won all my money — give me an ounce to get back to the mines with." Without saying a word, the gambler handed him back sixteen dollars, and the victim returned to his toil again.

Even boys of twelve and sixteen years of age were sometimes seen betting. But little else could be expected, from the extent of the demoralizing influences thus set before them.

In passing down to Sacramento through some of the mining settlements, I could not but observe the march of refinement which was going on, or, more properly speaking, the comforts, which were introduced. Crockery and table-cloths appeared on the tables of the hotels along the road ; glass tumblers, and even wine glasses, were used ; berths, similar to those on steamboats, were made around the rooms, and occasionally spare blankets could be found, so that on the principal thoroughfares it was no longer necessary to sleep on the ground, nor carry one's own plate, knife, and tin cup ; and as early as July, 1850, a line of stages commenced running from Sacramento to Marysville, which the following year became a very important and well-regulated route, from which, in 1851, lines diverged to various points in the mines.

During the winter of 1849 and '50, one of the greatest floods occurred which had ever been known in the valley of the Sacramento. From the top of a high hill on the left bank of

Feather River, not far from the Table Mountain, where I could command an extensive view of the valley, I estimated that one-third of the land was overflowed. Hundreds of cattle, horses and mules were drowned, being carried down by the rapidity of the current in their attempt to reach higher ground; and Sacramento City, then being without its levee, was almost entirely submerged. A small steamboat actually run up its principal streets, and discharged its freight on the steps of one of the principal stores, (Starr, Bensley & Co.'s) But at that time the limits of the city were not more than a third equal to its present size. A vast amount of property was destroyed, and many of its lighter buildings washed away.

The number of dead carcasses of animals, which floated down and lodged as the waters retired, produced a most loathsome effluvia, and it was the work of several days to rid the city of their putrid remains. All intercourse with the mines was suspended, and although it was predicted that the prosperity of the city was ruined, the substantial improvements which followed soon showed that the ardor and energy of its people could not be checked, even by an extraordinary catastrophe.

By the 29th of March I was once more at Dawlytown, but as the water still continued too high for mining operations, I resolved to go to Marysville, and endeavor to get into some business which would at least afford me the means of living. Of all the money I had received, but thirty-two dollars remained — enough to sustain me one week, as the price of board then ranged. A man may be placed in circumstances where all the ingenuity he is possessed of may be called forth, and this was emphatically my case. In vulgar parlance, I was *strapped*, and it was necessary that I should do something to raise the *quid pro quo*. Having a little skill in drawing, I took some crayons and drawing paper, and a few days saw me installed in town as a miniature painter, doing a thriving business. For three weeks I plied my pencil in copying the outre phiz and forms of the long-bearded miners, at an ounce a head, when I found myself the wealthy recipient of four hundred dollars; but wishing to make money a little faster, I played the speculator, purchased paper town lots, and —— lost nearly half of my earnings in the operation! It was, however, at this period that one of the most interesting events of my California life began. The rage for town speculations was still rife, when a friend proposed that we should make a claim twenty miles above Marysville, on Feather River, lay out a town, and get rich by selling the lots. We proceeded accordingly, made our claim, laid off the lots, and in a few days I was installed the patroon of our new village, with a fine stock of goods, cheap enough, if customers could only be coaxed to that really beautiful, but isolated spot. But that was a difficulty not easily overcome. My friend, by adverse circumstances, was finally compelled to give up the speculation, and I called my town an addition to one which my nearest and only neighbor, Captain Yates, had laid out. Captain Yates had been in the country nine years, and was a fine specimen of the old Californian. He was an Englishman by birth, and formerly a sea captain— brave, open, and generous — and though he was somewhat rough in his outward deportment, he possessed so many real sterling qualities, I really respected him. Though it may be supposed that our interests clashed, we lived together in the utmost harmony, and finally parted with mutual good will and esteem for each other. He lived half a mile above me, and near him was a large village of Indians, over whom he acquired complete control, and who were much attached to him; while

on my plot, and within ten rods of my house, was another village, of the tribe of Oleepa, and over which it was my good
fortune to acquire a like control, with their good will, which
continued during the three months I lived near them. It is
true, I took every occasion which offered to conciliate them,
isolated as I was, and completely in their power, had they been
disposed to be hostile. An incident occurred soon after my arrival among them, which gave them an idea that I was disposed
to justice, and to respect the law of *meum* and *tuum*. When
we were surveying our town we wanted stakes to mark out the
size and boundaries of the lots, and proper timber to make
them of was very scarce. In searching along a low spot on the
river bank, we found several cedar logs, which had floated down
during the flood, and which we supposed had drifted to the place
where they lay. Our axe-man mounted one for the purpose of
splitting out stakes, but scarcely had he struck a dozen blows,
when we heard a shout from the direction of the village, and
twenty Indians came running down, shouting in Spanish,
" *Canoa, canoa!* " accompanied by excited jesticulations, and
a volubility of words which we could not understand. Seeing
that something was wrong, I called to the axe-man to desist,
when they came up, and with much interest, began to examine
the cuts he had made. Fortunately he had cut near the end,
and had not injured it. They made us comprehend that they
had picked up these logs for making canoes, and to them they
were very valuable, for nothing but oak timber grew in that
vicinity. I assured them, as well as I could, that it was a mistake on our part, and that we would not interfere further with
them. As timber was scarce, however, the axe-man got upon
a log, declaring with an oath, he would cut them, and that
there was no use in coaxing such Indians. They seemed to un-

derstand his intention, and again appealed to me to save them. I insisted that the axe-man should not strike another blow, and made him come down. I then took a piece of paper, drew a picture of a canoe, with two Indians and a white man in it, and gave it to the one who seemed to be a leader. This they interpreted as my sign-manual that I would protect their property, and peace and harmony was at once restored, and they frequently repeated in Spanish, "*Bueno, bueno,* (good, good,) *Bueno Americano.*"

While the axe-man was gone after sticks, I sat down on the grass and began to converse with them by signs, which they easily comprehended. Taking out some medicines, I made them understand that I was a physician, (Heaven help me for the deceit!) and if they got sick I would cure them. I explained as well as I could the use of quinine and opium, and gave each a small pill of the latter, which they readily swallowed. Then I told them that I should make my "camps" near them, and we would be very good friends. They seemed delighted as they comprehended my meaning, and *Bueno, bueno Americano,* was again echoed all around.

CHAPTER XX.

INFLUENCE OVER THE INDIANS — THEIR CHARACTER AND HABITS — BURIAL
RITES — AFFECTION FOR THE DEAD — THEIR LANGUAGE — FOOD — SELEC-
TION OF MARRIAGE PARTNERS — GOVERNMENT — DRESS — THEIR PROPEN-
SITY TO GAMBLE.

It can hardly be expected that in three months I could gain
a perfect knowledge of the Indian customs and superstitions,
without understanding their language; but it was my chief
amusement to study their character and language while I remained, and I thus learned more of them than I could have
done by simply passing through their country. It was my first
business to cultivate their good will. An occasion was not
long wanting to turn a little circumstance to my advantage.
Owing to their extreme filth and dirt, they are very subject to
an eruption of the skin, which commences first by painful swel-
lings, and then suppuration ensues, which, on its discharge, irri-
tates whatever portion of the body it touches, producing large
and disgusting sores, so that not unfrequently their body and
limbs are covered with scabs and running sores. This has been
sometimes mistaken by the common observer for venereal
disease, but justice obliges me to declare that this assertion is
wholly unfounded, for I never in my life saw an Indian afflicted

with this vile disease, where they had no intercourse with de based whites. I found that the most simple remedy soon restored them to perfect health.

Soon after I had got my house erected, mercantile and house-keeping arrangements completed, I strolled one evening into the village, and saw the chief sitting by the fire in front of his house, apparently suffering from pain. I inquired by signs if he was sick. He put his hand just back of his ear, and signified that he had been in such pain that he had not slept for two nights. Feeling the spot indicated, I found a tumor gathering, when, returning to my house, I got some strong volatile liniment, with which I rubbed the affected part well, and giving him a pretty good pill of opium, I directed him to go to bed, assuring him that he would sleep. When morning came, the swelling had nearly subsided, and he felt much better. I then washed the place with Castile soap and water, and made a second application of liniment, and by the second morning the poor savage was completely restored to health. This was wonderful; and my credit as a medicine man was established at once. I continued my practice on others with complete success, and very soon my reputation became so high that every sore toe and scabbed skin was submitted to my inspection; and if it had been a matter of dollars and cents, my fortune had been surely made; but, unfortunately for me, they neither had nor understood the value of money. I was soon looked upon as a friend, and for aught I know recognized as of the tribe of Oleepa. When I first arrived, the men manifested no interest in me; and on drawing near the houses, the women and children almost always retired, as if in fear; but my uniform kindness soon dispelled this feeling, and when I went among them I was surrounded by numbers, with the utmost cordiality, and always invited to share their meals, or to partake of their luxuries, and they never seemed weary in showing me little attentions.

It has been supposed that they are taciturn in their dispositions. This may be so in their intercourse with whites and others with whom they are not acquainted; but among themselves, and with those in whom they confide, a more jolly, laughter-loving, careless and good-natured people, do not exist. The air resounded with their merry shouts as we sat around their fires at night, when some practical joke was perpetrated, or funny allusion made. And they were always ready to dance or sing at the slightest intimation, and nothing seemed to give them more pleasure than to have me join in their recreations. To each other they were uniformly kind, and during the whole of my residence with them, I never saw a quarrel or serious disagreement.

I soon began to get hold of their words, and to aid my memory, wrote them down. They were very fond of instructing me — repeating each word slowly and distinctly until I caught the sound. It was not long before I comprehended enough to make myself understood on common occasions. Whenever I was at a loss for the word, I referred to my glossary, and it was a matter of wonder to them that the paper could tell me how to speak. They frequently took it in their hands and looked at it every way, turned it upside down and around, but they could make nothing of it. Sometimes they would take my pencil, examine it closely, and then try to write, but in their hands it would not go off, and with a long drawn *waugh !* of wonder, they returned it to me.

For intelligence, they are far behind the Indians east of the Rocky Mountains, but although they are affectionate and kind to each other, as is the custom among all civilized tribes, their

M*

women are held to be inferior to the males, and are reduced to unmitigated slavery. The men are idle vagabonds, and spend most of their time in lounging; occasionally shooting birds and small game, or spearing fish, and, as it seemed to me, more for amusement than from any desire to be useful to their families. While thus engaged, the women were almost constantly occupied, either in gathering nuts, seeds or wood; cooking, pounding acorns, weaving blankets, or in some way providing for the comfort of their lords. I have often seen a woman staggering under a heavy load, attended by her husband, who never offered to relieve her. Yet this is not always the case, for on a long march, and when human endurance is not sufficient to stand longer under the burthen, an Indian will take the load on his own back, and relieve his squaw for awhile. And yet these very men can be employed by whites, and will carry, frequently, over an hundred pounds on their backs, with the package fastened by a strap, which passes across their foreheads, and in this way will climb long and steep mountains with apparent ease, when a white man would tire at once.

Their chief aim seemed to be to get enough to eat. Usually, about nine o'clock in the morning, half the squaws in the village, attended by the young girls who were old enough to work, and one or two men, to act as a kind of body-guard, start out with their baskets hanging on their heads, by a strap from their foreheads, to gather seeds, nuts, or anything to support their miserable existence. They are usually thus employed till three or four o'clock in the afternoon, when they return to cook and prepare acorn flour. Weaving baskets occupies the rest of their time till nearly sundown, when there is a general suspension of labor, the evening being generally spent in sitting around fires in groups, talking and laughing, or on moonlight nights in dancing.

Sometimes they procured enough to last two or three days, and then a large number of the women have but little to do, and are at liberty to be idle; but this does not very often occur. The men and women never eat together, and each congregate by themselves. Even around their fires at night, it rarely happens that the males sit in the same circle with the females. Sometimes men will be standing around, and now and then condescend to laugh and joke a little, but it is not common, and as a general thing they seem to prefer the society of their kind, rather than mix in social chat as we do. Even little boys and girls do not play together, and the latter are brought up to yield obedience to the former from childhood. Frequently a bevy of little girls would come to my store, and though timid and shy, liked the *kiethta* and *loopa* (bread and sugar) of the *Americano*, when, if the boys came, they would all retire at once; and I have seen a dozen women retire in the same way, at the approach of a single man of their tribe. Yet there seemed nothing like jealousy in the men, for I often sat down in the circle with the women while they were standing around, and such little familiarity seemed to give pleasure rather than annoy them. I recollect sitting thus one beautiful evening, when they were endeavoring to learn me to pronounce their words, and laughing immoderately at my uncouth mistakes, when a young man approached, and looking at me, said something good-naturedly, and then gazing around, he saw one of the best looking squaws, full of frolic, at the farther side of the circle. He approached, seized her, and dragging her along, placed her in my lap, saying that she was my sweetheart. There were several Indians standing near, and among them the husband of the squaw. The men and women set up a joyous shout of laughter, and passed several jokes, which seemed to mortify the poor squaw, and she soon returned to her former seat. All seemed affectionate and kind to each other, and readily shared a tit-bit. When laying out my plot, I employed a young Indian to carry stakes. At dinner I gave him an ample plateful, when two other Indians came along, and sat down without ceremony, and shared his meal as readily as if it had been their own. For the purpose of trying two boys who came into my store, I would give one of them a single cracker, when he would invariably break it in two and give half to his companion.

I could never learn much about their ideas of a Supreme Being. That they have some ideas of a Spirit superior to themselves, is certain; for at times they have peculiar dances in honor of the moon, and a superstitious reverence for their dead. At intervals, as often as once a year, they have large bonfires, and spend the night in wailings, and sometimes in peculiar dances and ceremonies, not only to lament for their departed friends, but to propitiate a good Being in their behalf. Different tribes have peculiar customs, but this seems to be universal, both among the mountain and valley Indians. The valley Indians usually bury, while those of the mountains burn their dead. I was one day talking with the war chief who belonged to the upper village, (who, by the way was a frank, open-hearted, generous fellow, and intelligent beyond his people,) when near my own village I observed a small rail enclosure, like that around graves in some of our pioneer settlements. I asked him what it was. We had been talking together gaily, but the moment I propounded the question, his whole manner changed to sadness, and sinking his voice to a whisper, he said it was bad, very bad. I told him I would go and see what it was — that I did not think it could be bad. "No, no," he continued, "do not go; it is bad," and stooping down, he scraped a little hole in the ground, putting a chip in it, carefully covered it with dirt, and pointing expressively to the enclosure, made me understand that one was buried there. Of course I respected his feelings, and did not visit it.

I attended the burial of a young man who died at the upper village. The body was bent into a sitting posture, and closely wound with cord, so as to form a kind of ball, after which some squaws dug a pit about four feet deep, and ten feet in front of the father's door. The corpse was then put therein in a sitting posture; two squaws got in, and while the dirt was being thrown in, they trod it down hard around the body, till the hole was nearly filled to the surface, when they retired. Up to this time not a tear was shed, nor a lamentation uttered; but when the ceremony was completed, the old man took a little broom and commenced sweeping the ground over the grave, and in front of his house, till a large space was cleaned, accompanying his labor by a long and loud wail, which at regular intervals was responded to by the women and children in the house, while the tears streamed down his face as if his heart was nearly broken. Their lamentation was continued nearly all night long, and at intervals for several days, until they gradually ceased, and the burial rites were concluded.

Captain Yates told me an affecting anecdote of a mountain Indian, which strongly illustrates their affection and never-dying love for the memory of their friends. A few years since Mr. Johnson, late proprietor of the ranch which bears his name, at the foot of the hills on Bear River, brought up an Indian boy and girl from childhood. They were educated as well as the circumstances of the country would permit, and while the girl was instructed in the domestic arts, the boy was taught the science of agriculture. Both were trusty and faithful, and Mr.

Johnson became much attached to them. In process of time they grew up, and the boy wanted a wife. Mr. Johnson proposed to him to marry the girl, which being perfectly in unison with their feelings, their marriage was celebrated with the usual rejoicing, and they lived together in the utmost harmony. In a year or two the boy was taken sick and died. Mr. Johnson, to testify his regard for his adopted children, desired to have a somewhat expensive funeral. Numerous guests were invited, and he gave his Indian relatives new clothes, and purchased a new hat for each, for which he paid eighteen dollars a piece, in order that they might make a decent appearance at the ceremony. Mr. Johnson intended to bury the body in a beautiful spot on his farm. But the poor girl begged him to let her lay her beloved husband beside the bones of her fathers in the hills. Of course he at once consented, and when all was ready, he set out, accompanied by his guests and retainers, to escort the body to the mountains. They were met by the rude mountaineers, with every demonstration of sorrow, who placed the body on a pile and set fire to it. As it was consuming, the Indians began to dance around it with a slow and measured tread, accompanied with songs of lamentation, each casting into the flames some precious offering, while the widow stripped herself completely of her civilized garments, and threw them into the fire, and Mr. Johnson's domestics each pulled off his hat and cast it into the burning pile of his deceased fellow and friend. When all was consumed, the Indians gathered up the ashes in their hands, and scattered them to the winds.

After the ceremony was concluded, Mr. Johnson told the young widow that her mule was ready, and they would return, but she refused to go. "My husband, my heart, is dead; I will stay in the mountains with him; I will watch his ashes on the hills, and his spirit shall be with me. I am an Indian now. I love you, my father, but I will go no more to the valley. I will be an Indian till I die."

It was in vain that she was promised new clothes, a life of ease and comfort, and the wants and miseries of a savage life exhibited to her. She would not go. "Her heart was here now. His bones were with her father's. Hers should be with his;" and no entreaty could prevail on her to change her determination. She assumed the usual grass apron worn by the squaws, and remains with them now.

Their language does not consist of as great variety of words as our own; they are comparatively few and simple, yet sufficiently expressive, and, like those of Indian tribes in general, they use some metaphor in a lengthened address. Of course, they have no terms of their own for things to which they are not accustomed; for instance, in articles of dress — they use the Spanish words for hat, coat, shirt, shoes, &c. I append a few of their common words, giving the sound by letters as near as possible :

ENGLISH.	INDIAN.	ENGLISH.	INDIAN.
Bread,	Ki-eth-ta.	House,	Koom-ballum.
Acorn bread,	Mah-tee.	Man,	Wah-nah-mah.
Acorn or wh't flour,	Hi-de-e-nah.	Woman,	Maam.
Wood,	Charp.	Boy,	Yah-mush-tim.
Fish,	Mocco.	Girl,	Cola.
Salmon,	Mi-eemh.	Captain,	Hoko'm.
Hair,	Oleem.	Come here,	Upeah.
Ground,	Cowepe.	Go away,	Wanok.
Work,	Tow-wal-te.	Good,	To-pe.

Although there seems to be a general language, by which

many of the valley tribes can communicate with each other, and even with the mountain Indians; yet the provincial dialects are so different, that those separated only fifteen or twenty miles seem to speak almost an entirely different language, and the examples which I have quoted above might not be understood by tribes twenty miles distant.

The Indians of California are more swarthy in complexion, and of smaller stature than those east of the Rocky Mountains; and although they may be placed in situations where they will fight bravely, they are less bold, and more cowardly in the main, than those on the great plains west of the Missouri; while they are more gentle in their natures, and become willing slaves to those who will feed and clothe them, if they are not overworked. They have more of the Asiatic cast of countenance than the eastern tribes, and are easily controlled if properly managed. Strict justice, and a uniform but firm and gentle behavior, will conciliate them, and gain their good will and respect. The mountain and valley tribes are in perpetual warfare, and rarely venture into each other's possessions, unless in considerable force, or by stealth.

Their staple article of food is acorns. These they gather in the proper season in large quantities, which constitute their principal supply of winter provisions. Before each house cribs are built, which will hold from thirty to fifty bushels each, and these are filled by the industrious squaws. None are thrown away from being worm eaten or mouldy, but good and bad are pounded up together, in holes worked in rocks, having a long, round stone for a pestle. The flour, if it may be so called, is put into a place scooped out of the sand, and wet with water and formed into a kind of paste, frequently mixed with the pulp of clover, or with wild berries, and then dried in the sun, or baked in hot ashes.

Were it not for their abominable filth in preparing it, this kind of bread would be very palatable. In addition to their acorn bread, they gather several kinds of grass seeds, one of which resembles mustard seed in its outward appearance, but on being pounded, is converted into a coarse, white flour, agreeable to the taste. Fish, birds and insects are also used, being baked on hot stones covered with earth; and their fastidiousness does not prompt them to take the entrails out. Everything which can be eaten is saved. I have frequently seen them eat handfuls of fresh clover. I was one day sauntering along through the village, when I discovered a new dish, which appeared to be some kind of nut, nicely browned. I took one in my fingers, and was about conveying it to my mouth, when I recognized it as the chrysalis of a caterpillar. I dropped it with some signs of disgust, when an Indian exclaimed, " *To-pe, to-pe;*" and to convince me that it was good, he ate a handful before my face. I replied that it might be good for an Indian, but it was not for an " Americano."

Their habits are filthy — frequently in the extreme. I have seen them eating the vermin which they picked from each other's heads, and from their blankets. Although they bathe frequently, they lay for hours in the dirt, basking in the sun, covered with dust. They generally wear their hair short, and their mode of cutting it is somewhat primitive. They either burn it off with ignited sticks, or turn it over a piece of wood and *saw it off with a clam shell!*

They manufacture but few articles, and in these they exhibit considerable ingenuity. Their baskets, made of willows, are perfectly water-tight, and are of the different sizes that may be required.   Their bows are of cedar, about thirty inches long, covered on the outer side with deer sinew, and will throw an arrow with amazing force.   The arrows are a species of reed, pointed with flint, or volcanic glass, and are made in two parts. When it enters the body, the short piece, containing the point, is left in the wound, from which it is impossible to extract it, thus leaving it to fester and rankle till it produces death.   Their spears are pointed with bone, with which they are very expert in striking salmon.   A line is attached to the spear, and after striking the fish they gradually draw him in as he becomes exhausted by his struggles.   Their houses in form resemble pits made for burning charcoal.   An excavation is made in the ground, a frame work is set up, tied together with raw hide ; this is covered with small pieces of wood and brush, and then covered with earth a foot or more deep.   A hole is left at the top by which smoke escapes.   The door is simply a hole, about two feet square, into which they crawl on their hands and knees.   A net work of small poles and willows is made overhead, which serves them for beds.   Some of these houses are quite capacious — and are cool in summer and warm in winter, but dark, dingy with smoke, and abounding with vermin.

The form of marriage among the Oleepas resembles, in some respects, that of the Tartars.   When a young man has fixed his affections on a girl, he makes a proposal to the parents, and with their consent, which is easily obtained, she goes out and hides.   The lover then sets out in search, and if he finds her twice out of three times, she is his without farther ceremony. But if he fails he is on probation for about three weeks, when he is allowed to make another trial, when, if he does not succeed, the matter is final.   The simple result is, that if the girl likes him, she hides where she is easily found, but if she disapproves of the match, a dozen Indians cannot find her.

Their government is patriarchal. There is a civil chief, who has control of the affairs in the village in time of peace, and a war chief, who takes command of war parties. To these the Indians yield obedience, as a son to his father, and the authority exercised is more that of love than of terror. I never saw their commands disputed, nor their authority unduly exercised; and it was more like one large family of dutiful sons and daughters, having but one general interest in common, than that of many familes, with conflicting tastes and interests.

Unless they have been brought into contact with the whites, where articles of dress can be procured, the Indians of California wear no clothes. The men go entirely naked; but the women, with intuitive modesty, wear a small, narrow, grass apron, which extends from the waist to the knees, leaving their bodies and limbs partially exposed. Still they adopt the American dress when they can get it, and in or near the settlements it is a common thing to see the men and women with simply a shirt on. Some, who have had better luck, are arrayed in pantaloons, with or without the shirt; and sometimes a coat, or vest, without either shirt, pants, or hat — making a more grotesque appearance than in their native nakedness.

They are most inveterate gamblers, and frequently play away every article of value they possess; but beads are their staple gambling currency. They have two or three games; one of which is with small sticks, held in the hand, which being suddenly opened, some roll on the fingers, when the opposite player guesses at a glance their number. If he guesses right, he wins, if wrong, pays the forfeit. Another is with two small pieces of bone, one of which is hollow. These they roll in a handful of grass, and tossing them in the air several times, accompanied with a monotonous chant, they suddenly pull the ball of grass in two with the hands, and the antagonist guesses which hand the hollow bone is in.   They have small sticks for counters, and as they win, or loose, a stick is passed from one to the other, till the close of the game, when he who has the most sticks is the winner.   They will sometimes play all day long, stopping only to eat.   I gave the chief a shirt and pantaloons, with which he was delighted.   About an hour after, I saw him strutting about entirely naked, and asking him where his clothes were, he replied, with perfect coolness — " Oh, another man got 'em.   I lost 'em gambling ;" and my shirt and pants were actually worn by three different Indians the same day !

CHAPTER XXI.

DISPOSITION AND CHARACTER OF THE INDIANS — THEIR HONESTY — CRUELTY
AND INJUSTICE OF THE WHITES — INCIDENTS — THEIR CONFIDENCE —
NUMBER OF WIVES — ANECDOTES — THEIR FINAL EXTERMINATION.

THE Indians of California are regarded as being treacherous, revengeful, and dishonest. This may be so to a certain extent, when judged by the customs and laws of civilization; but it should be qualified by the fact that they are governed by their own sense of propriety and justice, and are probably less likely to break the laws which they recognize as right, than are the whites to break theirs. Living in a state of nature, surrounded continually by enemies, emphatically the children of Esau — "their hand against every man, and every man's hand against them" — they are taught from necessity to be watchful and wary, and to look upon all men as enemies whom they do not know to be friends. Being in a state of perpetual warfare, they hold it to be a virtue to steal from those with whom they are not in alliance, and to avenge an insult upon those whom they do not regard as friends. They do not steal from their own people, and during my residence with the Oleepas, I never saw a quarrel; and I firmly believe that nine-tenths of the troubles between the whites and Indians, can be traced to imprudence in the former, in the first instance. Thus revengeful feelings are instigated, and being unable to distinguish between the innocent and the guilty, it being their custom to visit the insult of an individual upon his tribe, they take vengeance on the first white man they meet, as they do on the first Indian of a hostile tribe. Looking, too, on the whites as encroachers upon their territory, and as doubtful friends — their cupidity tempted by an unusual display of articles useful to them — they look upon it as a merit to steal; and they are sometimes forced to take cattle, mules and provisions, to eat, when a poor season limits their own supplies.

Renegade whites and Mexicans, in whom they have confidence, are not wanting to stir them up to acts of hostility; and this has been one fruitful source of their wars with the whites. It cannot be denied that there are evil-disposed Indians as well as white men; for human propensities are alike in all ages and climes; but the dogma of visiting vengeance upon the innocent as well as the guilty, widens instead of heals the breach. In their wild state they are, from the force of circumstances and education, suspicious, and like wild beasts, they must be tamed and enlightened, before they can fully understand *our* laws, and our notions of right and wrong.

I was completely in their power, and might have been killed or robbed at any moment; but while I was with them I am not aware that I lost the worth of a dollar, although I had five thousand dollars' worth of goods with me at one time. Yet they would steal from passers-by. I sometimes had occasion to be gone all day from home, but leaving my house and goods in the care of the chief, or some of the old men, I invariably found everything safe on my return. My confidence was never abused. I never abused theirs. I was uniform in my conduct with them, never but once making a promise I did not perform. In that instance it was unavoidable, and was explained to their satisfaction. If I was leaving my store, although a hundred Indians were in, every one followed me out, unless I told some one to stay, when *all* would remain.

The indiscretion of some of the whites was strongly exemplified in the spring of 1850, on the middle fork of Feather River. It had become common to charge every theft of cattle on the Indians. A party of miners missed several head of oxen, and a cry was raised that the Indians had stolen them. Fifteen men were started out, well armed, swearing vengeance. Proceeding to a rancheria, about twelve miles higher in the mountains, they found a few bones, which they considered proof positive of the guilt of the inhabitants. They immediately surrounded the huts, when the Indians came out, and seeing their hostile attitude, without understanding the cause, and impelled by the instinct of self-preservation, attempted to fly. A deadly discharge of firearms was made, and fourteen Indians fell dead. After demolishing the houses, the brave whites set out on their return, with the glory of having taken signal and successful vengeance on the mountain robbers. When they had nearly reached home, their sense of justice was a little shaken, by seeing every ox which they had supposed stolen, quietly feeding in a somewhat isolated gorge, whither they had strayed in search of grass. Had the Indians, under similar circumstances, killed fourteen whites, an exterminating warfare would have ensued.

Captain Yates related an anecdote, which is a further illustration of the want of discretion often shown by the Americans. An Indian visited a miner's camp, and begged for something to eat. The miners told him to chop some wood, and they would give him some bread. He accordingly took their axe, commenced work near the brink of a creek. The axe being loose, worked off the helve, and flew into a deep hole, which, owing to high water, could not then be gotten out. Fearing that the miners would charge him with theft, he ran away. On discovering their loss, the men swore vengeance against the Indian, and having armed themselves, they were proceeding towards the rancheria, when, being met by Yates, it was with much difficulty that they were persuaded by him to desist, assuring them that if the Indian had stolen it, he could recover it. He sent for the chief, and a true statement of the case was elicited. When the water had subsided, the captain took the Indian to the spot, and making him dive into the hole, the axe was brought up. Thus, by a little forbearance and common sense, a cruel wrong was avoided. They are impulsive because they have not been taught reflection.

At the first settlement of Grass Valley, in Nevada county, a general war was at one time apprehended, from a difficulty which resulted in the murder, by the Indians, of an innocent and good man. Two brothers, named Holt, had erected a sawmill, four or five miles from where the town now stands. Their uniform kindness and justice had secured the Indians' friendship, and they all lived on amicable terms. Not far off lived a heedless and dissolute miner, who one day took a squaw into his cabin, where he kept her two or three days, to gratify his lustful passion. This incensed the Indians so much that they determined to take revenge, and not being able to find the perpetrator of the outrage, with characteristic sense of right, they determined to take vengeance on any of the white man's tribe they could find. The elder Holt was one morning busily at work in his mill, while his brother was out a short distance, when a number of Indians advanced with their usual friendly demeanor. They suddenly commenced an assault on poor Holt, who fell under their murderous weapons. He could barely cry out to his brother before he fell, to save himself. His brother, seeing the attack, fled, receiving two arrows, but succeeded in making his escape to the cabin of Judge Walsh, at Grass Valley, and gave the alarm. Walsh had one man with him, and at night was joined by three miners, who had been out prospecting. This little band prepared themselves in the best manner they could, resolving to sell their lives as dearly as possible. They watched all night, momentarily expecting an attack; but Indian vengeance was appeased, and they did not appear. The miners in the neighborhood were aroused, and stood upon the defensive; but a talk was held, and the affair happily compromised. Thus the indiscretion of one man had nearly caused the death of many. Reversing the picture: Had the outrage been perpetrated by an Indian on a white woman, her kindred would quite as likely have taken revenge on the whole tribe, by killing or driving them off.

Soon after I got my plat surveyed, a gentleman named Gray became my neighbor, and built a house adjoining mine. He was of a pleasant, jovial disposition, but at times, when depressed, could not maintain his equanimity of temper; and though he frolicked and laughed occasionally with the Indians, and they, on the whole, liked him, yet when he was vexed, he did not hesitate to repulse them with some rudeness. Of course, although some Indians liked him, others did not. One day I had gone to Marysville, leaving my store in his care. He had imprudently given some of the Indians liquor, and when they became excited, they wanted more, which he refused, and drove them off. I did not return till the second day, after nightfall. On my way up, I met Captain Yates, who told me there was trouble in my village, and that the Indians were much incensed at Gray, and he feared it would not end well. It was nine o'clock

N

in the evening when I rode up to my store, and had scarcely got off my horse, when a large number turned out as usual to welcome me; and while one took the bridle, another took off the saddle, and a third led my horse to grass, and a fourth brought me fresh water. But Gray was not to be seen, and on inquiry, the Indians could not tell me where he was. Striking a light, I stepped into his store, and as I went in, I saw an Indian dodging out of the back door in a rather equivocal manner. Soon I heard the gurgling sound of running liquor, and on looking about, I discovered that the plug was pulled out of his brandy cask, and a pail was standing under, which was nearly half full. Comprehending the matter at once, I poured the liquor back, put in the tap, and broke it off— telling the chief that he had a bad Indian, and that he must be accountable if anything was lost, after which I quietly went to bed and slept soundly till morning.

About nine o'clock Gray came in, and after expressing surprise that I should have the hardihood to sleep there, told me about his difficulties: When the Indians found that he would give them no more liquor, three of them laid a plot to murder him that night. Soon after dark, while he was unconscious of his danger, a squaw rushed into his tent from the back way, and, much excited, told him to go into the woods to sleep, for the Indians intended to kill him; saying which, she hurried out in a round-about way, and gained the village unperceived. Her husband was to be one of the murderers. Gray went up to Captain Yates', and spent the night; and the Indians, not finding him, meant to make sure of the liquor before I came; but fortunately I arrived in time to prevent it. Why they did not steal mine, or my goods, at the time, I do not know, for they had every opportunity.

In illustrating their confidence in individuals who are fortunate enough to secure it, I will record one of the many incidents which occurred to me.

A party of ladies and gentlemen from Marysville came up on a steamboat one day on a pleasure excursion, and while the most of them were at Captain Yates', near whose house they had landed, I was walking with one or two gentlemen over my plat, discoursing (eloquently, of course) on the beauty of my situation, and hoping, by the way, to sell them a share, when my attention was drawn to my village, by seeing the women, with their children and such valuables as they could carry, flying in consternation towards a place of concealment near the river. Satisfied that something unusual had occurred, I called out to inquire what was the matter, but the only reply I could get was, " Steambota, malo steambota ;" and they continued their flight. Presently, a little boy who lived with me came running by, wild with affright, and catching him by the arm, I inquired what it all meant. In the utmost excitement he cried out, " O malo steambota, malo steamboata, it will carry us all off; our homes will be lost; our mothers stolen; our children killed." " No — no," said I ; " there is a mistake. It is not so ;" and directing one of the gentlemen, who could speak their language better than I could, to call them back, he spoke to an Indian, who called after the fugitives, and they again stopped. I soon learned the cause of their alarm. Two drunken fellows had gone into Captain Yates' village, and in a frolic told the Indians that the steamboat would carry off all the women. The word was soon passed, and an Indian came running down to our village with the horrid news. I went towards the trembling fugitives and told them that the story was false, and that the steamboat was soon going away, and would sleep about a mile below, on the opposite bank, and that I would protect them. At length, confidence was restored, and they returned to the village. It was near nightfall when the gentlemen went again to the boat, and I returned to the village, in order to allay any latent fears of my Indian friends. A great crowd gathered around me with noisy pleasure, the children came up to take me by the hand, and mothers passed their infants from hand to hand for me to fondle, and in a little time peace and quietness was restored. As the boat started from her moorings, I went to the bank to see her pass, attended by all the little boys, who had hold of my hands, arms and coat, as many as could gather around, while others held to those nearest to me. Just before the boat reached us, the fireman stirred up the fire, making a brilliant display of sparks in the dusky shades of night, when, in sudden fright, the children threw themselves into my arms, or grasped my legs, crying, "Upeah steambota," (the steamboat comes,) and I had hardly time to say "it would not come," before it shot swiftly past, and their excited fears were put to rest. But their affectionate confidence thrilled my heart, and I am not ashamed to confess, betrayed me into unusual emotion.

Polygamy is practised among them. But it sometimes happens that there are more males than females in a village, when they content themselves with one wife. Indiscriminate cohabitation is never practiced.

I was one day talking with the civil chief, and he asked me how many wives I had. I told him but one. He only inquired if women were scarce in my village.

"No, they are as numerous as the leaves on the trees."

"Wah!" he exclaimed with surprise, and holding up his fingers and pointing to his koomballum, he signified that he had four.

" Well, you old Solomon, (I said this in English,) what do you do with so many ? "

" I make them gather acorns, make bread, pick up wood, and work for me."

" And I work for myself," said I.

" Humph ! " said he, contemptuously. " Good for nothing. Does your wife dress like you ? "

I could have added that she did not exactly wear the breeches, but I told him that she wore a long shirt, shoes and stockings, and a kind of hat.

He thought I must have " much clothes, or I was a very great fool to spend so much on one woman."

They can be learned to plow, to herd cattle, and perform manual labor very well. But I was once somewhat amused at the awkwardness of an Indian in a (to him) new branch of business. A sack of sugar had been landed for me about half a mile below, on the opposite bank of the river, and taking two Indians, I went after it. I found it too heavy for them to carry, so I borrowed a wheelbarrow and set them to wheeling it to the landing. As I expected, they made awkward work of it, but by dint of perseverance, one of them made out to keep the one wheeled wagon in the track, and we managed to get it to the landing. Thinking the other Indian would find no difficulty in wheeling back the empty barrow, I directed him te return it. He stood a moment, looking irresolutely at it, when, calling for the aid of his companion, he hoisted it on his head, and deliberately marched off with it.

At the close of my residence with them, when making arrangements to return to the mines, I had saved from my stock, which had been sold out, a summer's supply of provisions, and it being necessary for me to visit Marysville, I packed all securely up, and going into the village, told the chief and some of the old men that I was going to Yuba, that I should be gone some days, and that I wanted them to take care of my house and goods until I came back, to which they gave their usual assent. It so happened that I was obliged to go to Sacramento City, and I was unwell a day or two, so that I did not return until the thirteenth day. I came back on the opposite side of the river, and calling to the Indians, they came over on their log canoes and conveyed me across. On ascending the bank, the men of the village came out as usual to see me, but I observed this time that they kept a little back, instead of coming around me as they generally did. In a moment an old man advanced, and slowly, and with much dignity, addressed me with,

"Wah-ne-mah, when you left us you said you would be gone so many sleeps," and holding out a string, he showed me seven knots tied in it. "You have been gone so many," and slipping his hand along he showed me thirteen. "How is this?"

"I explained to him that I was seven days at Yuba, two days I was sick, two days I had to go to Sacramento, and it took me two days to come home.

"It is good," said he, "it is all right."

When this important matter was explained, the others came up and greeted me cordially, and I stood upon my usual footing.

"Come," said I, let us go to my house," and I led the way, when on reaching it I saw that they had piled the door full of limbs and brush, which, according to their custom, signifies that the owner is absent, and no one enters. Pulling these away, we entered, when I discovered that all my provisions were gone; not a single article was left. At first I was a little startled, but

I exhibited no surprise. In a short time I observed, " Come, let us go to the village, I want to see the women and children." I was followed by the crowd, and going into the town, I found the chief, sitting on a beef's hide, and he invited me to sit beside him. After a due pause, and explaining the cause of my long absence, I observed, " Well, you have taken good care of my house, did you take care of my goods ? "

" Yes."

" Are they all safe ? "

" Yes — all safe."

" Good," I replied, " where are they ? "

" There," said he, pointing to his house.

" Very well — I have come home now, you may take them back."

He sprang up, and going on the top of his house, he called several Indians together, and gave them directions, when they went to work, and in thirty minutes every box, every sack of flour, was taken out, and piled up precisely as they had found them in my house, and even a hatchet and a dozen nails were returned to me, unasked. The faithful Indian had removed them to his own house for safe keeping against straggling whites and vicious Indians. " Honor to whom honor is due."

I could relate many anecdotes of what transpired during my brief sojourn with the untutored savages, which would present them in a favorable light, but it is probable the reader is already tired, and I forbear. I do not mean to appear as their apologist, but I do think that their character is not well understood by the mass of people, and that their good will might be gained by conciliation, kindness and justice, if they can be kept free from malign influences, and that the principles of civilization may be instilled into their minds. But this will never be. Once in contact with the whites, they learn their vices without understanding their virtues; and it will not be long before intemperance, disease and feuds will end in their extermination, or complete debasement, and these once powerful tribes, like those upon the Atlantic shores, will have passed away, or be but a wreck of miserable humanity. They are already dwindling, for the fire-water and rifle of the white man are doing their work of death, and five years will not pass ere they will become humbled and powerless — a wretched remnant of a large population. I have been told that the valley of the Sacramento, fifteen years ago, contained from fifteen to twenty thousand, but a fatal disease breaking out, in one year destroyed many thousands — in fact, reduced them more than one half; and this I think quite likely; for during a trip which I made last fall to the upper Sacramento, I passed a multitude of old deserted villages, which I was assured was caused by desolating disease. But the two races cannot exist in contact, and one must invariably yield to the other; and it was justly remarked by Governor Burnett, in his annual message of January, 1851 : " That a war of extermination will continue to be waged between the two races, until the Indian race becomes extinct, must be expected. While we cannot anticipate this result but with painful regret, the inevitable destiny of the race is beyond the power or wisdom of man to avert."

CHAPTER XXII.

PETER THE HUNTER — AT THE BATTLE OF WATERLOO — HIS ADVENTURES — HIS DAUGHTERS — JIM BECKWITH — HIS DARING ACT AMONG THE BLACK- FEET, AND ESCAPE — SOUTHERN INDIANS — INFLUENCE OF THE CATHOLIC MISSIONS — CHANGE OF QUARTERS — MINERS IN SEARCH OF THE GOLDEN LAKE — THE RESULT.

WE sometimes find in California, hanging around the out-skirts of civilization, animals of the biped species, which differ doth from the natives of the soil, and those of a higher grade in human form — those who are far removed from the savage state, yet want the refinements and accomplishments of civil-ized society. While living at Yateston, I became acquaint-ed with one of the *genus homo* who was something of an original, with all the peculiarities of the class to which he belonged.

Peter the Hunter was a half-breed, of the Sioux nation, his father being a French trapper, his mother a squaw; and when I became acquainted with him, he was about fifty-eight years of age. His tall, gaunt, attenuated frame, his restless black eye, his thin, sunken cheeks, attested a life of hardship and exposure, while his roving disposition proclaimed him of that class of men who are frequently found hanging around, and often beyond the farthest verge of civilization. He followed the chase for a liv-ing, and with great success — for Peter was a capital shot. And although he could accumulate such property as is deemed

N*   21 valuable with his class — horses, mules, furs and skins — he had not tact enough to come in competition with the more wily trader, and was generally cheated out of his property as fast as he gained it, and always remained poor. Without education, and notwithstanding his isolated and roving life in the wilds between the Rocky Mountains and the Pacific Ocean, he still had a good idea of the proprieties of civilized life, and took much pains to instill his crude notions into the minds of his children. In short, he was a curious compound of civilization and barbarism — a man of considerable observation, and much good sense. He spoke English and French fluently, as well as the language of many of the tribes in the wilds of America.

In his youthful days, being in Montreal, he was impressed into the British service. Thus forced from his home on the Platte, he served seven years as a soldier in the British ranks, and was at the battle of Waterloo when Bonaparte was overthrown. His relation of that event was vivid and correct; and his eye would sparkle with animation as he recounted various evolutions during the battle, and the fire of youth seemed to flow again in his veins.

After the restoration of the Bourbons, and when peace was declared, Peter, with many others, was sent to the mouth of the Columbia, in Oregon, and discharged. There he married a Catholic squaw, by whom he had four children — three girls and a boy — when his wife died. Although he always led a roving life, and seldom remained long in one place, his children were brought up in the Catholic faith; and with the use of the lasso, the rifle, and the hunting knife, in which they were perfectly expert, his girls were taught morning and evening to bow in reverence to Almighty God. Two of his girls were young women grown; the third, and youngest, was about eight years old. The boy was dead. His girls were as fearless riders as I ever saw, and could throw the lasso with unerring aim when riding at full speed, and it will be seen that in the use of the rifle they could not be excelled.

Peter was ardently attached to his wife, and often spoke of her in the warmest terms of affection; but when his boy died, who was his pride and hope, it almost broke his heart.

"My wife was a good Christian," said Peter, "and took good care of the children. She loved me, and was faithful, and I loved her; but she was growing old, and I knew of course she must die sometime. But my boy was young, and active beyond his years. My girls are smart, and are good shots, but they can't begin to do with a rifle what he could. He never missed his aim. I was proud of him — too proud. I thought he would live; that he would be a man, but —— "

Peter's lip quivered, his eyes filled with tears, and he could not go on. Some little kindnesses which I had it in my power to bestow, won his confidence, and he frequently unburthened to me his overcharged heart. Now, he only lived for his family. To protect them seemed to be his only care — his only ambition. When he came to the valley he had twenty-seven horses, but he had been robbed of all but three, and all attempts to recover them proved unavailing.

"Did the Indians steal them from you, Peter?" said I.

"No," he replied, with some energy; "it was the cursed whites. Indians will steal sometimes, but not from me, where they know me; and I don't fear *them*. I can take care of myself among them, for I know their ways, but these white men are robbers, and they have so much bad law that they can cheat the scalp off your head, and you can't help yourself.

Here is all the law I want" — and he slapped his rifle — "and if I could meet some of the thieves on the plain, I'd give 'em an argument they couldn't answer. I can trust an Indian further than I can a white man.

One day Peter came to me with some perturbation, and told me that a gang of thieving Frenchmen, who lived a few miles above us, had threatened to carry off his daughters — in fact, had attempted to insult one of them in his presence, but he had beat them off.

"I do not care for myself," said he. "If I am killed, it matters nothing, but who will protect my children?"

"Pitch your tent by mine, Peter," said I "and if they make an attack, let the girls run into my house, and I think that you, Gray and I, with the aid of our Indians, can give them such a reception that they will be glad to sheer off. They must walk over our bodies before they succeed, and on a pinch the girls can fire a shot. He grasped my hand without saying a word, and in a little time his camp was removed in close proximity with my own. Our evenings were often whiled away around his camp fire, in listening to him, recounting many of his strange adventures. He had been wandering through the mountains of California and Oregon for twenty-five years, among the fierce and hostile tribes that inhabited them, and his descriptions of the scenery and country have been proved correct by subsequent explorations. He described the Klamath Rogue River, and Trinity Indians as more bold and warlike, and highly advanced in the scale of improvement, than those of the south — a character that travelers subsequently gave them. He said that their houses, though rough, were built of wood, above ground, and that they took more care to provide against want in winter, by laying in supplies of fish and meat, than the valley Indians, and that they wear a covering of skins — facts which have since become known. He had penetrated to the sea at the mouth of the Klamath, and described the extreme broken mountain country on Trinity and Scott's Rivers, with vivid correctness. My table was bountifully supplied with bear meat, venison and antelope, while we remained together. With the peculiar customs of the wild tribes near us, and the strange hunter, who was my companion, I have always looked upon this part of my sojourn in California as the most interesting.

Peter had been most desperately wounded, a short time before I became acquainted with him, and his head was still bound up, the wound not being fully healed. He was still weak. The incident is one of thrilling adventure. About twelve miles nearly west of us, a solitary butte rises from the plain, from fifteen hundred to two thousand feet high, and whose broken, craggy and pointed ridges seem to kiss the clouds. It stands nearly in the centre of the plain, equi-distant from the coast range and Siérra Neváda, and can be seen at a great distance on either side, frowning in gloomy majesty, a beacon and guide to the weary and bewildered traveler.

It was one morning in the spring of 1850, that Peter saddled his horses, and as usual, accompanied by his daughters, all armed to the teeth, set out on a hunting excursion towards the buttes. Nothing material occurred till they arrived at the solitary mountain, and had ascended some distance, when coming to a nearly perpendicular point, they dismounted, and Peter climbed alone through the bushes toward a shelving rock, for the purpose of taking an observation for game. With much difficulty he gained the foot of the shelf, and setting his rifle against the rock, he climbed over the ledge, when, to his

horror he found himself facing a huge grizzly bear. The monster sprang upon him at once, and he instinctively drew his
knife, as the bear rushed upon him and seized his arm. Quick
as thought, he plunged his knife in the animals side, who now,
enraged, seized him in his grasp, tearing his scalp from his
head, and biting him in a fearful manner, when in the struggle
they both fell off the rock, and together rolled down the hill.
Peter, in the meantime, making the best use of his knife possible, inflicting several severe wounds upon his adversary. His
girls witnessed the fearful struggle, and the eldest stood paraly-
zed with astonishment, but the second one, with the impulse of
one inspired, sprang towards her father, and as the combatants
became momentarily separated in their fall, she raised her trusty rifle, and with unerring aim, discharged it at the bear. The
bullet took effect in the monster's head, and he fell, stunned if
not dead. Instantly she ran and seized her sister's rifle, and returning placed it against the bear's ear, and what little of life
remained soon passed away. He was dead, while she, the he-
roine, the noble girl, was the savior of her father's life. Bleeding and wounded, they carried their poor father to the camp,
and many weeks elapsed before he recovered. " She is a brave
girl," said Peter to me ; " and I don't fear the Frenchman on
her account, for she can defend herself; but her sister is more
timersome; and then, the little one ————." Suffice it to say,
the Frenchman never made the attempt.

"I have had many offers," said Peter, " from white men, to
take my girls and give them and me a home, but they would
not marry them, and I know that by your laws and customs
it is not creditable for a man and woman to live together un-
married. They can't be respectable, except they are married,
and I love my girls, and want them to be well settled, as much

as the whites do their own. I had rather live in the way we do, and my girls take care of themselves alone, than become paramours to beastly whites; and they shall, too, as long as I live."

Like all of his class, he sometimes indulged too freely in the use of ardent spirits, and when under its influence was quarrelsome and bad. "I know it is bad, it makes me a bad man when I drink it," he said, "and I wish I never could get a drop, but I can't always resist the temptation when it is offered to me. But sometimes, when I find the fit coming on, I go off where I can't get it, for the sake of my family." I thought his example might be imitated with advantage by those who could boast of a superior education, and more refinement.

One morning I got up, and casting my eyes in the direction of Peter's camp, I found his tent gone, and all signs of him had disappeared. He had gone off very early, and I never heard of him afterwards.

Among that reckless, daring class of men, who are met among the savage tribes west of the Missouri, was Jim Beckwith, a mulatto, who was in California about the same time. For many years he had lived among the Rocky Mountain tribes, and had led a life of wild adventure, and his history is one continued scene of reckless daring and hair-breadth escapes. He became a chief of the Crow nation; but he had lived with the Blackfeet, and had a wife among them, and of course stood on friendly relations with them. Being on one occasion out upon some excursion, he met a war party of Blackfeet going against some belligerent tribe, and on their invitation he joined them. They were victorious, taking a number of scalps, and among them was that of a French trader, whom some of the Indians had killed in the skirmish.

On their return, the Blackfeet held a grand festival, to cele-
brate their victory; but in this Jim did not join, but sat moodily by the fire in his lodge, little heeding the uproarious cries
without. In the wigwam with him were three French traders,
whose curiosity attracted them to the door to witness the dancing and antics of the Indians. Jim sat leaning his head upon his
hands, holding communion with none but his own thoughts, when
suddenly looking around, he observed the Frenchmen gazing
at the crowd, when he ask them stearnly,

"Why do you stand there, looking on that scene?"

"Because we like to see them dance," they replied.

"Do you not know that they have the scalp of a white man?
And can you see them rejoice over the death of a white man?
I never did; and," he added, with emphasis, "I never will. If
you know what is best for you you will come in."

They knew him too well to dispute his admonition, and they
closed the door, but at the same time inquired, "If you dislike
it why do you allow your squaw to join them?"

"Is she there?" asked Jim.

"Yes; and she dances more merrily than any of them."

Without making any reply, he strode into the savage crowd,
seized his wife by the flowing hair, and dragged her into the
lodge. "I told you not to join in the dance. The scalp of a
white man is there. There must be no rejoicing by me or
mine over that. Now go and bring me some water."

The reply of the irritated squaw was that of a free-born
woman: "If you have a slave, send her — I am no slave."

Without deigning a remark, he took a hatchet, clove her
skull, and she fell a corpse at his feet.

Several squaws who had followed them, ran out, screaming,
and communicating the attrocious act to the already excited In-

dians. In the mean time, Jim coolly took down his rifle, pistols, knife and tomahawk, and turning to the amazed whites, calmly observed, " Now you must fight or die — you will hear from it soon."

" For a few moments there was an appalling stillness, which contrasted strangely with the horrid din which had been ringing without. "Ah, ha!" ejaculated Jim, "do you mind that?" Directly a long, loud, savage war whoop was sounded, with a yell that might have made the stoutest heart tremble, and then came the thought to the caged Frenchmen, that they were surrounded by hundreds of enraged Indians, from whom escape was impossible. Death seemed inevitable. The yell was repeated. "I told you so," said Jim, betraying no sign of fear. "It is for life you have to fight now."

"Why did you kill her?" asked the white men, shuddering.

"I told her," he replied, "that I never rejoiced over the scalp of a white man, and that she must not. I never did, and I never will. No squaw of mine shall ever do it. I forbade her, and she disobeyed me."

A rush was momentarily expected, and the whites looked upon themselves as doomed by Jim's rashness. The door of the lodge was slowly opened, when, instead of a throng of savage Indians, an old man, the father of the murdered squaw, appeared, and with a slow and dignified tread he advanced to the fire and sat down. After a pause he turned to Beckwith and addressed him:

"My son — why did you do this? Why did you kill my daughter?"

"She forgot her duty. She disobeyed me," said Jim, fearlessly. "It was my right." Another pause ensued, which was at length broken by the old man.

"My son, you did right. She should have obeyed you. She had no ears. You did right! I have another girl; you shall have her for a wife. She has ears, and will hear." Savage as the act was, Jim had only availed himself of the prerogative of Indian law.

The old man arose, went out and explained the circumstances to the Indians, who, though dissatisfied, acquiesced. That same night Jim married the other daughter of the old man, and for the present the matter was compromised. But he knew too well that their vengeance would overtake him at the first convenient opportunity, although he was safe so long as he remained under the protection of his father-in-law. When he proposed to leave them, the old man gained the consent of the Indians to give him an hour the start from a certain designated point, when, after that, if they caught him they would kill him. On arriving at the place of departure, Jim left them, walking leisurly along till he was out of sight, when he began to run with all his might, for he knew that speed alone could save him. By great exertion he succeeded in making his escape, and finally reached the Crow nation and his home in safety.

The Indians in the Southern part of Upper California are farther advanced in civilization, if it may be so called, than those farther north. They are more provident and wear some clothing. While the country was under the dominion of Mexican rule, the Catholic Fathers established several missions below San Francisco, and with their usual kindness, they instructed the Indians in some of the ruder branches of labor, together with the proprieties of civilized life, so far as circumstances would permit. Those who came under their influences, and were christianized, adopted, in some measure, their habits, and were thus improved. When the missions were suppressed, or when the tide of conquest by the Americans destroyed them, the result of this training was not wholly lost, and it may have had its effect among the still wilder tribes in proximity with them, in the mountains.

I do not mean to say they were civilized, for this could not be effected in one generation; but they attained a knowledge of making themselves comfortable beyond the tribes higher up the valley. I am disposed to give the Fathers of the Catholic Missions credit for their efforts; for, so far as my knowledge goes, they did much to lessen human suffering, and to improve the moral as well as physical condition of the miserable race of natives over whom they could exercise authority and control. And among these, the result of this training may not have been wholly lost. Those who look for a sudden and perfect transformation in uncivilized races, will be disappointed. Notwithstanding the unceasing efforts of missionaries in the Sandwich Islands for the last sixty years, and although a great change has been produced in the character of the people, it has been found impossible to eradicate wholly all old prejudices and predilections. Subject as the natives are to influences which cannot be controlled, it is a change which will require the efforts of more than one generation to perfect.

In closing this chapter, I may be permitted to remark that speculation in town lots ceased as suddenly as it arose. From one end of the valley of the Sacramento to the other, innumerable towns were laid out, which would have required the concentration of the population of California to supply with inhabitants, and it soon became apparent that it was a merely speculative operation, though undoubtedly many were sincere in the belief, that their town was eligibly situated, and would be improved. Many did not realize the expense of surveys from the sale of lots, and finding myself nearly in this category, (though to this day favorably impressed with the advantages of its site, if it could have been improved,) after living solitary and alone about three months, the unwelcome truth became apparent to me, that, like Death in Doctor Hornbook, " I maun do something for my bread." I reluctantly left my quarters, after getting my claim recorded, and placing it on as sure a foundation as the law of the time required.

In May, 1850, a report reached the settlements that a wonderful lake had been discovered, an hundred miles back among the mountains, towards the head of the Middle Fork of Feather River, the shores of which abounded with gold, and to such an extent that it lay like pebbles on the beach. An extraordinary ferment among the people ensued, and a grand rush was made from the towns, in search of this splendid El Dorado. Stores were left to take care of themselves, business of all kinds was dropped, mules were suddenly bought up at exorbitant prices, and crowds started off to search for the golden lake.

Days passed away, when at length adventurers began to return, with disappointed looks, and their worn out and dilapidated garments showed that they had " seen some service," and it proved that, though several lakes had been discovered, the Gold Lake *par excellence* was not found. The mountains swarmed with men, exhausted and worn out with toil and hunger; mules were starved, or killed by falling from precipices. Still the search was continued over snow forty or fifty feet deep, till the highest ridge of the Siérra was passed, when the disappointed crowds began to return, without getting a glimpse of the grand *desideratum*, having had their labor for their pains. Yet this sally was not without some practical and beneficial results. The country was more perfectly explored, some rich diggings were found, and, as usual, a few among the many were benefitted. A new field for enterprize was opened, and within a month, roads were made and traversed by wagons, trading posts were established, and a new mining country was opened, which really proved in the main to be rich, and had it not been for the gold-lake fever, it might have remained many months undiscovered and unoccupied. The character of the newly discovered country will be given in the progress of the following chapter.

CHAPTER XXIII

DEPARTURE FOR THE GOLD LAKE COUNTRY—MEXICAN MULETEERS, AND PACK MULES—A CALIFORNIA LION—ARRIVAL AT GRASS VALLEY—SETTLERS AND GAMBLERS—A QUARREL—LOSS OF MULES—SUBLIME MOUNTAIN SCENERY —ONION VALLEY—DIFFICULT DESCENT FROM THE MOUNTAINS—MULES PRECIPITATED DOWN THE STEEP BANKS—ARRIVAL AND SETTLEMENT AT INDEPENDENCE—UNCERTAINTY OF BUSINESS OPERATIONS AT THE MINES— A STORM—SUDDEN DEPARTURE OF THE MINERS—A LOOSING BUSINESS.

ON the 10th of August, a little over a month after the death of my flourishing town speculation, I made an arrangement with some gentlemen in Marysville, to establish a trading post somewhere in the Gold Lake region of country. We purchased twelve beautiful Peruvian mules, with necessary arapahoes, (Mexican pack saddles,) besides a riding mule, and engaged an American who could speak Spanish, and a Mexican who did not understand a word of English; and selecting a desirable stock of necessary goods, on the afternoon of the 14th we were ready to start. Accompanying us on a similar adventure, was a Mr. Brinkerhoff, a merchant of Marysville, a good companion, as I soon found, who had also engaged a Mexican for a driver, who had the care of seven mules, making our number twenty animals in all, not including my Mexican, who proved to be more of a beast than either of the quadrupeds.

Our first setting out was inauspicious. Our mules had been unused to labor — preferring rather to *lay down* on their dignity; for as soon as one was packed, he would saunter off a little way and lay down, and it being impossible for him to rise again without help, in his struggles he would disarrange his load so much, that they had to be repacked, much to the vexation of our drivers, as well as ourselves. But at last we got them all on their feet, and our caravan moved off. We could not go ten rods before some rascally mule would either lay down, or stray off, in spite of all we could do, and while we were running and shouting after one, another was sure to tramp off in a different direction — for of all mulish animals under the sun, a mule is ——; but I wont swear! — only we found a mule to be a mule.

By dint of hard labor, and much *hippahing*, at sunset we actually found ourselves a mile and a half from the plaza of Marysville, from whence we had set out at two o'clock in the afternoon. Taking off the packs, we turned the animals out to grass, and leaving Billy, the interpreter, and the two Mexicans, to guard the property, Mr. Brinkerhoff and I went back to town, like the boy in the story, to stay the first night. I could not help thinking of the rule of three, viz : If it took half a day to go a mile and a half, how many days would it take to go the hundred which were before us ? On going out the next morning, we found that one of my very best mules was missing. We spent half a day in search, and had to give it up. He had probably been stolen, as we never found him. Sending his load back to town, we started forwards. We had gone but about two miles, in our unusually pleasant manner, when one of the best mules, (of course,) having an axe tied to his pack, took a fancy to lay down, and in his struggles to get up he managed to get the axe under him, which cut an artery of his fore-leg, so that he bled to death in a little while. I put his load on my own mule, resolving to walk, as I had done on the plains. The second day we managed to get four miles, and staid the second night a little over five miles from town. The fact was, our mules had not been driven for so long a time, that they would not keep the road; and it is only when they are constantly driven that they are manageable. Besides, ours were so fat, that although it seemed as if they were girted to suffocation, the loads would slip easily if they laid down, which they often did; or the packs, if not exactly balanced, would turn, when the mule must be stopped, and the pack rearranged.

On the third morning we were stirring early, but it took the Mexicans nearly three hours to pack the mules, and get them fairly in motion, for the fellows did not work with much spirit. Our animals began to travel better, and to keep the road, and now we really began to make some headway; the greatest difficulty being the occasional slipping of a pack, or now and then a mule lying down, when we had to assist him to rise. I was trudging along in the hot sun and dust, when the pack of one of the mules began to turn, and I stopped him in the road, waiting for my Mexican, who was behind, to come up and right it. Billy, the interpreter, was forward, and when the Mexican came up, he asked me by signs to assist him. There is nearly as much rigging about a loaded mule as there is about a ship, and these were the first mule cargoes that I had ever seen stowed; but being willing to render all the aid I could, I took my station on one side, while he took the other. He tried to tell me what he wanted, but I could not fully understand, though I knew it was something about jerking, so I got hold of a cask on my side, while he took hold of one on his. He jerked one way then I jerked. It was wrong. "Malo! malo!" said he, standing on his toes and peeping over the load, and added a direction which I could not understand. We tried it again, but with the same success. Finally he got the load balanced himself, and then came the handling of the ropes. He came around and gave me particular directions how to pull, and then returned to his own side, and sung out. He pulled, and I pulled. Every pull I made was wrong. "Malo, malo! — no bueno!" he shouted, and I tried it again. He vociferated an oath in English, which was the extent of his vocabulary in that language. Then he came around to my side, his eyes fairly snapping with vexation and impatience, and took hold of the rope and showed me how to pull. This time I thought I was right, and when he gave the word I pulled with all my strength, and — it was wrong! It was so perfectly ridiculous that I could not help laughing, while the driver became almost furious at my awkwardness; and throwing up his hands in despair, he uttered a long volley of oaths, in which I could distinguish "d——d Americano!" in every sentence. Finally he went to work alone, and secured the ropes properly, and when we overtook Billy, he swore he would not go another step with such an "awkward American." This being properly interpreted, only increased my mirth, while I acknowledged its justice. But it was finally arranged that Billy should keep near him to assist, when the matter was settled, and all the Mexican's gas evaporated. We now had fifteen miles to go without water. The day was extremely hot, our pace slow, and our thirst became excessive; but, as many months of training had inured us to hardship, we did not grumble, though when we reached a spring in the gorge of the first hills, men and animals rushed to it together, to slake their burning thirst. The serious difficulties with our mules

O 22

were now over; they were " broke in," and except the occasional slipping of a pack, we had little difficulty.

As we reached the mountains, by degrees they became more steep and difficult, and by five o'clock, footsore and exhausted, I lay down in the shade of a mansinieta, about two miles from where the train proposed to encamp. After resting an hour I plodded on, and found them encamped in a narrow valley, with a beautiful stream flowing through it, having made about twenty miles — a very fair day's drive. We went early to bed, and were indeed tired enough to sleep sound. About two o'clock in the morning I was awakened by a strange noise near us, when, raising my head above my blankets, I saw within three rods of us a huge California lion, standing and gazing at us, quietly frisking his tail; but as he did not appear to assume a belligerent attitude, and my companions were sleeping heavily, I did not alarm them, when the animal, probably having satisfied his curiosity, turned off in another direction, and I laid down and soon went to sleep again.

The following morning, the Mexicans packed the mules, and Mr. Brinkerhoff and I kept them in motion, as fast as loaded, which prevented their laying down; thus we were enabled to start in good season, with our Mexicans in good spirits. On account of grass and water, our drive was only ten miles — through a narrow but pleasant valley, with high hills on each side — and we reached our camp ground early, when I had a chance to give my blistered feet some rest. Our general course from Marysville was north-east. The formation was granite, in which feldspar predominated over quartz, with a superabundance of mica; yet quartz veins were frequent, and no basaltic or trap rock is visible through this range, which is the case generally, from north to south, in this range through the mountains.

The following day was to be one of toil, as we had twenty miles to go, over a rough country, before we could find forage for our animals. Making an early start, we left our valley trail, our path now leading along a sidling hill, occasionally over ledges of granite rock, towards the dividing ridge between the waters of Feather River and the Yuba, ascending all the while, till at noon we found ourselves upon the summit of a hill, which overlooked the hills below, and the Sacramento valley far beyond, forming a beautiful view. The timber had been chiefly evergreen oak, but now we were amidst the most magnificent pines and cedars I ever beheld. I estimated many at two hundred and fifty feet in height, perfectly straight, and eight feet in diameter at the base. The hills were covered with pumice and lava for miles, incontestibly proving that somewhere in the vicinity there had existed, at some time, an active volcano. The granite formation now changed to talcous slate, the soil a deep reddish brown, (per oxyd of iron,) and the indications of gold much greater than below. For many miles we passed over a mountain plain, sparsely covered with trees, but on which there was a heavy growth of chaparral, which would have made it a work of much labor to make a road over, in any other than the way in which it had been done, which was thus: Before the snow had melted, and while it was firmly packed, waggons began to pass over. A track was thus marked out, and as the snow receded, the tops of the bushes were gradually worn down, when occasionally, with the use of an axe, the path was cleared out, merely cutting away around the rocks which were found to be too great to be passed over.

We had long been traveling without water. Mr. Brinker-hoff and I were some distance ahead of the train, when, near the road-side, amid a dense cluster of beautiful pines, we discovered a sparkling spring. He spurred his mule to a gallop, and weary as I was, I started on a run, and to my satisfaction I reached it first. It was a delicious draught, and we lingered till we could drink no more, and then proceeded on our journey. We began to descend, and a mile and a half traveling brought us to the verge of a steep and difficult mountain, at the base of which lay the Grass Valley, where the South Fork of Feather River heads. This valley lay embosomed in the hills, and was about half a mile wide, by five or six in length ; but its high altitude makes it very cold, with heavy frosts every night during the warmest summer weather. It is a beautiful green spot of earth, enclosed by high red mountains, like the fabled happy valley of Rasselas, with dark out-crops of slate, nearly devoid of vegetation, while the rippling current of the river, here only a pretty brook, flows through its whole length, and is lost in the deep cañon at its western extremity. A little higher up, on the northern side, a singular bald peak, probably two thousand feet high, lifts its naked head above the surrounding hills, without a tree or shrub to enliven its bold prominence, while at about two-thirds of the distance to its summit large projections of slate rock, hundreds of feet high, stand towering out from its sides, like huge portals to some subterranean castle.

Here, in this strange valley, where two months before there was not a living soul, and where the snow was twenty feet deep, we found a cluster of cabins, and cloth stores, with groceries and hotels, and the usual concomitants of a mining town — scores of monte banks. Where the miner goes, no matter how difficult the transit, the gambler follows, to tempt him to part with his hard earned gains in a game of chance, and they too often find willing victims to their nefarious practices. Here, too, we found families of women and children, who, despising the fatigue and dangers of the trip, left the safer and more luxurious comforts of the older towns, to grapple with the golden god.

We encamped on the green sward by the bank of the stream, and notwithstanding the night was cold, we slept soundly till morning. On collecting our mules, we found one to be missing, and we spent the day in looking for him. He was found at night, having wandered off about three miles from our camp. Before we started the next morning, a difficulty occurred between my Mexican and Billy. The latter reproached him with lagging behind, and being inattentive to his duty, which was true, and not unfrequently gave us trouble in arranging the sliding packs; often delaying our progress. A few words passed between them, when the Mexican sprang to his feet, his eyes glistening with the venom of a serpent, and drew his knife, with a motion to stab the interpreter to the heart. Billy instantly presented his pistol, and coolly told his adversary to advance if he thought best; but finding him prepared, and not at all cowed, and deeming " discretion the better part of valor," the Mexican turned upon his heel and walked off. As he was an ugly and quarrelsome fellow, I discharged him on the spot, for I believe a greater scoundrel never went unhung. Mr. Brinkerhoff's muleteer was a quiet, orderly man, and I made an arrangement with him to assist in packing our animals, and Billy and I turned drivers. Another mule had now disappeared; and after spending half a day in an unsuccessful search, (although we subsequently recovered him,) his load was packed on Billy's mule, and at noon we got under motion. Our route lay up the valley a few miles, passing the base of the bald mountain, when we began to ascend a hill longer and steeper than any we had yet found. In passing along we saw a high ledge of glazed and vitrified rock, glistening in the sun like glass, which appeared as if it had scarcely cooled from the fire; and when at length, after hours of toil, we with difficulty reached the summit, a most magnificent scene opened upon our view. We were upon a lofty ridge, completely shut in by mountains, where there seemed to have been a grand breaking up of the Universe. On either side there was a deep abyss which the eye could not fathom; above, below, all around, high, broken, rocky mountains towered to the skies; chain after chain was thrown up in vast confusion; deep gorges were shadowed forth at their base, while at the extent of vision, on the south-east, and above the other peaks in that direction, a huge and nearly perpendicular table mountain, with its cone-like outline, lifted its bald, rocky crest in defiance of a thousand storms, like a monstrous watch-tower, from which the Genius of this barren and isolated region could view the work of desolation by which he was surrounded, while on the east, still higher, the lofty crest of the Siérra Neváda rose in solemn grandeur, white with everlasting snows. A simple mule driver as I was, and familiar with the varied scenery from the Rocky Mountains to the Pacific Ocean, I could not look upon this grand display of Almighty Power without wonder and awe, and I confess that the most solemn impressions stole over my mind, on beholding this sublime scene, which I had never seen equaled. Would that I could depict with my pencil, what my language fails to describe; as it is, I can only feel my own impotence.

Following the ridge for three or four miles, we began gradually to descend towards Onion Valley, a small valley so named from quantities of wild onions growing in it, although ice is formed in pools at night all summer long. On the side of the mountain overhanging the valley, we found large quantities of snow still remaining, which was indeed grateful to our parched tongues; and descending the steep mountain side, night found us tired and hungry enough to enjoy our suppers and blankets to the full.

We had not decided where to establish our post. My friend, S. B. Gridley, Esq., formerly from Ottawa, Illinois, had established himself at the mouth of Nelson's Creek, six miles beyond, and in the morning I proposed to walk forward and consult with him about a location, while the train should follow, to which Mr. Brinkerhoff assented, and I set out. The trail ascended for about a mile, to a ridge having on the right a branch of Nelson's Creek, and on the left the stream which, flowing through Onion Valley, found its way by a deep gorge to the Middle Fork of Feather River. From the top of this ridge the path descended by a series of benches, five miles to the river. For a mile or two the descent was not extremely rapid, but then it became so precipitous for the rest of the way that it was threaded only by short zigzag paths, like winding stairs, which made it extremely laborious, and at one place there was a narrow pass over rocks for several rods, not more than three or four feet wide, sometimes by steps, when, if a mule lost his balance, he would inevitably be hurled to destruction on either side, over smooth and shining rock, into a gulf probably two thousand feet deep. The ridge terminated at the river in a point five or six hundred feet high on the sides, and at the end was a perpendicular cliff of rocks, a hundred feet in height, overhanging the river. On the right, in a narrow gorge, Nelson's Creek united with the Middle Fork, where Gridley's tent was pitched, and on the left was a little flat, where several traders had made a station; for this was on what had now become a thoroughfare to the mines in the mountains still beyond. From a consultation held with Gridley, I thought it advisable to go to Independence, about four miles up the creek, the road to which turned off about half-way up the hill that I had just descended.   Brinkerhoff, in the meantime, came on, but accidentally took the left-hand trail, instead of the right, to Gridley's, and descended to the flat.   When we got ready to move, I went forward to find the Independence trail, which was rather obscure, where I was to wait till Mr. Brinkerhoff arrived with the train, I sat down on reaching it and waited two hours, when, finding they did not arrive, and fearing some accident had occurred, I retraced my steps.   I found indeed that my forebodings had proved correct.   Mr. Brinkerhoff, under the impression that the path leading from the flat to Gridley's would be the easiest one up the hill, started the mules across in that direction, when one of his own, loosing its foothold, slid off the precipice, and was dashed in pieces in the fall.   He had no sooner succeeded in picking up the fragments of the cargo, and started up the trail above Gridley's, than one of my mules made a false step, just as he reached the ridge, and rolled over and over with his load into the creek, staving a part of his cargo, but not seriously injuring himself.   When he finally got them up the hill, with mulish perverseness, they turned to the right, (as they were then going up,) and went down the trail to the flat again, which they had so recently left.   It was at this juncture that I arrived, and finding it too late to go on that night, we encamped, and as there was no grass, we were compelled to pay thirty-two dollars for barley enough to feed our mules at night and in the morning.

The next morning we again attempted to get up the hill, when four of the mules, in a sudden freak of amiability, in spite of "*hippah ! mula*," and "*arriva ! arrea*," stepped out of the track upon the soft, yielding earth, and in a moment were turning somersets to the bottom, making a most dismal clattering among our furniture, smashing pans and basins, making mincemeat of bottles and pickles, and bursting two kegs of brandy. It was noon before we succeeded in getting them on to the first bench, and night before we descended the deep gorge to Independence, only four miles from the mouth of the creek.

Such is the difficulty of driving mules, and of taking supplies into the distant mines of California, before time is given to survey more eligible roads ; and in some places these cannot be found. Verily, the muleteer, as well as the miner, earns his money. "Confound this mule driving," said Brink, sadly. "*Ohe jam satis*," responded I, in the same tone ; and, dear reader, are you not satisfied too ?

I beg leave to introduce a few more incidents, which were characteristic of the uncertainty of business operations at this time, and to show how slight a thing may ruin a man's hopes, even by prudent management. Brinkerhoff and I soon had our stores established, and our first stocks sold readily and well. There were from one to two thousand men in the neighborhood, and the diggings generally paid well. We immediately ordered a new and good supply of provisions, but it was nearly three weeks before they arrived. In the meantime Mr. Brinkerhoff was violently seized with bilious fever, when I took him into my tent, and attended him to convalescence, though this time I did not pursue my Indian practice. On the 16th of September, a few days before our new supplies arrived, the first storm of the season fell, though this was snow on the hills and rain in the gulches. Knowing

O*

that in the mountains the snow fell many feet deep, remembering the inclement season of the previous year, and being unprovided with provisions for the winter, when supplies could not be obtained, the miners became alarmed, and fearing they would be caught in the impassable snows, they hastily abandoned their claims, so that in less than a week there were but twenty men left on our populous bar. As they left our goods came. We had plenty of goods but no customers. "We're in a fix now, Brink," said I. "What is to be done?" "Give the confounded goods a dose of calomel, as you did me, and work 'em off," said he, gruffly. But as that would not pay, I did not follow his advice. After selling what we could at Independence, we procured mules and took them to the mouth of the creek, paying five cents a pound for transportation, where, at length, we closed the sales, I and my partners loosing about a thousand dollars in the operation ; and had the storm held off two weeks longer, we probably should have cleared double that amount.

"He attempted to seize it again, drawing his pistol on the gambler, when the latter shot him dead."—p. 352.

CHAPTER XXIV.

NELSON'S CREEK — INDEPENDENCE BAR — THE CLIMATE — MOUNTAIN LIFE — STRUGGLES OF THE MINERS — THEIR DISAPPOINTMENTS — POPULATION — MINING LIFE — GAMBLING AND DISSIPATION — HORRIBLE MURDER — ROBBERIES — VOLCANIC REMAINS — CHANGE OF LOCATION — NEW ACQUAINTANCES — DEPARTURE FOR SAN FRANCISCO.

NELSON'S CREEK rises about fifteen miles above Independence, near the base of the main ridge of the Siérra Neváda, and like nearly all the streams in that high region, flows through a deep gorge till it disembogues into the Middle Fork of the Feather river, about sixty miles in a direct line from where the latter unites with the main or North Fork. Independence Bar was first located in June, 1850. Enormous hills rise on each side, exhibiting a highly volcanic appearance, based upon a talcous slate formation, and the country is highly auriferous. In the deep dell of the bar, the sun does not make his appearance above the mountains till eight o'clock in the morning, and disappeared behind the western hills a little after four in the afternoon. Although the nights are cold — the ice frequently forming in our buckets — the days are hot, and oppressive. Scarcely a night passed in which we did not hear rocks rolling from the hills into the gulf, which were loosened from their beds by the action of frost, rain and sun; and egress and ingress was over steep hills by means of zigzag paths, difficult, and often dangerous.

As a description of mountain life may not be wholly uninteresting, and as it possesses a general character in these isolated wilds, I shall give a brief description of some of the occurrences which transpired there. And again I beg the reader to remember, that my object is to exhibit the struggles that all miners first undergo, at new points, through the whole length and breadth of California, though frequently diversified in their character.

From the mouth of Nelson's Creek to its source, men were at work in digging. Sometimes the stream was turned from its bed, and the channel worked; in other places, wing dams were thrown out, and the bed partially worked; while in some, the banks only were dug. Some of these, as is the case everywhere in the mines, paid well, some, fair wages, while many were failures. One evening, while waiting for my second supply of goods, I strolled by a deserted camp. I was attracted to the ruins of a shanty, by observing the effigy of a man standing upright in an old, torn shirt, a pair of ragged pantaloons, and boots which looked as if they had been clambering over rocks since they were made — in short, the image represented a lean, meagre, worn-out and woe-begone miner, such as might daily be seen at almost every point in the upper mines. On the shirt was inscribed, in a good business hand, "My claim failed — will you pay the taxes?" (an allusion to the tax on foreigners.) Appended to the figure was a paper, bearing the following words: " Californians — Oh, Californians, look at me! once fat and saucy as a privateersman, but now — look ye — a miserable skeleton. In a word, I am a used up man. Never mind, I can sing, notwithstanding,

" O California ! this is the land for me ;
  A pick and shovel, and lots of bones !
Who would not come the sight to see,—
  The golden land of dross and stones.

     O Susannah, don't you cry for me,
     I'm living *dead* in Califor-*nee*."

Ludicrous as it may appear, it was a truthful commentary on the efforts of hundreds of poor fellows in the "golden land." This company had penetrated the mountain snows with infinite labor, in the early part of the season, enduring hardships of no ordinary character — had patiently toiled for weeks, living on the coarsest fare ; had spent time and money in building a dam and digging a race through rocks to drain off the water ; endured wet and cold, in the chilling atmosphere of the country, and when the last stone was turned, at the very close of all this labor, they did not find a single cent to reward them for their toil and privations, and what was still more aggravating, a small, wing dam, on the very claim below them, yielded several thousand dollars.   Having paid out their money, and lost their labor, they were compelled to abandon the claim, and search for other diggings, where the result might be precisely the same.   The only wonder is that the poor fellows could have courage enough to sing at all.

The population of Independence represented almost every State in the Union, while France, England, Ireland, Germany, and even Bohemia, had their delegates.   As soon as breakfast was dispatched, all hands were engaged in digging and washing gold in the banks, or in the bed of the stream.   When evening came, large fires were built, around which the miners congregated, some engrossed with thoughts of home and friends, some to talk of new discoveries, and richer diggings somewhere else ;

or, sometimes a subject of debate was started, and the evening was whiled away in pleasant, and often instructive, discussion, while many, for whom this kind of recreation had not excitement enough, resorted to dealing monte, on a small scale, thus either exciting or keeping up a passion for play. Some weeks were passed in this way under the clear blue sky of the mountains, and many had made respectable piles. I highly enjoyed the wild scenery, and, quite as well, the wild life we were leading, for there were many accomplished and intelligent men; and a subject for amusement or debate was rarely wanting. As for ceremony or dress, it gave us no trouble: we were all alike. Shaving was voted a bore; the air holes in our pants were *not* "few and far between," and our toes were as often out "prospecting" from the ends of our boots as any way, and two weeks before my last supplies arrived I was barefoot, having completely worn out my shoes. At length a monte dealer arrived, with a respectable bank.

A change had been gradually coming over many of our people, and for three or four days several industrious men had commenced drinking, and after the monte bank was set up, it seemed as if the long smothered fire burst forth into a flame. Labor, with few exceptions, seemed suspended, and a great many miners spent their time in riot and debauchery. Some scarcely ate their meals, some would not go to their cabins, but building large fires, would lay down, exposed to the frost; and one night, in the rain. Even after the monte dealer had cleared nearly all out who would play, the game was kept up by the miners themselves in a small way, till the fragments of their purses were exhausted. There were two companies at work near me, who, when I first went there, were taking out daily in each company, from one hundred to one hundred and fifty dollars. This they continued to do for more tha two weeks, when it seemed as if the gold blistered their fingers, and they began a career of drinking and gambling, until it was gone. Instead of going to work on their claims again, they were seized with the prospecting mania, so common at that time among miners, and after spending some days in looking for other diggings, in snow and rain, finally went to the valley — many not having money enough to pay small bills against them. Among the miners was one who lost nine hundred dollars, another, eight hundred — their whole summer's work — and went off poor and penniless. The monte dealer, who, in his way was a gentleman, and honorable according to the notions of that class of men, won in two nights three thousand dollars! When he had collected his taxes on our bar, he went to Onion Valley, six miles distant, and lost in one night four thousand, exemplifying the fact, that a gambler may be rich to-day, and a beggar to-morrow. Gambling at that period was more prevalent in the mines than it is now; and it is but justice to say, that very many men did not play at all, nor incline to dissipation; and that at this time, (1852,) a great reformation has taken place throughout the mines, although gambling is carried on to some extent.

We were startled one morning, with the report that two men had been murdered a short distance above us. On repairing to the spot, a ghastly spectacle presented itself. Two men, having their heads cut open with a hatchet, lay in the creek, perfectly dead. The circumstances were these: Three men from near Vergennes, Vermont, named Ward, Lawrence, and Luther, lay in a tent on the bank of the creek, at the foot of a high, steep hill. Their bed was a flat rock, and their feet reached within a few inches of the water. As they all lay asleep, about ten o'clock at night, Ward was suddenly awakened by a noise, when looking up, he saw a man standing over him with a hatchet, in the act of striking.   Instantly he sprang to his feet, and encountered another man, who made at him, but he turned and ran out at the lower end of the tent, and clambering over a pile of rocks, escaped, and continued his flight in the dark towards a cabin about forty rods distant, shouting "murder!"   Reaching the cabin, the inmates turned out as soon as Ward was able to give a distinct relation of the affair; and on reaching the scene of slaughter, they found that the assassins, after completing their work of death, had robbed their victims of about four hundred dollars each, and then had thrown their bodies into the creek and escaped.   As the parties were going down, they heard the sound of somebody scrambling on the hill-side, over head, but in the gloom of night, and from the nature of the country, pursuit was impossible.   Suspicion naturally enough fell on poor Ward, but an investigation being held, all circumstances were in his favor, and he was fully acquitted.   Indeed, his terror, and his almost miraculous escape, scarcely allowed him to sleep for many nights.   They were industrious, prudent men, and esteemed by all who knew them.

Robberies, too, occasionally occurred.   One poor fellow's cabin was robbed of fifteen hundred dollars while he was at work.   Thus in a moment he was stripped of the result of months of hard labor.   He could scarcely suspect the author of his misfortune.   At a gambling house near the mouth of the creek, a man who had started for home was induced to try his luck at the monte table, when under the influence of liquor, and in the excitement of having lost his money, he attempted to seize it again, drawing his pistol on the gambler, when the latter shot him dead! He had previously written to his family that he was about starting for home, but this one thoughtless and imprudent act cost him his life, and his family would look long and in vain for the return of the husband and father, and probably without ever learning his sad and discreditable end.

About four miles below Nelson's Creek, on the Middle Fork of Feather River, arose to a great height an old extinct volcano, which curiosity impelled me to visit. Crossing the river at the mouth of the creek, I commenced a toilsome ascent of the steep mountain, and after half a day of hard climbing, I gained the summit of what had once been its crater. Vast quantities of lava had been ejected, which, mixed with quartz and volcanic *debris,* formed a mass of flint-like hardness, and it was heaped up and piled around the apex of the mountain, in rough, columnar shapes, resembling in some measure rude pillars and cones, while in cavities the action of the flames seemed to be as fresh as if it had been recently done. In one place was a deep, narrow chasm, which the eye could not fathom, and on throwing down a stone, a sound was heard as though it was striking against rough points, till gradually it was lost to the ear, without apparently reaching the bottom. It appeared as if the flames had burst forth, throwing out the rock in a melted state, which had cooled without forming a regular crater, leaving the lava in a cemented mass, with chasms which reached to a vast depth in the bowels of the earth. On the side next the river, projections had been thrown out, and a little farther east, on the southern slope, the sides were smooth and shining, and a miss step would have precipitated the unfortunate traveler a quarter of a mile down its sides, before any jutting would have caught his mangled and bleeding form. The panorama around was beautiful and sublime, and I counted in the view no less than five volcanic peaks in the wild, broken range of the wonderful Siérra. My thirst prevented the full indulgence of my curiosity. I gladly would have spent the night in this elevated and inspiring situation, but I was reluctantly obliged to descend. Taking a circuitous route — indeed the only practicable one in that direction — I commenced a descent towards Rich Bar, which lay at its base. It required nearly two hours to accomplish the descent. Indeed, the labor was quite equal to the ascent. The bar at its base proved to be one of the richest which had been discovered, and a large amount of gold was taken from it. One man took out of a pocket fifteen hundred dollars at one panfull of dirt. This, of course, was only a single instance, for as at every other bar through the mines, while some were richly rewarded, others scarcely got enough to pay expenses.

Mr. Gridley had sold out his stock before Mr. Brinkerhoff and I removed to the mouth of the creek, and had gone below. Messrs. Lathrop, Rockwell and Fish, from Jackson, Michigan, were the purchasers; and after we had closed our sales, Mr. Brinkerhoff, availing himself of an opportunity, went to Marysville, and as his health continued bad, subsequently to New-York. I took up my quarters with Messrs. Lathrop & Co., with whom I had a cheerful time, for, isolated as miners are, they are disposed to avail themselves of every little circumstance which may provoke mirth, and the eight days I stayed with them, waiting a chance to ride to the valley, forms one of the pleasantest reminiscences of my mountain life. If these pages should ever meet their eyes, it will call to mind many a story and jest, which whiled away our long, cold evenings, at the foot of that five-mile mountain, which towered above the Middle Fork of Feather River.

A few weeks later found me a resident, and a man of business, in San Francisco, without anything occurring sufficient to interest the reader; and from this period personal adventure will be merged in a more general history of prominent events as they occurred in the State, some of them taking place under my own eye.

CHAPTER XXV.

ARRIVAL AT SAN FRANCISCO — ADMISSION OF CALIFORNIA AS A STATE — EXCITEMENT AND REJOICING OF THE CITIZENS — STATE OF THE COUNTRY — INDIGNATION AT THE DELAYS OF CONGRESS IN ADMITTING HER INTO THE UNION — THE NEED OF LAWS — PREVIOUS GOOD ORDER OF THE INHABITANTS — COMMENCEMENT OF CRIME — PARTICULAR CASES OF CRIME — INSECURITY OF LIFE AND PROPERTY — INDIGNATION OF THE CITIZENS — BOLD ROBBERY AND APPREHENSION OF THE CRIMINALS — EXECUTION OF STUART AND WILDRED — PUBLIC SENTIMENT — IMMENSE MEETING ON THE PLAZA — THE VIGILANCE COMMITTEE OF SAN FRANCISCO — EXECUTION OF JENKINS — RESOLUTIONS TO ESTABLISH THE PEOPLE'S COURT — SALUTARY EFFECTS.

It was in September, 1850, that the joyful tidings arrived that California had been recognized by the Congress of the United States, as a younger sister of the Union.

Hitherto public expectation had long been excited. And when one steamer after another arrived, bearing the unwelcome intelligence, that the subject of her admission was still protracted by the useless debates of demagogues — that the question had been merged into a subject wholly irrelevant, — and when it was considered, too, that she had complied with all the requirements of the Constitution, and that the condition of her affairs (then just emerging from the unsettled chaos of territorial government,) demanded a speedy settlement of the question, and the establishment of a regular system of local laws, for the security of her citizens — a degree of intense impatience prevailed, in consequence of the dilatoriness of Congress in awarding rights to which she was justly entitled.

Previous to this — in the full expectation that she had only to ask, and receive her just right, when it was ascertained beyond question that she had nearly three times the population required by law for her admission, and that the Constitution she adopted was in accordance with that prescribed by the General Government — the people, owing to the necessity of the case, had elected a Governor and a Legislature, with Judges, and all the appendages of a State Government, under the confident belief that Congress would not hesitate to confirm their acts, and cheerfully accord to her, what it was in duty bound to do, and what was by former precedent established to be her right. For months she had been in doubt and distrust. Every act passed by her Legislature was subject to be contested in the United States' Court; the decisions of her own courts might be considered illegal; the collection of debts under the laws, as questionable; the assessment of taxes for the support of her own government, an unwarrantable assumption of power; her local laws for the protection of life and property might be declared null and void, and society return to its original elements, where the power of the sword would triumph over the weak. The feeling was becoming general, and freely expressed by many, that whether recognized or not the people would stand by their State Government, until they were overpowered by the force of arms. And this was at a moment when she was pouring into the lap of the older States, and into the treasury of the General Government, through her miners and shipping, a larger revenue, and when she offered a market many times greater for her home produce, than any young State had ever done — and even at that moment far beyond a majority of the older States. Under such circumstances, it is not strange that a feeling of disgust was created at the selfish conduct of politicians at home, who were willing to sacrifice their brethren in California to their own selfishness, and sectional or local affairs. California has become a by-word for dishonesty and crime. One cause of it may be looked for in the unsettled condition of things, by the dilatoriness of Congress in not putting her into a condition, at once, to arrest the evil before it had taken root; for I believe it is a truth established by time, that when an example is set by governments of laxity of principle, the people will follow, to a certain extent; but where justice is speedily and promptly rendered, individual as well as public rights will be readily respected.

The announcement, then, that Colifornia was finally, though grudgingly, admitted as a State, and that the acts of her people were confirmed, was hailed with joy, and bonfires were kindled, artillery pealed, and acclamations resounded in every town throughout the length and breadth of the land — for the people of California loved their brethren at home, and above all, the glorious Union of States which bound them in one common tie; and also ardently desired the " star spangled banner " should wave over her mountains and plains, a symbol that this too was " the land of the free, the home of the brave." San Francisco took the lead, and processions, orations, odes and illuminations, and general rejoicings were the order of the day. The thousand ships which proudly floated in its magnificent harbor, were gaily decked with streamers; gun after gun boomed over its placid waters. In a moment all feeling of irritation ceased, and could our Atlantic brethren have witnessed the general joy, they would have gladly joined in the prolonged shout of " the Union, now and forever! "

But an evil had taken root, which grew out of the previous existing state of things, and which at one time threatened to overturn all law and order — in fact, government itself. The gold of California had attracted to its shores the dissolute and dishonest from all countries of the civilized globe. Situated within reach of the penal colonies of Great Britain, as well as being in proximity with the semi-barbarous hordes of Spanish America, whose whole history is that of revolution and disorder, it was soon flooded by great numbers from those countries, who were accomplished in crime, and who, without feeling any sympathy for our institutions, and contributing nothing for the support of our government, their only aim seemed to be to obtain gold, by any means, no matter how fraudulent; and owing to the weakness of the constituted authorities, joined to the vicious among our own people, they succeeded in their frauds and crimes to an amazing extent, and rendered the security of life and property a paradox on legislation, hitherto unprecedented in the annals of modern history.

During the year 1849, a robbery was of rare occurrence, comparatively speaking. Boxes and bales of goods were left open and exposed, with impunity, in the crowded streets of the new towns. Gold did not seem to tempt the cupidity of men to dishonesty, and stealing from miners was rarely heard of. Horses, mules and cattle were safe on the ranches, or by the road side, and it was a general subject of remark by letter writers at the time, that property was safer in California than in the older States at home. The recent emigrants had not so soon forgotten the principles under which they had been educated; and rights and property were respected, as they had been accustomed to respect them at home, although there was no law to coerce them. Even as late as June, 1850, I was one of a jury in the mines, to decide on a case of litigation, where one party sued another before a self-constituted miners' court, in the absence of higher law, for flooding the water on a river claim, and thus preventing its being worked. The court was duly opened, the proofs and allegations adduced, and the costs of the trial *advanced*. Judgment was rendered against the plaintiff, in favor of the oldest occupant of the adverse claims, when the plaintiff submitted without hesitation, and paid $102, costs, with as much cheerfulness as if it had been done by a legally constituted court of the United States.

In the early part of the winter of 1850, however, some of those who left the mines early for fear of starvation, or because they preferred the comforts and pleasures of the town to a winter seclusion in the mines, being unable, perhaps unwilling, to obtain employment, gave loose to their vicious propensities; and about that time, too, Sydney convicts began to arrive, when affairs began speedily to assume another aspect, and it became necessary to guard property with as much care as in towns of the older States. The laxity of government — in fact, the want of an effective government — was a grand stimulant to the perpetration of crime; because when there is no acknowledged head, it can be done with more impunity. It continued to become more frequent, until a State government was formed, and then, by a strange course of events, the law was perverted so that it was made oftener to shield the guilty, than to punish the offender.

In the winter of '49 and '50, stealing cattle commenced with some degree of system. The wild cattle on the plains were, by some, considered as regular game, and the old inhabitants began to have their cattle killed, and much complaint was made. Some, however, did not stop at this, but took cattle and mules indiscriminately, sometimes to sell, sometimes for use, and the miners thus lost whole teams, or had teams broken up. At first the Indians were charged with these thefts, but when many were subsequently recovered, having passed through various hands, it was not long before it was understood that the white savages were worse than the red. Things grew worse fast, until the spring of 1851, when it became past endurance. Robberies and murders were of daily occurrence. Organized bands of thieves existed in the towns and in the mountains. I was privately informed by a young man of my acquaintance, that he had been offered seven hundred dollars a month to steal horses and mules. Although he was a wild, daring fellow, he had too much principle to engage in nefarious practices. The daily papers of the day are records of crime, and scarcely a morning paper appeared that did not chronicle the perpetration of a robbery or murder. The report of a grand jury from San Francisco, in June, 1850, showed that there were at that time sixty individuals awaiting trial for criminal practices, in that single county, ten of which were on indictments for assault with intent to kill. I shall only mention a few cases among the many hundred which occurred.

While I was at Marysville, in March, 1850, a cloth house was cut open with a knife, and a trunk stolen, containing $1,000. The thieves were arrested as they were preparing to go down the river, taken before the alcalde, and sentenced to be whipped, which was at once carried into effect on the plaza. Only a portion of the money was recovered. About the same time two men in Placer county went into a tent, and finding a woman alone, her husband being out at work, bound and gagged her, and then robbed the tent of fifteen hundred dollars. The thieves were arrested, and as there were no prisons in the country, they

P

were whipped, and again turned loose. Daily accounts of such outrages were received. In December, 1850, the custom house at Monterey was robbed of $14,000, while the collector was absent from his office about twenty-five minutes. Five individuals from Sydney were arrested, and a portion of the money found. Two others were arrested at San Juan, as being accessory, and also for mule stealing, when it was found that one of the mules they had stolen belonged to Judge Ord, who was counsel for them on the first charge.

In January following, the sleeping room of Captain Howard, of the police, in San Francisco, was entered, and a trunk, containing $2,100 in scrip, and $3,000 in gold, was abstracted. So adroit had the thieves become, that they actually went into a store about ten o'clock at night, and while men were at work overhead, they actually blew open a safe, and took $700, which it contained, and escaped. Cases even more bold and daring than any of these, might fill these pages. Such became the insecurity of property, from the hordes of villains prowling about, that men scarcely felt safe under any circumstances, and no man slept in a building without having firearms within reach, well loaded, to protect himself against these ruthless midnight villains. It was dangerous to buy a mule of a stranger, for fear the property had been stolen, and might be claimed by another party. In addition to other crimes, was that of arson. San Francisco was four times burned, and every principal city in California suffered severely from fires, when subsequent disclosures proved that some, at least, if not all, were caused by the fiendish incendiary, to gratify a desire for plunder, or from a horrible spirit of revenge.

In addition to this state of things, another evil existed, which had crept in through the demoralizing influence of an inordinate desire to acquire wealth by any plausible pretext, to which the unsettled condition of the government, and the consequent laxity of moral principle, afforded facilities, and men taking advantage of this, when not wholly destitute of moral principle themselves, too often gave their talents for the sake of high reward, to shield the criminal by the technicalities of the law, and the power of office.

When the history of California shall be written, after time has mellowed the asperity of passing events, the occurrences of these days will form a singular but strange chapter for the perusal of the statesman and philanthropist. In a country whose people are proverbial for their love of justice and order, where the force of early education, and of public example, has tended to the observance of law, for the preservation of order, and the protection of those rights which belong to free citizens, a condition of things existed, which threatened at one time to dissolve the social compact of the community; and, in fact, they had arrived at the point when strong individual combinations were required, to protect life and property from organized bands of desperadoes and assassins, who made the existing laws only an instrument to protect them in crime and high-handed villainy. If this was the state of things in a single town, city, or district, the evil might in time have worked its own cure, through the agency of an improved moral principle, and the law itself; but strange to say, the whole length and breadth of California was now beset with unprincipled men, who set law, order, and justice alike at defiance; or who used the first, by its technicalities and subtleties, to subvert the others; so that, for the peace of society, a general revolution became necessary. On every side there was distrust of men and authorities. In the cities, as well as in the mountains, it was unsafe for men to go unarmed after nightfall; and even in San Francisco, the largest town in the State, in the principal thoroughfares, at a late hour of night, men chose to take the middle of the street, fearful that the first man they met might be a robber, or an assassin with a slung shot or a pistol. That reverence for law, which is almost an intuitive feeling with Americans, induced them to await its action, in the hope that its just administration would rid society of its pests and excrescences; but when it was at length seen, that the Executive pardoned crime in its most glaring deformity — that criminals almost universally escaped punishment. and with more than two hundred murders in less than a year, but a single legal execution took place in the whole State — that the police force was wholly inefficient for the amount of crime committed — that witnesses notoriously perjured them-selves to screen their companions in guilt — that abandoned men were allowed to give testimony in courts where they were of notoriously bad character—that public officers in some cases were guilty of peculation and malfeasance — and that if the guilty were in any way condemned to prison, the insecurity of the jail only afforded them an easy mode of escape; in short, when it was found that under the administration of the law, the insecurity of life and property increased instead of diminished, the people became aroused to a sense of their own wrongs, and, convinced that there was no other mode of redress, they resolved to take the punishment of offenders into their own hands, and to do what the administrators of the law could not, or would not do — protect the honest part of community from the dep-redations which were daily and hourly committed upon them. It had not unfrequently been the case, that offenders were admitted to bail, which proved to be worthless, and when the trial came off the culprit was gone, and was still at large, to prey upon community. Numerous murders had been committed in San Francisco, and if some of the murderers went through the farce of a trial, they were suffered eventually to run at large, and bullied the courts and citizens with impunity, till it became a by-word and reproach, when a notorious offender was arrested, that "he will escape by the law." Incendiarism in the cities became so common, that when the citizen laid down at night, his papers and valuables were placed in a situation where he could seize them at a moment's warning; and the thought was constant, that before the dawn of another day he might be a houseless, homeless, ruined man. This state of things could no longer be endured. Patience was no longer a virtue. Self-preservation rendered it imperative that the first law of nature should be observed, and that unless some united effort was made, society must resolve itself into its primitive elements, and brute force become the only defence against aggression and violence.

Every ship from the penal colonies of Great Britain, only swelled the number of English convicts already here; while the vicious from all nations seemed to find a rendezvous in California, and hordes of the most accomplished villains in the world, who had passed through every grade of crime, found a home and congenial spirits in this devoted land.

In February, 1851, the city of San Francisco was thrown into a fever of excitement, by one of the most audacious robberies which had ever been committed in the town. Two Englishmen, convicts from Sidney, went into the store of a Mr. Janson, near the corner of Washington and Montgomery streets, at eight o'clock in the evening, and inquired for some blankets. While Mr. Janson was in the act of showing them, one of the scoundrels struck him a blow on the head with a slung shot.

He fell prostrate on the floor, when they jumped upon him and again struck him. They then broke open his desk and robbed it of nearly two thousand dollars, and effected their escape. In a short time he recovered sufficiently to crawl to the next door, and give the alarm, but the villains were gone. This outrage was perpetrated on one of the most crowded streets in the city, and it being done so early in the evening, evinced the hardihood and desperation of the robbers. A few days after, a police officer of Sacramento recognized one of them as a fugitive from justice, for crimes committed in the mines, and arrested him, together with a companion. Some circumstances gave suspicion that they were connected with the robbery of Janson, and upon their examination an attempt was made by their counsel to prove an alibi, as usual, but the notorious character of the witness excited a feeling of indignation in the audience, that such testimony should be received by the court. A row ensued, in which the people attempted to seize the prisoners; but they were rescued by the police and a company of the Washington Guards, and conveyed to the prison. This was on Saturday, and intense excitement prevailed. The Washington Guards were hissed, and in the exasperation of the moment, the people determined to destroy the armory. A rush was made in that direction; a few windows were broken, when Captain Bartol came out and addressed the crowd, telling them that the company had acted only in obedience to law, and that if the prisoners were guilty, and if required by the authorities, he would march out and assist in hanging them. His address was received with favor, and the crowd acted with more coolness and deliberation. They organized a meeting, and appointed a committee of twelve to consult with the city authorities, and to guard the prisoners. A meeting was called for the next day

On Sunday, the 24th, as the hour approached, crowds began to gather around the City Hall, the streets were soon filled, and the roofs, windows and balconies of the adjoining houses were occupied by the people. Probably ten thousand persons were present; when the mayor, as well as several other gentlemen, came forward to address the multitude, advising them to leave the matter with the proper authorities, and pledging themselves that justice should be administered. They were frequently interrupted with cries of "no more quibbles of law — no straw bail — the criminals all escape — give us justice." Although the excitement was intense, and there was a diversity of opinion with regard to executing the prisoners, the people finally yielded, when, in a few days the prisoners broke jail, and these men escaped, with others.

A man was subsequently taken and put into jail at Marysville, supposed to be Stuart. Some doubts arising, his conviction was postponed for additional evidence, and in the meantime, the real Stuart was taken, who proved to be the robber, and he was hung by the Vigilance Committee of San Francisco, together with Wildred, his accomplice in crime, who confessed his guilt. But the appearance of the two men was so nearly alike, that it forms a singular episode in the history of criminal jurisprudence and circumstantial evidence.

The papers of the day only echoed the sentiments of the people, and they spoke out frankly and boldly. The Alta California, one of the best papers in the State, held the following language, on the 23d of September : " We do not wonder that the whole city is excited, that every honest man feels indignant against the vile miscreants who have fired our houses, robbed our citizens, and murdered them. This feeling is natural. And the present apparent and expressed determination to take the administration of the law into their own hands, is the inevitable result of a shameful laxity in the administration of our lower courts. To them alone, is chargeable the present state of public feeling. Examinations, and trials of criminals have been a miserable tissue of trifling, quibbling, and nonsensical distinctions, and deductions unworthy to be used by a respectable bar, unworthy any consideration by the judges. Any persons have been allowed to testify. Not one of the thieves and robbers who infest our city, but has witnesses enough to swear an alibi, and such evidence has been allowed." And still further: " Every means, too, has been taken by unscrupulous advocates, to postpone, and stave off trials, knowing that delay would absolutely destroy all criminating evidence."

Up to the 10th of June, things continued in an uncertain state, no improvement having been made in conducting trials, or in punishing offenders, notwithstanding the complaints of the people, and the earnest appeals of the papers. The Daily Courier of that date (June 10) speaks as follows : " It is clear to every man, that San Francisco is partially in the hands of criminals, and that crime has reached a crisis when life and property are in imminent danger. There is no alternative now left us, but to lay aside our business, and direct our whole energies, as a people, to seek out the abodes of these villains, and execute summary vengeance upon them." Every paper has been compelled, as a faithful journalist, for months, to record a daily amount of crime, which showed beyond contradiction that the law, as administered, was completely nugatory and void. It could be borne no longer. Forbearance had ceased to be a virtue, and the time for action had come. On the 11th of June, a notice appeared in the Courier and Alta California, requesting the citizens to assemble on the Plaza at three o'clock

P. M. ; and what was more startling, the morning of the 11th discovered the spectacle of a man hanging by the neck from the porch of the adobe house on Portsmouth Square. It was not generally known that an association had been formed, composed of the most substantial, and some of the best men in the city, as a Vigilance Committee, who were determined to take the execution of justice into their own hands, and see that it was surely and promptly administered ; and this was the first result of their organization. On the night of the 11th, a man, named Jenkins, a Sydney convict, was taken in the act of robbing a safe. A jury was selected, indubitable proof of his guilt was adduced, and he was hung immediately, about two o'clock in the morning ; and this was the commencement of the reign of justice in the criminal code of California. At the hour appointed for the meeting, a vast concourse of people assembled on the Plaza, composed of the most respectable class of citizens. The meeting was duly organized, and several among the most highly esteemed citizens addressed the people, briefly stating the condition of affairs, and advocating the necessity of taking steps to arrest the career of crime. The existence of a Vigilance Committe was announced, and when a resolution was offered, approving their acts in hanging Jenkins, it was received with loud acclamations, and with only one single dissenting voice, and that from a lawyer whose interest it undoubtedly was to perpetuate this unwarrantable condition of things in community. The meeting adjourned over to the next day, at the same hour and place, when, it was understood, a series of resolutions would be presented.

At the appointed time, the Plaza was again filled with anxious but not excited citizens, and there was a determined calmness in their demeanor, which plainly told that it proceeded from

P*   24

long suffering, and that they would coolly, deliberately, and surely protect themselves from further insult and outrage. The resolutions were then offered. After a preamble, touching the necessity of the case in a dispassionate manner, it continued :

Resolved, That while we deprecate the occasion, and regret the necessity which calls us to decide, yet on account of circumstances over which we have no control, we are constrained to believe that the crimes of grand larceny, burglary and arson, should be punished with death, disclaiming the right to inflict this penalty after a proper time has elapsed to obtain the voice of all the people, through the ballot box.

Resolved, That a committee of seven be appointed to call an election of the citizens in each ward, to decide whether or no these crimes shall be punished with death, appoint the officers of the election, and define the form of the ticket.

Resolved, That at the same time and place, a judge and sheriff shall be elected, (unless one of our judges and sheriff will serve,) who shall enforce the will of the people in punishing the guilty, who shall have jurisdiction only on those criminal cases above-mentioned.

Resolved, That we pledge our lives, our fortunes, and our sacred honors, to protect and defend the people's court and officers, against any and all other jurisprudence.

Resolved, That any person charged with crime shall have a fair and impartial trial by jury, nor shall he be deprived of the privilege of giving any evidence he can bring to prove his innocence.

Resolved, That in case of any doubt as to the guilt of any person, he shall have the benefit of such doubt, in accordance with established usage.

Resolved, That the people's court shall have no jurisdiction after the next legislature has been convened five days.

Resolved, That all expenses of such court shall be paid by the contribution of citizens.

These resolutions were passed by acclamation, although opposition was offered by the Hon. David C. Broderick, and a few who looked upon him as a leader. Thus a political revolution had taken place, as much justified by the state of affairs as was the revolution of '76, when the Colonies revolted from the oppressions of Great Britain. From this time, the Vigilance Committee held sway, and their ranks were swelled by a voluntary enrollment of great numbers of the best and most effective citizens, and although opposition was offered at various times by those in authority, and by interested lawyers, who were losing a fruitful source of revenue in the defence of scoundrels, they maintained their ground, and within ten days the good effects of their administration was seen and felt. An effective and active police was thus formed, the rogues were either caught or banished, and the city was soon relieved from the thralldom of their presence.

This change was not felt in San Francisco alone. In all the towns throughout the State, and in the mines, committees of vigilance were organized, guilty offenders summarily punished ; and within thirty days, a security of life and property was felt throughout the whole length and breadth of the land, which had not existed since 1849. When, at length, order had been restored, and the courts began tardily to administer that justice for which they were designed, the Vigilance Committe, instead of executing the law themselves, acted as a people's police, to aid the constituted authorities in detecting villains, and left their condemnation and execution to the conservators of the law, and this was particularly the case when the following Legislature passed an act making the crimes above-mentioned capital offences. This was one of the most exciting periods in the history of California ; and may God grant that there may never be cause to have it repeated.

CHAPTER XXVI.

RESOURCES OF CALIFORNIA — UNCERTAINTY OF MINING — PROBABLE EXTENT OF THE GOLD REGION — WHERE GOLD IS USUALLY FOUND — HINTS TO PERSONS PROSPECTING — TALC BEDS — AURIFEROUS QUARTZ VEINS — CAUSE OF FAILURE IN MINING — CRUSHING THE ROCK AND SEPARATING IT FROM THE GOLD — THE CHILIAN MILL — PROCESS OF SEPARATION — THE MINES INEXHAUSTIBLE — ENTERPRIZE OF THE MINERS.

SINCE the discovery of gold, the mountains of California have attracted the attention of the civilized world, from the vast amount of mineral wealth they contain. An amount of treasure hitherto unparalleled in the annals of mankind has been taken out, which threatens at no distant day to have an important bearing on the commercial and financial operations of the world. The character of the mines is too well known now to require a particular description, but notwithstanding the repeated failure of thousands, after months, and even years, of faithful labor, to realize a competence — notwithstanding the multitude of letters which have been written back, giving glowing and truthful accounts of the difficulties and uncertainty of mining, with a full description of the labor necessary to get even a little — it is a matter of surprise that so many should continue to leave comfortable homes, and a good business, to try their fortunes in the uncertain occupation of mining. There are indeed considerations which might tempt men to make a permanent residence in California, but I do not hesitate to declare that no man should emigrate, unless with the intention of making it his home for life. Gold is not equally distributed in the earth, and the idea of picking up lumps in the mines, like gravel stones, is preposterous. Even in the most auriferous sections, there is only a comparatively small portion which pays the laborer abundantly ; and while now and then one miner may make a good strike, by far the greater number will make scarcely day-wages. In an early day men were not content with doing well, and were not satisfied with a fair remuneration. Ten dollars per day was looked upon as not sufficient to pay. Now the mines are better understood, and generally, if a miner finds diggings which pay from three to five dollars, he continues to work, and it sometimes happens that he strikes a rich bed, which amply rewards his patience and perseverance. Still, it cannot be denied that he sometimes fails altogether ; and men can be found who have labored faithfully and diligently for years, who have scarcely made their board.

It is impossible, in the present stage of mining, to lay down arbitrary rules for prospecting ; but after all, there are general principles which may be observed with advantage, such as the shape of the hills, the color of the soil, the nature and character of the rocks, the depth and shape of the ravines. I believe that the best diggings are generally found where the formation is talcous slate, or, where there is an abundance of auriferous quartz — where the soil is covered with per oxide of iron. Sometimes rich earth is found, where the earth is not highly colored with iron, but there is a superabundance either of slate or quartz in its vicinity, and miners are in the habit of remarking, that where there are good quartz veins there are almost invariably good placer diggings ; but the rule will not, so far as is known, bear to be reversed always. Sometimes detached portions of slate and quartz are curiously blended. I have seen near Nelson's Creek, pieces where they ran into each other with so delicate a shade that it was impossible to determine where either began, and these were found in a section of country highly auriferous. As a general thing, the largest quantity of gold is found resting on the bed rock, or in the dirt nearest to it, and shafts have been sunk even as low as a hundred feet, before the deposit was reached, and then followed by drifting under ground, but it is sometimes found on the mountains, mixed with more compact earth, at various depths of one foot or more; but this was probably deposited from time to time, by extraneous causes. Gold being the heaviest metal, always sinks to the lowest depths, until arrested by some stationary cause. At Grass Valley, Neváda county, in February, 1852, a shaft was sunk in a mountain slide to the depth of forty feet. At this depth trees were found, which were partially carbonized, and a bed of talc passed through, when a vein of auriferous earth was reached, combined with a greenish, partially decomposed quartz, which paid in some instances seven dollars to the bucket. The hill had at some period of time been undermined by a little stream, which flowed beneath it, and which had been gradually receiving its deposit for ages. The hill in its fall had covered up this deposit, carrying with it fragments of a vein, which passed through it, thus increasing the richness of its deposit, to reward the patient labor and perseverance of the lucky miner.

Talc beds are good indications, for gold is not unfrequently found richly imbedded in them, yet this is not always certain, for I have found veins of talc adjoining quartz veins which exhibited no indications of gold. Still, wherever I found a bed of talc, I should always try it. At Neváda some of the shafts of deep placer (or, as they are termed in California mining parlance, *cayote*) diggings, are eighty feet deep, and the auriferous earth is found mixed with green quartz, while in some of the southern mines it is found with yellow quartz. In giving my opinion with regard to gold being found in its various forms in the mines, I beg the reader to remember that it is entitled to no more weight than the opinions of perhaps hundreds of others, for there are various theories, all based upon valcanic hypothesis, and my own explanation is clear to myself, and to me accounts for more phenomena than any other.

Gold is found in particles from the fineness of impalpable powder, to masses of several pounds in weight. When the explosion occurred, which brought it to the surface, I suppose that portions were raised by the concussion in the primitive form of dust, other particles were melted, and running together like molten lead, cooled in lumps, or masses, in its upward passage, or as it fell, in the shape it is found. I think that the veins of quartz were ejected in a melted or fluid state, from the centre of the earth, and came in contact with particles of gold, which sunk into it in various shapes and sizes, by their specific gravity, and when the rock cooled it held the gold embedded in the mass, precisely as it is found. When the melted quartz came in contact with large quantities of the dust, more, of course, was imbedded; hence some portions of rock are very rich, while others are less so, and some have none at all. And what goes further to prove that the mineral is not equally distributed below, is the fact that many veins contain no gold, not having passed through any in its upward passage to the surface of the earth. The reason that rich placer diggings are found in the neighborhood of auriferous quartz veins, is because, in addition to what is thrown up loose by volcanic force, the quartz is sometimes either wholly or partially decomposed by chemical, gaseous causes, the climate, or otherwise, and the particles which are held in it are released, in the course of centuries, and find their way down the slopes to a final resting place. Small pieces of quartz are often found strewing the ground, and many times these can be traced to the ledge itself. And this leads me to the consideration of the quartz veins.

In the absence of a clearly established theory, (having never seen anything like a treatise upon the subject unconnected with California,) I must depend upon my own observations. I have traveled the mountains for about three hundred miles, between the American River and the Cascade Mountains, and have examined specimens taken from various parts of California, even from the desert east of the Siérra, and also from various parts of Oregon, and can pretend to nothing more than giving my own impressions. Having been a sufferer by the fire in San Francisco, on the 4th of May, 1851, my time for a year after that event was spent chiefly in quartz mining, or gold working, and I was among the first who engaged in the then new business.

Through the whole range of the Siérra Neváda in California, and the continuous chain in Oregon, innumerable veins of quartz extend, bearing a general parallel with the principal chain; but branches, or lateral veins, shoot off in various directions, generally diagonal, but occasionally at right angles. These vary in thickness from a few inches, even a single inch, to fourteen feet — nay, I have heard of their being twenty feet thick, but I never saw them. They are found dipping in various directions, but not unfrequently are perpendicular, the heavy veins being more generally so than the lighter ones. So far as my experience goes, those of from four inches to three feet thick are the best, and in the heavy ledges the gold bearing vein can be distinctly traced, sometimes only an inch or two wide, while other portions of the quartz contain little or no gold. Sometimes these veins come above the surface of the ground, then again they are found only at the depth of several feet. The best veins abound in pyrites, or sulphuret of iron, and the best quality of ore is of a dull brownish red, which varies in its shade, being colored with oxide of iron. There are four qualities of rock, which will pay expenses of working, viz: the red, the green, yellow, and a certain shade of white, which I cannot describe. Practice, however, is necessary to determine, for some of the red has merely a coating of per-oxide of iron, which is not diffused through the rock. As a general thing, I have found those veins dipping to the east, and laying at an angle of from forty-five to sixty degrees, to pay the best; but it is not always so, nor do I understand why their dipping to the east should have any effect; and this, after all, may only be a provincial superstition, but is true, in most cases, to the best of my recollection. Some perpendicular veins certainly pay well, as, for instance, one of those in Mariposa, and some dipping west may probably be good. The only reason I can suppose why a dipping vein should be richer than a perpendicular one, is because it passes along a greater surface of earth, taking more gold in its course; and the thinner a vein is, the sooner it will cool. According to my theory, a heavy vein would be found richer at a great depth than a light one, for so long as the quartz was in a melted state, so long would the gold settle, and would only be held when the rock became too hard to allow it to fall further down, and the greater the body of quartz, the longer it would remain in a fluid state.

Quartz veins generally have a parallel vein of granite, yet it sometimes happens that the quartz dislocates the granite, and passes through it, and sometimes it will pass under a granite ledge; but if prospecting for veins, when they did not appear above the surface, I should certainly take the parallel range of granite for a general guide. I cannot call to mind a single instance of a regular quartz vein, where it has not had an attendant granite ledge on the surface, though it may be several rods distant, and sometimes it may have a granite range on both sides. I cannot lay it down as an infallible rule, that when there are granite ledges there are quartz veins also, but quartz and granite appear to hold companionship. I look upon quartz rock as an indication of gold, but it is by no means certain that because good specimens are found in the top of a ledge, that the whole vein will pay. To this I charge the great number of failures in quartz mining. In its early history men were much deceived by not properly prospecting their veins. No man is a sufficient judge of the quality of the ore without trying it. Probably seven-eighths of the failures of mills in California, proceeded from not fully prospecting the ledge. The vein, in its upper progress, may barely touch a deposite of gold, taking enough to furnish a few specimens, while the great body does not contain enough to pay for working. Many a good man has been wofully deceived by a mistake which I should once have fallen into myself. To prospect a vein thoroughly, shafts should be sunk in several places, as low as the water, and the rock tested from time to time, from top to bottom, not by any chemical process, but by grinding the rock, and washing it in the common way with a pan, and by the result thus obtained one can judge with much certainty of the character of the vein. This should be done before the expense of machinery is gone into. It is better to lose a few hundred dollars in prospecting, than thousands in erecting machinery which will be of no use.

Men of experience can tell at a glance, whether rock contains gold or not, but they cannot tell the amount it contains with sufficient certainty to warrant the expense of erecting machinery till they try it.

When veins are highly crystaline, or when the mass of rock is chiefly composed of palpable crystals, there is no use in looking for gold, for although the vein may exhibit good specimens, it will not, as a whole, contain enough to pay for working. After all that can be said, practical experience is necessary to ensure success, and if men would employ practical miners in prospecting veins, it would be a saving of time and money in the end.

The most approved mode of crushing the rock, and of separating the gold, is either by stampers, or the improved Chilian mill. Except in the mode of crushing, the *modus operandi* is nearly the same in both. The first is by heavy stampers, weighing from two to six hundred pounds, which strike upon a heavy bed-plate of iron, enclosed in a tight box, having an iron plate pierced with holes, through which the pulverized rock escapes when fine enough, and is then passed over by a current of water. The Chilian mill is a series of heavy, upright, cast-iron wheels, which run in a circular groove, or trough of cast-iron, and this groove has sieves, somewhat similar to the stamping box, for the escape of rock, when sufficiently pulverized. By this method the rock is crushed, and ground by the weight of the wheels, and it is, in my opinion, the best, because it crushes the rock finer than the stampers, will wear much longer and needs fewer repairs. The stampes will wear out, and require to be duplicated in a month, while the wheels will wear a year. The rock then passes from the crushers, by long troughs, into an amalgamator, which is a box with two or three parti-

tions, the whole being five or six feet long, by sixteen or twenty
inches wide.   In the first partition is a bed of quick-silver, on
which the crushed rock falls, being carried by a current of water flowing from the crushers into the amalgamator, through the
troughs.   Here the gold unites, or amalgamates with the mer-
cury, while the rock passes onward by a proper motion being
given to the amalgamator.   When the rock has been thus run
through, the quick-silver is strained through a thick buckskin,
in which is left the gold and quick-silver in a .mass, now called
amalgam, which, after being carefully washed and cleaned, is
put into a retort, when the quick-silver escapes from the gold, in
the form of vapour, and is condensed, and falls into another
vessel, ready to be used again, while the gold remains pure in
the retort.

My impression is the mines can never be exhausted.   They
are distributed over such a large extent of country that hundreds of years must elapse before the ground can be dug over;
and, besides, the veins of quartz are so deep   that a single mine
may be worked, by the aid of pumps, many years.

I cannot dismiss the subject of the mines, without adverting
to the vast work undertaken and completed by individual enterprise, in overcoming the natural barriers of the climate, and
face of the country, in gold digging.   Where water is not
found in isolated places, canals are dug, sometimes forty   or
fifty miles long, by which water is carried from some permanent stream along stupendous hill-sides, over ravines and gulches, and around rocks by sluices and flumes, often at vast expense
of labor and money — thus attesting the skill, energy, and enterprise of the people who are delving among the mountains;
hoping to acquire a competence to smooth the down-hill of life,
and render old age comfortable.

CHAPTER XXVII.

CALIFORNIA — HER RESOURCES — MINERAL WEALTH — CLIMATE — TILLABLE
LAND IN THE VALLEYS — RICHNESS OF THE SOIL — PRODUCTIONS — WA-
TER-POWER — TIMBER — RAPID INCREASE OF POPULATION — HEALTH —
CONCLUSION.

WITH regard to the resources of California, Nature has indeed been bountiful, and if they are properly developed, no
State in the Union can present a greater amount of real wealth.
California extends from about the thirty-second to the forty-
second degree of latitude, and embraces within this space of ten
degrees, almost every variety of climate. It is a country of
mountain and plain, but its greatest area is mountainous. On
the east the Siérra Neváda, with its everlasting snows, stretches
from one end of the State to the other, presenting peaks from
ten to fourteen thousand feet above the level of the ocean ; and
on its western borders, the coast range is bounded entirely by
the Pacific Ocean. Between the Siérra and the coast range
lay the valleys of the San Joaquin and Sacramento, making
one continuous plain, five hundred miles in length, while many
minor valleys in the foot-hills of the Siérra, and probably in
the coast range, also, make collectively a large area of arable
land. From the main ridge of the Siérra, the country declines
to the principal valleys of the Sacramento and San Joaquin,

by a series of foot-hills, which, though often high, and extremely broken, presenting much grand and sublime scenery, abound in glades and small valleys, which are proved, by experience, to be highly susceptible of cultivation — the soil being equally as rich as that of the lower valleys. In my opinion there is arable land enough in these mountain valleys, if properly cultivated, to supply the whole mining population with vegetables, fruit and grain, while the larger valleys can raise enough not only to supply its population, and that of the cities, but also a surplus for exportation. I have, been induced to change my preconceived opinion with regard to the agricultural capacities of the country by actual demonstration. On my first arrival very little farming was done. Nearly all the vegetables, flour and grain, were derived from foreign ports, and little had been done to develop the agricultural capacities of the country. The long drowths seemed to render it impossible for grain to grow without irrigating the parched earth, where the grass withered and became crisp under the burning sun; but the energy of man soon demonstrated that California had its regular seasons, as well as the Atlantic States, and that grain put into the ground in season to have the benefit of the winter and spring rains, grows rapidly in the prolific soil, and matures before the summer sun withers it; and that crops are as sure in California as on the Atlantic coast.

Two years produced an important change: vegetables were produced in sufficient quantities, not only to supply the demand, but the prices were infinitely reduced, and their importation ceased; and it was found that small grains thrived well, and yielded three-fold what they do at home. Oats are indigenous, and miles of dry plain are yearly covered with a luxuriant growth; and I venture to predict that within two years wheat enough will be raised to stop the importation of flour completely. In the South, sugar cane, cotton and tea can be raised, while the talc lands seem as if designed by nature for the cultivation of rice; and portions of the valley which are overflowed annually, will eventually, by means of dykes and levees, be valuable for their productions. In the South the grape is cultivated with infinite success; peaches grow in perfection, and I cannot see why apples will not succeed well in certain districts of the mountain valleys.

In the mountains, water-power is abundant for all mechanical purposes, and the noble pines, made into lumber, will form a source of wealth equaled only by its mineral treasures. It is true, there has been a vast deal of individual suffering, more, perhaps, than usually occurs in the settlement of a country.

Approached only by a wide and barren desert on one side, and by a long and perilous sea voyage on the other, the immense emigration of the two first years — in a measure cut off from home supplies, in a country which was untried, and too new to afford ample means of support within itself, at once, without a superabundance of funds to purchase such supplies as were brought in — necessarily experienced suffering, hardships, and sometimes death. But politically, the country rapidly advanced. Its population increased to an unprecedented degree. Houses and towns were built, roads opened, the country explored, the mines worked, commerce established, a government organized, and the foundation laid for future prosperity and greatness; and it only requires the fostering care of a firm, yet liberal government, which will fully develop its resources, to make California one of the richest and most prosperous States in the Union.

The climate is delightful and salubrious. Although the days

in summer are hot, yet the evenings are cool; and the laborer, though exhausted by the heat of the day, is refreshed with a good night's sleep, without the sultriness of the Atlantic summers; and the dryness of the atmosphere in summer soon withers the vegetation, and prevents the malaria of damper climates.

The upper part of the valley of the Sacramento, however, is less free from bilious diseases than the southern part. Chills and fever are more prevalent than farther south; and though there is no apparent cause for this, it may probably be found in its being situated nearer the coast, the Siérra Neváda range approaching to unite, and the extremes of heat and cold being greater between night and day; but cultivation and habit may eventually change this in some measure, as it is found to operate favorably in new States at home. Emigrants are frequently subject to bilious attacks on their first arrival, but these are not dangerous, if properly attended to in season; and after being acclimated, with common prudence in avoiding unnecessary exposure, and the vices now too prevalent, a man may maintain better health than in the older States on the Atlantic.

In conclusion, I beg leave to say, that there are many subjects of which it would have given me pleasure to speak; particularly of the geological structure of the country, and of the statistical facts with regard to its mines, and its agricultural productions; but the nature of this work, and its already lengthened proportions forbid. The most that I can hope for, is, that the reader may find amusement, and understand some of the trials encountered by the early emigrants to California, especially by the miners, whom I know to be an honorable and intelligent class of people.